Praise for
The College Student's Guide to the Law
by C. L. Lindsay III

"This book is your get-out-of-jail-free—and stay off of *COPS*—card. A little practical knowledge is far superior to abstract theory when it comes to the law."

—**John Langley**, cocreator and executive producer, *COPS*

"College students, this book is a must-have. You are an adult now and the law will definitely hold you to it. This one-stop law reference will save you time and money, and it quite possibly will keep you out of trouble—and not just while you're reading it."

—**Kim Ossi**, editor, KRT Campus, Knight Ridder/Tribune Wire Service

"Lindsay explains the crucial difference between university policy and student legal rights as if you were having coffee in the student union. This book is a must for college and university administrators—and for those students who wish to remain forever unknown to them."

—**Michael Gamer**, undergraduate chair of English,
University of Pennsylvania

"A funny and incredibly useful handbook for college students—whether they're at a giant state school or a small, private university. It's got everything students need to know to make it through their college years legally unscathed, from dealing with administrators to understanding how to navigate the legal system."

—**Nick Seaver**, Yale University sophomore and chair,
ACLU, Yale University Chapter

"What a great book. It's funny, but more importantly, it's well written and extremely informative. Lindsay takes complex legal concepts and makes them understandable and even enjoyable. Now I know what to get my nephew for his high school graduation."

—**Christopher W. Timmons**, assistant solicitor-general,
DeKalb County, Georgia

the College Student's GUIDE TO THE LAW

the College Student's GUIDE TO THE LAW

* Get a Grade Changed,
* Keep Your Stuff Private,
* Throw a Police-Free Party,
* and MORE!

C. L. LINDSAY III

TAYLOR TRADE PUBLISHING
Lanham * Dallas * Boulder * New York * Toronto

Some images provided by retroart.com.
Grade-change decision tree created by Zoli Design.

Published by Taylor Trade Publishing
An imprint of The Rowman & Littlefield Publishing Group, Inc.
4501 Forbes Boulevard, Suite 200
Lanham, Maryland 20706

Distributed by National Book Network

Library of Congress Cataloging-in-Publication Data

Lindsay, C. L., 1971–
    The college student's guide to the law : get a grade changed, keep your stuff private, throw a police-free party, and more! / C. L. Lindsay.
      p. cm.
    Includes bibliographical references.
    ISBN 1-58979-089-8 (pbk. : alk. paper)
    College students—Legal status, laws, etc.—United States. 2. Universities and colleges—Law and legislation—United States. I. Title.

    KF4243.Z9L56 2005
    344.73'079—dc22   2004025901

Contents

Acknowledgments

There are so many people who have supported me, each in their own way, and in their own time, in this effort: Leah Evanski, Kevin Blalock, Brandy Pryor, Barb Tompkins, Shāna Phipps, Kerri and Alex Hoyt, my sisters Chris and Anne (and their good for nothing husbands Pat and Tony), Bob Jacobson, Chris Messina, Margaret Kohr, John Martin, Tony Inscor, Chuck Bennett, and Bob Seith.

To all of you I offer heartfelt thanks.

There are also a few people who have stood by me every step of the way. Without them this book wouldn't have ever happened:

Mike Holloway for being an incredibly good friend and for his Herculean efforts in marketing and publicity.

Chris Mayer, Hellyn Sher, and Jeff Dine, all of whom I could always call up and say—in a desperate tone—"please read this" and get my copy returned quickly with thoughtful and decisive comments.

Averil VanGorder, Andy Gardiner, and Zoli Design for countless hours of free design and even more hours of sincere counsel and emotional support.

The entire, extended Faure family, Blake, Blaise, Brittany, Hans, Brooks (not Catherine), Steve, Gene, Betsy, Barbara, and Michel for listening to me drone on about this project for hours on end over the past two years.

Michael Garner and Elise Bruhl who edited my work in its earliest (and most embarrassing) stages, who offered compliments when I most needed them, and who always treated me as an intellectual equal, even though they could have very easily gotten away with doing differently.

Sean and Shelia Power—the former for unlimited tech support (the kind that Gateway and Dell never seem to offer) and the latter for feeding and entertaining me on a regular basis.

Serena Leigh Krombach, Judith Rothman, Katie Smith, Tracy Miracle, Brian Richards, Terry Fischer, Kimberly Ball Smith, Andy Brozyna, and

everyone else at the Rowman & Littlefield Publishing Group who worked so hard on this project.

The University of Michigan Law School and its incredible debt forgiveness program (and the deans and administrators there, who keep the program a priority), without which I wouldn't be able to do my job.

Jen Rice, for jump-starting the whole process by editing my proposal and for using her infinite charm and unlimited connections to pitch the project.

Barry Fetterolf, first for simply taking a random book proposal from a random friend seriously and, second, for making a pitch that actually worked.

Finally, a very special thank you must go to my father Carl L. Lindsay Jr. and to Carol Corbett who supported me, in both the figurative and literal sense, during this entire process.

This book is for the two of you.

Disclaimer

Every effort has been made to ensure that this handbook contains the most up-to-date, accurate, and effective information available. Still, even the best of books can't replace an attorney licensed to practice law in your state. Because it is written with the broadest possible audience in mind, this book addresses general legal issues only. So the information and advice given may or may not be appropriate to a specific situation. Further, laws and procedures change frequently and are subject to differing interpretations.

Nothing contained in the book is legal advice and should not be relied on as such. It is not intended to create, and does not create, a lawyer-client relationship. It is not a substitute for legal counsel in the relevant jurisdiction.

Introduction

If you're reading this page you are, most likely, a student. Probably you're at college or in graduate school. But you could also be a high school senior or junior and simply want to get a jump on understanding your rights. Obviously (as the title denotes) this book is written specifically with you in mind. So when I say "you" on these pages, I'm talking directly to, well, you.

But I'm also hoping that this book will find its way into the hands of members of the larger college community: administrators, professors, parents, student affairs and resident hall staff, really anyone with an interest in higher education. The law works best when all those involved—those subject to it, those charged with enforcing it, even third-party observers—have as much information as possible.

To all of you I say: Welcome and congratulations.

Why am I congratulating you? Because by opening up this book you've taken a proactive step to protect your rights. Although that may not seem like a big deal, it really is extremely important: Being an American is an *interactive* relationship. It requires action and vigilance on your part.

Most people, it seems, never figure that out. They think that their rights are draped around them like some kind of bulletproof vest, effortlessly defraying all abuses and challenges. In part, they're correct. We all do have rights that are guaranteed by the Constitution. But protecting them requires action. Sometimes it's a load of work; sometimes it's pretty simple—but it never happens without effort on your part.

So what do you need to do to? First, learn about and understand your rights. There's really nothing you can do to protect yourself if you don't.

Let's take the most famous—at least so far as television and movies go—rights of all as an example: the Miranda warnings. They're what the police are required to explain before they question you. We'll cover Miranda rights and all of their implications later on, so don't worry. But for now we can discuss them via their popular-culture persona.

We've all heard countless fictional policemen blurt out the Miranda warnings while handcuffing some poor slob on TV: "You have the right to remain silent. Any statement you make can be used as evidence against you" and so on. For an arrestee this is a great thing. The police—the very people who have the ability to abuse you in this situation—are required by law to explain your rights at the very moment you need to know them.

If there were similar laws covering all possible situations, you wouldn't need to know anything. Unfortunately, that's not the way the world works. Think for a minute about the many ways your rights could be compromised. Do you think an administrator at your school is going to sit you down and explain that you had a right to a hearing that you never got and that your expulsion was unconstitutional? Of course not. Will your landlord call to tell you that she's keeping your security deposit illegally? No. Even in the Miranda example, do you think that if the police want to unlawfully interrogate a suspect (and, unfortunately, such things do happen), they elaborate on his rights first?

You get the point.

You may be thinking, "I've made it this far without knowing this crap. Why do I need to learn it now?" For starters, you're probably going to be exposed to all sorts of new situations and have increased responsibilities over the next four years. In turn, your exposure to potential abuse is about to exponentially expand. This brings us to the most basic reason for knowing anything about the law: to protect yourself. Among other things, knowing your rights can help you keep money in your pocket, keep you out of jail, and keep you in school.

Let me give you an example of a time when I was able to turn to the law for protection. When I was a third-year law student, I went to an off-campus block party hosted by a few undergraduate friends of mine—sixteen houses on one street having simultaneous blowouts. Needless to say, it wasn't long before the cops showed up and started issuing open container, public intoxication, and underage drinking citations to the drunks foolish enough to stumble around out front.

After finishing with the street urchins, pairs of officers started to go from house to house. When they got to my friends' place, I met them at the door. One asked to come in, and I said, "No, we're not giving you permission to come in. Please step out onto the porch." Then I followed the two officers outside and shut the door behind me. I asked them why they thought they had reason to enter my friends' house, told them that I was

sober, that I fully understood the law, and that there was nothing illegal going on inside. "If you want to come in," I said, "I'm going to need to see a warrant."

Flabbergasted and visibly angry, they shuffled away.

Back inside, every woman at the party wanted to talk to me. It was the very first time that I thought that my considerable investment in a law degree might actually be worth it.

Now I'm not saying that reading this book will make people want to sleep with you. (I am, however, hoping that *writing* it will.) But I am saying that it's an incredible thing to identify when people are trying to take advantage and stop them in their tracks. And, more importantly, parties are only one of the countless things you can defend. Once you get the hang of it, you can expand your use of the law. You can protect the things you care about and even use it to change the world around you. Heady stuff, I know, especially for a book that you thought would just teach you how to keep the cops away from your kegger.

But that's my point: All of these things are part of the same world. There's really only the tiniest difference between organizing a demonstration to fight sweatshop labor and making sure your next frat party doesn't get shut down. And these skills, once learned, are translatable to almost every situation. They're something you can truly use for the rest of your life.

How to Use This Book

There's no real trick to it. Just read the damn thing.

Aside from that, I have a few humble suggestions:

First—please—read chapters 1 and 2 in their entirety. This book is designed to be used two ways. The first is to read it from cover to cover (this is what I'm hoping everyone will do). Taking time to read through all of the chapters—even the ones that don't seem relevant to you—will give you the fullest possible understanding of the law and your rights. Even if all you care about is the law pertaining to plagiarism, you'll still benefit from reading the sections on harassment and free speech. It might also be, if I do say so myself, enjoyable.

But I know many of you will primarily use this book as a reference to spot-check your rights in a specific area. If you plan on using the book in this way, please at least take the time to read the introductory chapters—"Your Constitution" and "Your College"—in their entirety. The rest of the book stands on the shoulders of the concepts introduced there.

Second, when spot-checking a particular issue, read as much of the surrounding material as possible—preferably the entire appropriate chapter. Legal concepts can rarely be reduced to a few sentences. Please don't make

the mistake of quickly reading a lone paragraph or two and thinking that you're fully informed.

Finally, have fun with this stuff. I know that sounds strange. "What's fun about the Bill of Rights or landlord/tenant law?" you're thinking. "So many things are so much more fun—like kittens, liquor, Las Vegas, watching people you don't like fail . . ." Trust me, while kittens and liquor have their charms, there's nothing more invigorating, exhilarating, and incredibly satisfying than standing up for your rights and winning.

CHAPTER 1

Your Constitution

A lot of what's in the Constitution isn't relevant to life on a modern campus. For instance, you shouldn't worry too much about having to quarter troops in your dorm room. Still, a surprising amount of what the framers committed to writing has a direct effect on today's college students.

Chapter Contents

You'd be hard-pressed to find a legal document more elegant or efficient than the United States Constitution. In just 4,400 words it lays out the basics of our government and establishes the groundwork for all of our civil rights. Its simple brilliance is, in a word, intimidating.

But, despite the minimalism in its drafting, the Constitution is also incredibly complex. You could dedicate your entire life to understanding its intricacies and not make much of a dent before senility sets in. Thankfully, this book isn't about the minutiae of constitutional law. I'm not qualified to write that text, and frankly, you probably wouldn't be interested in reading it even if I were. That said: It's worth a bit of your time to understand a little about how and why the Constitution was drafted. It's also essential to introduce you, at this early stage, to the high points of the Bill of Rights.

A Very Brief History of the U.S. Constitution

Think back to the Revolutionary War—fifes, drums, guys in funny pants. As I'm sure you know, on July 4, 1776, fifty-six men representing the thirteen colonies formally declared our independence from Great Britain by signing the (aptly named) Declaration of Independence. Actually, that's a bit of a myth. The Declaration was, in fact, signed over a long period of time beginning on August 2. The final language of the document was approved on July 4, but no one put their name on it for another few months. Some even signed as late as November. But since barbecues and fireworks aren't much fun in winter, we celebrate our independence in July.

Anyway, the colonists, or now, the citizens formerly known as colonists, had told King George to go blow—which was great. But there was a problem: Now England, the most powerful country in the world at the time, was really pissed off at them. Not so great. The colonists had to make preparations for war: raise funds, build an army, manufacture weapons. In short, they were badly in need of a central government.

Enter the Articles of Confederation. In 1777 a national congress drafted them. They were ratified by the states and went into effect in 1781. And the United States of America was born . . . sort of. This early form of our country was much different than the one we know today. It featured an

incredibly weak federal government. All the real power stayed in the hands of the individual states.

Of course, while all of this was happening, the Revolutionary War raged on. People ran up and down Bunker Hill (well, actually, Breeds Hill), hung around Valley Forge, and crossed the Delaware River (if you'd like a more detailed description of the war, please buy a different book). We won. The British surrendered in Yorktown in late 1781 and (other than the unpleasantness of 1812) haven't invaded with anything more formidable than the Beatles since.

Again, great. Now we *really* weren't under British rule. But, very soon after the war ended, things began to deteriorate under the weak Articles. The mini-government had served its purpose while the fight was on. But after Yorktown, without the common purpose of the war to bind the states, tension built and problems cropped up. There were arguments over which state owned what (there was almost a war over the Potomac River). States were printing money left and right, making all of it worthless. And, without a strong central government, there was no real way to deal with other countries.

It became clear that the U.S. government needed to be beefed up a bit or the states were going to destroy themselves from within. So in 1787, largely the same group that had gathered in 1777 drafted what is still today the main body of our Constitution. This new, stronger Constitution was quickly approved by the states, but in many cases by a very small margin, due to a general fear that we were putting into place exactly the type of government we had just fought a war to oust.

YOUR CONSTITUTION

That fear, of trading one dictatorship for another, is significant in understanding how the Constitution works, or better, in understanding how the Constitution works for you. The colonists had just come out of an era of fairly extreme governmental oppression (the slogan you learned in the tenth grade, "no taxation without representation," is a gross understatement of how bad things were). People wanted absolutely no part of being pushed around by some superpowerful government.

These fears and perceptions affected the drafters of the new Constitution more than you can imagine. In most critical areas, safeguards against oppression were included. They did a pretty good job at this. But even as each state government was debating and deciding whether or not to ratify, fears about the abuse of individuals under this new, powerful government circulated, especially given the intentionally vague terms of the document. Those against central power called for an explicit, simple statement of the rights guaranteed to each and every citizen.

This was the genesis of the Bill of Rights. Seventeen amendments were originally considered. Twelve were sent to the state governments for ratification. Ten made the final cut and became the Bill of Rights. That Bill is

✳ THE BILL OF RIGHTS IN A NUTSHELL ✳

1. You have the right to freely speak, assemble, practice religion, maintain the press, and petition the government.

2. You have the right to bear arms.

3. The government may not force you to house or feed soldiers.

4. The government may not unreasonably search your home or arrest you.

5. Those accused of a crime must be indicted by a grand jury, cannot be tried twice for the same offense, cannot be made to testify against themselves and are guaranteed due process. People must be compensated if the government takes their property.

6. Those accused of a crime must have a speedy trial, held where the crime was committed, in front of an impartial jury; have notice of the charges; have a lawyer and an opportunity to confront witnesses who testify against them.

7. In civil cases, you have a right to a trial by jury.

8. The government cannot impose cruel or unusual punishments or excessive bail.

9. This list is not all inclusive. Citizens retain many other rights not listed here.

10. All rights not granted to the federal government or prohibited still rest with the states.

your part of the Constitution. It's exactly what was called for: a list of things that the government may not do to you.

In the next part of this chapter, we're going to look at these amendments in more detail. And, yes, I will almost immediately muck them up a bit by talking about their limitations and the complexities of actual application. But please, as you work through them keep in mind the simple, basic meaning that each has.

Government Action Only One of the first things I want to point out seems very basic and obvious. But it's easy to forget when you're in the thick of a problem. *The Bill of Rights only applies to actions of the government.* Private entities are not bound by the rules set out there. In fact, as written, the Bill only applies to the federal government and not each state's local government. But over the years, using the Fourteenth Amendment as justification, the Supreme Court has held that most of these rules are also applicable to states.

Exactly what counts as part of the government, or what is a **state actor**, to use the legal vernacular, is a more difficult question than you might think. Of course all of the actual parts of the government are state actors— the police, the Internal Revenue Service, transportation authorities, public hospitals, and everything else you think of as the government. But sometimes seemingly private entities are, for constitutional purposes, also considered to be part of the state.

The state/private actor distinction is an exceedingly important one for college students. Whether you're at a public or private school has a huge bearing on your rights. Public schools are, without a doubt, state actors and need to adhere to all of the constitutional constraints. But private schools are a different matter altogether. Some of their parts or functions may make them state actors in specific areas, but not usually. So if you have a "constitutional-type" problem at a private university, you'll probably need to find a different reason to make them give you your due. We'll cover these issues on a case-by-case basis throughout the book. But it's good to keep in mind as we go along.

Vocabulary Lesson

STATE ACTOR—This term is a bit of a misnomer because it refers to both the government itself *and* to private entities that meet the test for state action. Whether or not something is a state actor is a complex question that takes a number of factors into consideration. But at its base, if a company, school, or other entity either *performs an exclusive public function* or *has significant state involvement in its activities*, it's a state actor and must follow the constitutional rules.

The Push and Pull of Your Rights

Before we get to the specifics of the Bill, I want to make something clear: With every right comes a responsibility—an obligation to, while exercising it, be wary of and protect the rights of others. In fact, our personal liberties extend only to the point where they interfere with someone else's. At that point, it becomes a question for the courts to decide which right trumps which.

This may seem somewhat counterintuitive on its face. "Doesn't free speech mean I can say whatever the hell I want?" Well, no. You can *believe* whatever the hell you want. But your right to articulate those beliefs is actually quite limited.

Think of Justice Holmes's classic example: "The most stringent protection of free speech would not protect a man in falsely shouting fire in a theatre and causing a panic." Of course it wouldn't. The right of the rest of the people to avoid being trampled easily beats out whatever right you have to exercise your vocal chords and yell "fire."

There are countless other examples: Sexually explicit speech in the workplace is one. You may really want to loudly describe your most recent exploit in your cubicle. But your coworkers have a right to work in an office that doesn't make them uncomfortable. Even in the classroom (although there aren't any actual laws about this), you have a right to speak your mind, but you don't have a right to be disruptive and impede the learning process of others.

These types of limitations apply to almost every basic right you have.

You probably feel hurt, confused, and a bit betrayed by this concept of limits. I know I was when I first figured out how unbelievably shifty the law can be. All I can say is, get used to it: In the law there really aren't that many absolutes. In fact, there is almost always an exception, caveat, exclusion, or extenuating circumstance. That doesn't mean the law is incomprehensible, it just means that there will very rarely be simple answers.

A Closer Look at the Bill Of Rights

FIRST AMENDMENT

Congress shall make no law respecting an establishment of religion, or prohibiting the free exercise thereof; or abridging the freedom of speech, or of the press; or the right of the people peaceably to assemble, and to petition the Government for a redress of grievances.

In the hierarchy of amendments, this one's the shiznit. Most of the major freedoms—those that truly define American freedom—are contained in this one amendment. We'll take them each in turn.

Religious Freedom You have the right to practice any religion you want, and the government can't establish a state religion. For the colonists, this was big stuff. But for you and me it seems like sort of a yawn.

Personally I view this as a victory for the framers (that's one for Team Jefferson, zero for King George). The concept of religious freedom has been so thoroughly embraced by the American government that in simple application it's a nonissue. Chances are no arm of the government has tried, or ever will try, to prohibit you from attending the church (or temple or coven . . .) of your choice.

But there are still some sticky problems associated with religious freedom. Sure, no one's going to stand in front of a mosque and tell you that you can't go in. But you may be asked to do things that conflict with your beliefs outside your place of worship. Whether or not you can be forced to comply is a First Amendment issue. We'll discuss one such application in chapter 5, "Animal Rights," in relation to vivisection and dissection. A student might be asked to harm an animal in conflict with his religious values. The First Amendment is the legal basis for objecting.

The Right to Petition the Government   Unlike the freedom of religion, I don't think petitioning rights are a hot topic to anyone. This clause guarantees your right to complain to the government. People do it every day in the form of letters to their representatives, petitions, protests, and so forth. Generally, unless you hire a lobbying firm in D.C., these complaints fall on deaf ears, but you have a right to speak up just the same.

Free Speech   We'll go into all the contours of free speech law in chapter 8, "Free Speech." Still, it makes sense to touch on at least the basics at this point. There are two main ways that the government can restrict speech: one, based on the **content** of the speech and two, based on the **conduct** of the speakers.

Restrictions based on **conduct**—sometimes called **time, place, and manner restrictions**—are the more common of the two. The government can limit speech in public places so long as the restrictions are content-neutral, narrowly designed to serve a governmental purpose, and leave open other channels of communication. For example, a city could require that the organizers of protests with more than five hundred people apply for a permit two weeks in advance. This would allow arrangements to be made for adequate crowd control, cleanup services, and safety measures. But a rule prohibiting political parties (content-based) or, even worse, prohibiting one political party but not others from assembling in the park would be unconstitutional.

The government can also, under *very* limited circumstances, regulate speech based on its **content**. For example, you have no right to use speech that will hurt other people. This includes words that will incite violence or a fight (sometimes called **fighting words**), obscenity, slander or libel (lying about someone else and hurting their reputation), or commercial fraud.

Freedom of Assembly   This is another concept that has become such an intuitive part of American life that it's hard to imagine why the framers felt the need to specifically incorporate it (that's two for Team Jefferson, still zero for King George). At the time of the revolution the British government didn't allow the colonists to gather to conduct business (which in all fairness was somewhat wise on the part of the British—the colonists were planning a revolution after all). Even today, many countries don't allow assemblies unless they are sanctioned by the government. But in America that's not the case. So long as you're not getting together to do something illegal or to incite violence, the government can't stop you (they can, however, make you get a permit or limit the time and place you do it—see above).

Freedom of the Press   The press has always been on the cutting edge of the First Amendment. They have pushed their rights to the limit and will fight and scrap for every last inch of leeway. Because of this, the law of the press—even the law of the student press—is very well developed and complex. It is, in short, far too involved a subject for the pages of this book.

For the average student, understanding that the press enjoys roughly the same freedoms as an individual should be enough to get you through. If you're an editor or reporter or work in any capacity at a school newspaper, you'll need way more information. Several excellent books about student press law are available. And there are some wonderful organizations, like the Student Press Law Center (www.splc.org), that can help you.

SECOND AMENDMENT

A well regulated Militia, being necessary to the security of a free State, the right of the people to keep and bear Arms, shall not be infringed.

This is one of the most hotly debated rights in the whole damned document. On one side are those who point to the statistics that show the relationship between the availability of weapons and crime. On the other is Ted Nugent, who says things like, "If guns cause crime, then all of mine are defective."

Whatever you think, the framers' intentions were fairly clear. They wanted to be able to protect themselves both from oppression and the wild elements.

Believe it or not, this issue has reared its ugly head on campus. The University of Utah has a rule that bans firearms on campus. But the state of Utah has a law based on the Second Amendment that allows those with permits to carry concealed weapons. At the time of the writing of this book, a legal battle was being fought between the state's attorney general and the university. It's being framed as an academic freedom issue by the school—they worry that students might not speak freely if they think that a classmate might pull out a gun in response. I guess that could happen: "Me and my .45 say that Shelley's portrait of Keats in 'Adonais' was psychologically false and shallow. *RIGHT*!" Where I went to college, people rarely stayed awake in class, let alone being moved enough to brandish weapons. Still, I see their point.

THIRD AMENDMENT

No Soldier shall, in time of peace be quartered in any house, without the consent of the Owner, nor in time of war, but in a manner to be prescribed by law.

Back in revolutionary times the quartering of troops was a big problem. The British enacted laws that specifically forced the colonists to provide living quarters, food, candles, and transportation to the British troops. There was even a clause in some versions of the law that required colonists to provide beer, cider, or rum mixed with water to soldiers who demanded a drink. Today the issue really isn't on the public radar. Still, I suppose it is comforting to know that some random soldier can't knock on your door, demand a place to sleep, and drink all your booze.

FOURTH AMENDMENT

The right of the people to be secure in their persons, houses, papers, and effects, against unreasonable searches and seizures, shall not be violated, and no Warrants

shall issue, but upon probable cause, supported by Oath or affirmation, and particularly describing the place to be searched, and the persons or things to be seized.

Under British rule, soldiers were basically allowed to search the private homes of the colonists and arrest people on a whim. They were given documents, called "writs of assistance," that were supposed to legitimize their actions. But even under British law at the time, the writs were, plain and simple, illegal.

This amendment is a direct affront to that practice. The police or any part of the government cannot search private property or arrest anyone without some evidence that a law has been broken. In the case of searches, a judge must issue a warrant based on information that the search will turn up evidence of a crime. In the case of arrests, either the officer has to actually observe the crime or a warrant needs to be issued.

The nuts-and-bolts of the Fourth Amendment are dealt with in detail in chapter 13, "The Police," and in chapter 9, "Dormitories and On-Campus Housing." There you'll learn the exact limits of police power and how to watch out for your rights when the authorities are cuffing you or knocking on your door.

FIFTH AMENDMENT

No person shall be held to answer for a capital, or otherwise infamous crime, unless on a presentment or indictment of a Grand Jury, except in cases arising in the land or naval forces, or in the Militia, when in actual service in time of War or public danger; nor shall any person be subject for the same offence to be twice put in jeopardy of life or limb; nor shall be compelled in any criminal case to be a witness against himself; nor be deprived of life, liberty, or property, without due process of law; nor shall private property be taken for public use, without just compensation.

Among amendments, this one's a bit of a celebrity. Almost every time a defendant is trotted into a fictional courtroom on TV the time-honored phrase "I plead the Fifth" comes from his mouth. We all sort of know what this means: He doesn't have to answer any questions because, well, he's pleading the Fifth. But very few people (Hollywood writers included) really understand the contours that extend beyond the self-incrimination portion of the Fifth Amendment—or even fully understand how that clause works.

In fact, there's quite a lot more packed into this amendment. Yes, much of it only applies to criminals, but within the Fifth are some much more subtle, and generally applicable, protections.

We'll take the clauses in order:

No person shall be held to answer for a capital, or otherwise infamous crime, unless on a presentment or indictment of a Grand Jury, except in cases arising in the land or naval forces, or in the Militia, when in actual service in time of War or public danger;

Capital and infamous crimes are ones that carry serious sentences—death and long terms of imprisonment, respectively. This portion of the Fifth places the decision of whether or not to charge a person with one of these high-level crimes in the hands of a jury, rather than one person. This jury hears evidence presented by a prosecutor and decides whether or not there is reason to proceed with a criminal trial. It's a sort of mini-trial before the fact.

As the clause says, military personnel serving during wartime are exempt. Soldiers accused of serious crimes are subject to a court-martial, which is generally held before a tribunal of officers. These courts can hand down very serious sentences, including death, without a prior grand jury indictment. The few, the proud, the convicted without a proper trial.

nor shall any person be subject for the same offence to be twice put in jeopardy of life or limb;

This clause is the B-List celebrity of the Bill of Rights. It's like Tom Arnold: You know about it, but it's generally not a headliner. Still, it's spawned its own set of movie and television show plots, most recently a miserable Ashley Judd vehicle where the heroine is convicted of her husband's faked murder and plans to hunt him down and kill him after she's out on parole. All because, as one of her fellow inmates told her, you can't be tried twice for the same crime. You "can walk right up to him in Times Square and pull the trigger, and there's nothing anybody can do about it," she explains.

Of course, that's not really how it works (and by the way, don't ever take legal advice from the woman who works with you at the prison cafeteria—chances are she doesn't really understand the Constitution all that well). The first "murder" would be considered a separate crime (albeit one that never happened) from the second subsequent one. Sorry, Ashley, you'd get tried again.

But the basic idea is right. You can't be tried for the same crime twice. Of course you can be tried criminally and civilly for the same incident (think: O. J.), or under your school's disciplinary code and the local police ordinances. And you can be tried under multiple criminal statutes for a single act. But once you've been tried and found innocent, or guilty, you can't be retried for the same offense.

nor shall be compelled in any criminal case to be a witness against himself;

This is the part we all automatically associate with the Fifth: the protection against self-incrimination. It's pretty simple. In a criminal trial (or a civil one, if there's a risk of later incarceration) a defendant cannot be required, or even asked, to take the stand and testify. And the fact that the defendant does not testify cannot be used to prove her guilt—prosecutors can't even mention it to the jury.

People who are simply witnesses, not the defendant, can be forced to take the stand. But they can still refuse to answer specific questions under the Fifth if they fear their testimony will incriminate them, personally, in a crime. But if a witness is granted adequate immunity from prosecution for those self-incriminating portions of his testimony, he can be forced to sing.

All of this applies to spoken testimony only—physical evidence, such as documents, records, bodily samples, and so forth, can't be kept out of court based on the Fifth. In other words, you can keep your mouth shut, but your urine can still be made to testify against you.

nor be deprived of life, liberty, or property, without due process of law;

This is referred to as the "Due Process Clause." These thirteen words pack a lot of import. They guarantee that in any situation where a person may lose life, liberty, or property, fair process and procedure must be followed. In practice this means, at the very least, an opportunity to make objections to a judge or other neutral decision maker.

While loss of life means the obvious—the death penalty—the definitions of liberty and property are a bit expanded for Fifth Amendment purposes: A loss of liberty not only includes imprisonment, but any physical restraint, like commitment to a mental institution. And it includes more obscure losses—in fact, any time a person is denied a right guaranteed by the Constitution or a statute, they have lost liberty and are guaranteed due process.

Property rights attach anytime a person has legitimate entitlement to something of value. The best example for you is your education. Pursuing a degree creates a property interest. Even if you're still countless semesters from graduation, you've still got a property interest in your diploma.

What exact form does due process take? It depends on the importance of the interest at stake. At the very least there needs to be fair procedures, an unbiased decision maker, and some sort of prior notice given. Depending on the circumstances, the actual procedure could be anything from an informal hearing to a trial before a jury.

nor shall private property be taken for public use, without just compensation.

The last little bit of the Fifth Amendment is somewhat unrelated to the rest. It has to do with public takings of private lands. Unlike the other clauses, it has nothing whatsoever to do with criminal procedure—maybe the framers didn't really know where else to put this stuff, so they just tacked it on here.

Here's what it means: The government has the power to take lands and property it needs. This is called eminent domain. For example, maybe traffic's gotten out of hand, and a new highway needs to be built. Unfortunately for you, they want to put it right through where your house sits. The gov-

ernment gets to take your land, but this clause guarantees that you'll be paid fair value for it.

There are all sorts of nuances to this part of the law: What exactly constitutes a taking? What if the government just builds something nasty nearby, like a nuclear power plant, and drains all the value from your land? What if they just want to run high-tension wires over your property? And what exactly is fair value?

Legally, these nuances are somewhat interesting. In the real world, they're boring as hell, and, more importantly, they're not even remotely likely to come up while you're at college. Enough said.

SIXTH AMENDMENT

In all criminal prosecutions, the accused shall enjoy the right to a speedy and public trial, by an impartial jury of the State and district wherein the crime shall have been committed, which district shall have been previously ascertained by law, and to be informed of the nature and cause of the accusation; to be confronted with the witnesses against him; to have compulsory process for obtaining witnesses in his favor, and to have the Assistance of Counsel for his defence.

This amendment proscribes when and how a trial must be conducted. Of course the money phrase in there is the "speedy" bit. This prevents the government from charging someone, then letting him rot in jail without ever giving him a trial.

But those charged are also guaranteed the following:

✓ an impartial jury,
✓ a trial in the geographic area where the crime was committed (this gives the accused a home-court advantage—remember, colonists were often shipped all the way back to England for trial—and allows for ready access to witnesses),
✓ prior notice of the charges so that a defense can be mounted,
✓ the ability to confront the witnesses that testify against them,
✓ a method of forcing witnesses to appear (i.e., subpoenas), and
✓ a lawyer.

Hopefully this amendment won't play a prominent role in your college career. If it does, I hope your coach finds you a good attorney.

SEVENTH AMENDMENT

In suits at common law, where the value in controversy shall exceed twenty dollars, the right of trial by jury shall be preserved, and no fact tried by a jury, shall be otherwise reexamined in any Court of the United States, than according to the rules of the common law.

There are two main facets to this amendment. The first is a person's right to a jury trial in civil (noncriminal) court cases. The founders set the bar for

this requirement at $20, and technically, if you really wanted to push the issue, I suppose you could constitutionally demand a jury trial over twenty bucks. Of course no one would go through the effort—mounting a jury trial costs tens of thousands of dollars in legal fees. Still, $20 remains the limit.

The second aspect of this amendment involves the inability of a federal court to second-guess a jury. The critical word in the phrase is *fact*—"no *fact* tried by a jury, shall be otherwise reexamined." This may seem wrong. Even the layest of laypeople knows that almost any court case can be appealed. True, but if a jury heard it, the case can only be appealed on the basis of errors of law rather than errors of fact.

What exactly does this mean? Issues of fact are the situational details that surround the controversy. Issues of law are the application of those facts to the relevant statute. Take a dog bite case as an example. Questions of fact would include things such as: Did the plaintiff provoke the dog? Did the owner have reason to believe the dog was dangerous? Was the leash used adequate? Once the jury decides these questions, no other court can overrule them. But a higher court can examine whether or not those facts were applied to the relevant laws correctly.

EIGHTH AMENDMENT

Excessive bail shall not be required, nor excessive fines imposed, nor cruel and unusual punishments inflicted.

As you will learn in chapter 13, "The Police," bail is a security deposit someone accused of a crime pledges to ensure they'll return for their trial. You pledge the money, and you're allowed to go free until trial. The Eighth Amendment guarantees that this security deposit will be proportionate to the crime. Imagine a system with no check in this area. A judge could set bail based on personal preference and keep low-level criminals in jail. In short, it would allow judges to circumvent the whole trial process and essentially punish people at whim.

The same fear is what motivated the prohibition against cruel and unusual punishments. Again, imagine a system where a judge could sentence you to fifty years, without parole, for speeding. Or could demand that your finger be cut off as punishment for a robbery conviction. Things could go amok pretty rapidly. States have sentencing guidelines and many criminal statutes contain maximum and minimum sentences to avoid such abuses, so there are more practical limits in this area. Even still, if a judge goes out of bounds, the defendant has constitutional recourse and can sue to have the sentence reduced.

Today, most of the discussion about cruel and unusual punishment revolves around the death penalty. The Supreme Court has gone back and forth on the issue over the last twenty-five years. They've stepped to the brink of

declaring the practice outright cruel and unusual, forcing revisions in how and when it can be administered, but have never banned it altogether.

NINTH AMENDMENT

The enumeration in the Constitution, of certain rights, shall not be construed to deny or disparage others retained by the people.

This is a cover-your-ass amendment. The framers feared that by listing specific rights in the Constitution it might be incorrectly assumed that the list was exhaustive. This amendment clears that up by stating that there are other rights retained by the people not listed here.

TENTH AMENDMENT

The powers not delegated to the United States by the Constitution, nor prohibited by it to the States, are reserved to the States respectively, or to the people.

This is the equivalent of the Ninth Amendment, but it protects the states' rights. Remember, in the postrevolutionary era, states' rights were hotly debated and vigorously protected. This reserves all functions and rights not specifically given to the federal government for the states.

What Really Is a Right or a Law?

That's the Bill of Rights—ten laws that set forth the most basic of American privileges. But what really is a law? It's seductive to simplify the concept by thinking it's nothing more than the rule that's written on the paper. But the statute itself is only a fraction of the story. Certainly, what's "on the books" and the drafters' intentions are the foundation of the laws as we know them. But the actuality of a law is the result of a long process that goes far beyond the static language. That's because laws are living, and constantly changing, entities.

Really, to understand a law is to understand the entire process that brought you to where you stand. Courts, from the smallest state court to the Supreme Court of the United States, constantly hear cases on, and thus redefine, the contours of what each law means. Governmental agencies and private actors then change their behavior based on their best guess as to what those redefinitions mean. But they're often no more than that—guesses.

This is because, when you get down to it, practical situations are unique. Laws are theoretical, and therefore, vague. In between the two, the theory of the law and its practical application, is this complicated, convoluted, and never-ending process of application and reinterpretation. Certainly there are bright line rules that need very little further explanation—we all know it's illegal to kill someone. But the majority of laws and situations are much

more obtuse. And even the seemingly simple laws, like those that prohibit murder, have very subtle and vague components.

The Bill of Rights is the perfect example of this. Take any clause of any amendment. Over the years it has probably spawned thousands, maybe hundreds of thousands, of court cases—each one further defining the application of the law to the real world, each one carving out yet another finite situation in which the law applies in a certain way.

To know the law is not just to know the words written on the page. It's a great start, to be sure. But to be able to really use the law, you need to know how those laws have been interpreted, limited, and defined in practice.

This is an important concept to understand as you read the rest of this book. The purpose of this text is to help you with the final, or most recent, step in this process—to help you make decisions about what to do and how to act in the face of a potential or actual legal dilemma. Whenever possible, I'll show you the bright line rules and say things like "don't ever do this" or "it's outright illegal to even think of doing that." But more often I'll offer guidelines and a brief explanation of this very process. I'll show you the basics of the theory so that you'll be able to apply it to your own situation. Yes, this places a little more of the burden on you. But by working this way, I'll be providing you with the fullest possible arsenal to protect your rights.

When to Make a Stand

There's a significant difference between having a right and being able to exercise it. Beyond that there is an equally large distinction between situations where it makes sense to exercise, or even mention, your rights and situations where it makes sense to save the argument for later.

Take voting rights, for example. Before the civil rights movement minorities in the Deep South had, ostensibly, the same right to cast a ballot as everyone else—guaranteed by law. But attempts to exercise those rights often fell flat, or worse, resulted in physical abuse. This is the classic example of the fact that all the rights in the world don't matter if the one person standing between you and your lawful due doesn't recognize them.

It's equally illustrative of the notion that there are times to make a stand for your rights and times to leave the battle for another day. Trying to explain the Constitution to a backwoods poll monitor with a shotgun would be foolhardy and dangerous. Likewise, a discussion of the fine points of the Seventh Amendment probably wouldn't deter a lynch mob.

Thankfully this example is largely a thing of the past. But there are still plenty of situations where the wisest and safest course of action will be to save a bold assertion of your rights for another day. In the law offices we used to call this knowing when to "lawyer up." We knew that in any argument—with the guy at the dry cleaners, the mechanic who fixed your

car, someone who keeps parking in your private spot—there was a specific time to play the lawyer card. If you did it too soon, sometimes your opponent would shut down and be more stubborn. Too late and you may have already lost. Sometimes it made sense not to let your foe know you were an attorney at all.

None of you are lawyers, but the same principles apply. When should you verbalize that you know your rights? Use common sense. Before you blurt out something along the lines of "I have rights," think about what you're doing. Think about whether or not that's actually going to help solve your problem. Sometimes it will. It's almost always a good idea to let the police know up front that they're dealing with someone who knows the rules. But often it will work against you. If you're talking with a professor about what you think is an unfair grade, leading with a Fifth Amendment argument will probably set an adversarial tone, rather than moving the negotiation to a place where you might get a good result.

And, of course, if you ever think that asserting your rights will put you in harm's way, protect yourself before your legal due. Rights are great, but not getting beat up is better.

CHAPTER 2
Your College

Your student handbook is a much better guide to life at college than the freshman facebook (although it's absolutely worthless when you're trying to identify who hit on you last night). You should get to know it—well. Until you graduate, those rules rank up there with the Ten Commandments.

Chapter Contents

If you've ever talked with an older person about their college days, you've probably noticed that—aside from the fact that everyone remembers his or her twenty-year-old self as smart, athletic, and good-looking—the campus atmosphere has changed drastically over the past few decades.

University students in the 1950s were subject to draconian rules and punishments. The school ruled with an iron fist both on and off campus. When my father was in college, possession of cigarettes was an offense that could result in expulsion. The administration even dictated which streets in the nearby town were acceptable places for female students to walk (no kidding).

Sometime in the sixties things began to change. The authoritarian role of the school slipped away and was replaced by an astoundingly laissez-faire attitude. Students were allowed to do almost anything they wanted. Alcohol and drugs were readily available and openly used. Outside of the classroom there were almost no rules whatsoever. (By the way, this is probably how it was when your parents went to college. So if they give you any crap about how you spend your time at school, you might want to ask some pointed questions about how they behaved during the years of tie-dye and other foolishness.)

Then, in the mid- to late eighties, another shift began. The schools began to regulate again, to make (and enforce) rules in an attempt to protect their students and decrease liability. In my years at college I watched this transformation take place right before my eyes. The administration was making changes on every front, but the ones we, the students, noticed most readily involved our social lives. The year before I started there was, essentially, no alcohol policy at all. Kegs were tapped on the quad, and students, be they sixteen or twenty-seven, could partake without fear of retribution. My freshman year saw a drastic change in the official line. We were told to "keep underage drinking in our rooms"—we didn't even have to close the door; we just couldn't cross the threshold into public space with an open container (talk about an arbitrary rule). By the time I was a senior, absolutely no underage drinking was allowed. RAs would literally bust parties and check IDs.

These changes in the college environment aren't particularly surprising. They closely reflect the broader cultural revolutions that each decade brought. Colleges and universities have always been on a separate, somewhat parallel, track of their own—a track that has, until very recently,

kept colleges practically immune from responsibility and almost entirely litigation-proof.

Pre-1960: The In Loco Parentis Era

From practically the beginning of the American educational system, colleges were thought to stand **in loco parentis** to their students. Since parents had almost absolute rule over their children, colleges and universities were afforded the same. To fully understand this legal doctrine you must remember that, for most of the history of America, parents were almost entirely immune from the law, both civilly and criminally, in regard to how they treated their children. Parents could do things like beat their children to death without any fear of criminal prosecution. Colleges were afforded almost the same immunity. Courts essentially stayed out of university affairs.

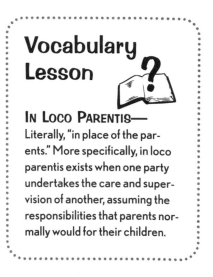

Vocabulary Lesson

IN LOCO PARENTIS—
Literally, "in place of the parents." More specifically, in loco parentis exists when one party undertakes the care and supervision of another, assuming the responsibilities that parents normally would for their children.

A 1913 case, *Gott v. Berea College*, illustrates this well. There, the college maintained a list of forbidden places in the student handbook. In the fall of 1911, a restaurant located directly across the street from the college was added to this list and students were told that if they went there they'd be expelled. During the first few days of the school year three students were actually kicked out for nothing more than enjoying delicious pancakes at said diner. Needless to say, after that, business at the diner dropped off significantly.

Justifiably pissed off, the owner sued the school, claiming they couldn't make a rule that forbade students from patronizing his business. The court responded with the in loco parentis justification, stating that colleges may "make any rule or regulation for the government or betterment of their pupils that a parent could for the same purpose" and said further that "whether the rules or regulations are wise or their aims are worthy is a matter left solely to the discretion of the authorities or parents, as the case may be."

Yes, believe it or not, the courts had armed universities with the kind of "because I said so" authority that had previously been the sole province of parents and schoolyard bullies.

What's worse, they gave schools this sweeping authority without attaching any liability whatsoever. When a rational person thinks about parental power, they generally consider the responsibility along with the control.

But that's a truly modern thought. It simply didn't apply to the 1920s, court-made college version of parenting. In fact, the most defining characteristic of the in loco parentis era was that colleges and universities were almost legally untouchable. Courts bent over backward to protect schools from liability. They often looked to the "stand-in parents" theory for justification, but when that didn't work, they offered colleges immunity from prosecution based on their status as charitable organizations or quasi-governmental institutions. Students lost limbs, eyes, and their lives and were expelled for talking to the wrong type of woman, going to the wrong store, and making too much noise in the dormitory halls. And, despite the fact that colleges had the ability to regulate the smallest detail of their students' lives, the courts held that the students (or their families in the case of the fatal mishaps) had absolutely no legal recourse.

Legally it was a strange era. But, thankfully, it didn't last much longer than the Edsel.

The Sixties and Seventies: Free Love, Free Speech, and More Freedom from Liability for Colleges

The advent of the sixties brought with it a student body that was of a very different mind than only a few years before. The hippies arrived and brought with them lava lamps and a new set of values. Their "hell no, we won't go" attitude was the seed for the modern era of student rights on campus.

At the same time, the laws surrounding families, charities, and the government were being reevaluated in the courts—in turn, changing the very models that courts had used to protect schools from legal liability. Parents were beginning to be held responsible for the well-being of their children, local governments were found to be legally accountable for negligent acts that harmed their citizens, and even charities—long entirely off-limits in the legal realm—were being sued for their wrongdoings and losing.

These two factors created a period of change and upheaval in higher-education law.

INTANGIBLE RIGHTS ON CAMPUS IN THE SIXTIES AND SEVENTIES

The first major victories for students were in the areas of constitutional rights and redress for economic harms (expulsion, discipline, etc.) on campuses—in other words, for intangible rights.

The first and most famous case involved six students who were expelled from Alabama State University for participating in local civil rights demonstrations. After the demonstration, the students were told in a somewhat vague letter from the president of the university that they had been expelled. There was never a hearing, or a meeting of any kind, where the students could present their side of the story. Even the letter that told them of their expulsion was silent as to why they had been kicked out. In short, they had received no process at all (remember this from the Fifth Amendment?). But then, why would a college grant a student due process before handing him walking papers? For 150 years schools had done as they pleased.

The decision in this case changed that forever. The court discarded the notion of in loco parentis outright and held that, since the college was a state entity, the Constitution full-on applied to their actions. This meant that the school owed the students some sort of process before expulsion or serious discipline. The decision left exactly what type of process would be put in place up to each school—certainly they weren't required to replicate the entire court system—but held that schools must give some chance for the student to be heard (we'll go into this in detail in chapter 10, "Disciplinary Proceedings").

Over time other courts expanded the idea to include free speech, free press, free assembly, and freedom from unreasonable searches and seizures. And soon thereafter, essentially the same guarantees were extended to private colleges and universities. The theories that brought these rights to the private sector are fairly cumbersome. In simple terms the courts reasoned that private schools were such an ingrained part of public life that they should be held to the same standards as public schools. They supported their findings with varying legal support—the inherent contract between the student and school, the amount of federal funding and support these private schools received, and the public perception of colleges as, well, public—but despite their differences, these cases consistently granted at least the most basic constitutional rights to students at private institutions.

LIABILITY FOR PHYSICAL INJURIES IN THE SIXTIES AND SEVENTIES

Imposing liability for personal student safety was more difficult. Despite some unbelievable actions on the part of administrators and professors, during the sixties and seventies and well into the eighties, schools were still held blameless for the injuries students incurred.

The facts of the cases of this time period read like scripts for gory movies. Students fell into crevasses after getting drunk on university-sponsored field trips, had grisly car accidents after boozing at on- and off-campus drinkfests, got their heads crushed in hazing rituals, and were injured or killed in any number of other gruesome ways.

In almost all of these instances, the colleges that bought the beer or failed to enforce state alcohol laws or encouraged fraternity antics got off scot-free. The theory was new: The courts were of the opinion that the students of this new era, with all of their fancy freedoms and rowdy behavior, were basically uncontrollable. But the outcome was the same: legal protection for the colleges from any kind of civil responsibility.

The Modern Era

This last vestige of protection, thankfully, didn't survive for very long. By the mid-1980s the process of erosion had begun. Only a decade later, with a few exceptions, colleges were being held liable for the harm they caused or should have prevented. The courts recognized the unique position and goals of the schools and afforded limited leeway based on those differences. But for the most part, universities could now be sued just like anybody else.

In legal terms the courts had, finally, recognized **duty** and therefore the possibility of **negligence** on the part of the universities. Negligence is probably a legal expression you've heard before. It's most often bandied in the context of slip-and-fall or other injury cases: the store was negligent because it didn't put signs up to warn me about the slippery floor; the landlord was negligent because he didn't properly salt my front steps and I fell; the bar was negligent because when I was trashed I tried to slide across the floor on a serving tray and went so fast that I hit the payphone on the other side of the room. And so on.

But negligence actually applies to a much larger portion of the **tort** suits than simply those where people fall down. Almost any time someone *unintentionally* harms another person the legal theory behind the lawsuit will be negligence.

Not surprisingly, most of what comes up in the college setting falls under the heading of negligence. Colleges don't often take affirmative steps to hurt their students. It's usually an error of some sort that results in lost eyes and such. The ins and outs of negligence can be very complicated, but at the base, four things have to happen for someone to be negligent. One, there has to be a duty.

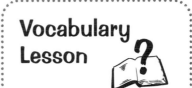

Vocabulary Lesson

TORT—Basically, anytime one person causes another any type of injury—physical, mental, emotional, monetary—a tort has been committed. Torts only exist in the realm of civil, not criminal, law. So while there are torts for injuring, or even killing, someone, the question at hand is: does the person who caused the injury owe the other any money for the damage they've done? Whether or not criminal punishments should be imposed isn't a part of the equation.

Two, that duty needs to be breached. Three, there has to be some sort of damage done. And four, the breach has to have been the cause of the damage.

☆ THE ELEMENTS OF ☆ A NEGLIGENCE CASE

1. A duty

2. Breach of that duty

3. Damage, which was

4. Caused by the breach

Take the first slip-and-fall case as an example. One, the grocery store has a duty to keep patrons safe. Two, they breached that duty by leaving a wet, slippery floor and not warning customers about it. Three, someone got hurt. And four, the store's failure to keep the floors dry is what caused the harm.

Simple, right?

The facts get more complicated. But when you get down to it, when you sue a school for harm it has done to you, this basic formula will almost always be applied.

When deciding one of these negligence cases courts usually look to off-campus legal theories to determine a college's duties and responsibilities. For example, students who live in a university-operated dormitory system have entered into something very similar to a landlord-tenant relationship with the school. Therefore, a school can be held liable for most things a landlord would: a robbery or assault due to an unfixed lock, an injury due to poorly maintained premises, damage to personal possessions due to broken plumbing. Case law about police forces and city governments inform decisions about campus safety and security. Where school activities are concerned, universities are treated as businesses and are required to use the same standard of reasonable care to protect their students, whether in phys-ed class, a chemistry lab, or on a field trip.

The one area in which universities have been able to hold on to some of their immunity from liability is alcohol-related injuries. Today, if a student is hurt any other way on campus, she has a very good chance of recovering damages. But if alcohol is part of the equation, the courts are much less likely to place blame on the college. Often the reasoning echoes the "students are uncontrollable" statements of the sixties. But a shift seems to be occurring. As time goes by, more and more students injured while under the influence are able to successfully sue their schools. But, overall, it's very hard for a drunken plaintiff to recover. The next decade will, likely, see a unified theory one way or the other emerge.

What Does All This Mean for You?

Here's where you stand:

CONSTITUTIONAL RIGHTS

As a college student in the new millennium, your constitutional rights are pretty well protected. This is more solidly established if you're at a public university rather than a private one, but the big hits of the Constitution—the First and Fifth Amendments—are usually enforceable.

SCHOOL LIABILITY FOR PHYSICAL INJURIES

In most other areas, your school's restrictions and responsibilities are evaluated based on how the school is acting. Courts look to off-campus models to define the higher-education law. Your school can act as many things over the course of a day. It is at once your landlord, your city government, a store, a restaurant, a business partner, and a transportation authority. You probably intuitively know what the limits of everyday businesses are. As a rule of thumb, try to think of your college on the same terms. The relationship is somewhat modified because of the school's lofty goal of providing you an education, but this methodology works as a very good starting point.

The Student Handbook: A Mini-Constitution

As you've probably realized by now, the legal foundations that establish your rights on campus are complex and somewhat murky. Higher-education law involves a mishmash of federal statutes, state laws, court decisions, and even British common law. Certainly there are large areas that are well-defined with bright-line rules. But for the most part, trying to determine the legal ramifications of a novel situation involves something akin to reading tea leaves. You do the best you can with the information you have and make a guess as to what the rules and liabilities are.

There is, however, one source of campus law that is definitive: the rules set forth in the student handbook published by the university. The student handbook is the single most important set of rules and regulations that you will encounter at college.

Strangely, most students aren't that familiar with their university handbook. Most have never flipped through it, let alone consult it on a regular basis. Don't be one of those uninformed people. Go get your handbook right now and keep it close. These rules are what you will be expected to live by and, if you're accused of something, they're what you'll have to show you didn't violate.

More importantly, the handbook forms a contract between you and the school. You can hold your college to whatever is published there. If, for example, it says students accused of cheating will be granted a hearing before being punished, then your school *has* to give you that hearing. If it says the school will protect the free speech of its students, then free speech rights *must* be afforded.

Do yourself a favor and take a look at your handbook before moving on to the next part of the book. Until you graduate, those rules are as important as the U.S. Constitution.

Part One
THE LAW IN THE CLASSROOM

CHAPTER 3

Your Professor

Don't ever think you'll be able to frighten, guilt, or bully a professor into changing a grade. He may seem like a pushover in class, but he has deep reserves of defenses that may surprise you. Do yourself a favor and don't go into a professor's office without substantial, credible evidence that your grade was undeserved.

Chapter Contents

Face it. Over the course of your college career, you're going to have a number of awkward and clumsy run-ins with your professors. I've certainly had my fair share of them, including one spectacularly embarrassing meeting with my Shakespeare professor, during which I absolutely blanked on, of all things, Shakespeare's name. I tried to cover by substituting phrases like "the author" or "him." Once I even referred to the Bard as "that guy."

Not my finest academic moment. But that's the point: We *all* get a bit tongue-tied when we're dealing with a member of the school's teaching elite. It's totally understandable. Professors are intimidating—they're old, smart, they've got degrees, elbow patches on their jackets. . . . But while respect and admiration are (sometimes) due, reverence and idolatry (and the anxiety that go along with them) generally aren't. So the next time you have to talk to one of your profs, try to put all that Intellectual Deity crap aside. Think of them as equals and peers—because believe it or not, that's probably how they think of you. Yes, they're really smart equals who expect you not to waste their time, but equals just the same.

General Guidelines on Dealing with Professors

That said, in the relationship between you and your professor, the prof is the one with almost all of the power. This may seem unfair. In fact, in many cases it is. But fairness doesn't change the dynamic. If you ever get into a struggle with one of your instructors, all of the presumptions will lie with him. This means that if you are to have any chance at all of getting your way, you're going to need to establish your position beyond any doubts.

I'm not saying that professors shouldn't ever be challenged. They're people just like everyone else. They make mistakes, sometimes are unfair, hold biases, let personal opinions get in the way, and do everything else any living, breathing person would do. What I am saying is this: If you plan on challenging a professor, be ready and be smart about it because when there's a doubt—and in many cases I mean only the tiniest scintilla of a doubt—the professor will be considered to be in the right. Centuries of submission to professors has institutionalized the practice. Depending on the issue, this is more or less true today. In the classroom itself, the professor's say is almost absolute, especially in the areas of pedagogy, curriculum, and grading. Outside, their power is a bit more reined in. But they still hold many of the cards.

This puts you, the student, in a significantly compromised bargaining position. You can't really threaten to raise hell with the administration because, chances are, they'll side with your teacher, not you. In practical terms this means that resolving a problem directly with a professor is usually your best bet for reaching any kind of satisfactory result. The list of things a professor might be willing to do for you is almost always much more extensive than those she can be *forced* to do for you.

So take the first rounds of negotiation—the first meetings with the professor herself—very seriously. Be very prepared. Be willing to compromise. Be open to ideas and suggestions. In short, do everything you can to resolve the situation at that point because the going only gets harder once you walk down the hall and engage the department chair or dean.

Here are a few specific tips to keep in mind the next time you've got a prof problem:

> ## Your Lawyer Says:
>
> **TRY TO WORK IT OUT!**
> The best bet for resolving most disputes with a professor is working it out between the two of you. Once you involve other people, like a dean or department chair, it may get much harder for you to "win." So be sure to prepare well and try hard at the one-on-one level because the going will only get worse as you move along.

DON'T BE CONFRONTATIONAL

This is almost always good advice. With a professor it's a downright necessity. Teachers at all levels are inundated with requests and complaints from students. The majority of these are, as you can imagine, unfounded. So when someone comes in and demands something, a professor's knee-jerk reaction will be to simply shut down and say no.

Imagine that you're talking to a professor about a grade you think is unfair. You could start the conversation by blurting out "I want my grade changed." But think about the climate that creates. It immediately puts the professor on the defensive. A much better approach would be to start with a question, like "How much did class participation factor into final grades?" Your professor will immediately know what you're getting at, but you'll have set the tone for a negotiation rather than an argument.

I know this all sounds like some sort of 1970s psychobabble "carefrontation" crap. But I'm not telling you to behave this way because it's nice or proper—I'm telling you to do this because it's the best way to get results. Like I said above, fights with professors are really hard to win, so don't fight. Talk.

This should almost go without saying, but never go in and try to resolve a situation with a hot head. Whatever the problem is, chances are taking a day or two to calm down will help you. Don't ever storm into your professor's office steaming mad (actually don't storm anywhere around campus; it's bad form). No one makes a good impression, or persuasive argument, when they're pissed as hell. So settle down before you do anything.

Finally, if you're planning on going to your professor to make one of those stupid, unfounded complaints like "I never got Cs in high school" or "So what if I was drunk in class? I still participated, didn't I?"—don't. You're just going to ruin it for the other guy who has a legitimate complaint.

STROKE THEIR EGOS

Professors are *almost* normal people—but, unlike the majority of the population, most of them have very healthy egos. Take this into consideration whenever you're trying to resolve a situation. Your prof's got a Ph.D., has been teaching for a while, and has probably published a bunch of articles and a few books. If you had been teaching for thirty years, or even thirty days, would you want some undergrad coming into your office and acting like they knew better than you? Of course not.

If you're going to do anything that could be interpreted as a challenge to a professor's area of expertise or method of teaching, do so very carefully. Taking the wrong tone could result in an instructor that's dug her heels in and a worse result for you.

It's a delicate balance to strike, but you need to subtly move your agenda forward while deferring to the professor's authority and ego. Try to confine your complaints to the specific matter at hand rather than make broad generalizations about your teacher's shortcomings. When possible, give her an out—a way to save face and maintain superiority while giving in to your requests. Easier said than done, I know. In fact, sometimes this type of maneuvering simply isn't possible. But when you're preparing for your meeting, take this into consideration and use it as a guide.

TAKE THE DEAL

If your professor offers a deal that's close to what you want, it's usually a good idea to take it. You aren't negotiating with a car dealer here. You can't simply go down the street to a competing dealership and see what they have to offer. You're stuck in negotiations with the guy across the desk and, as I've said before, the going will only get harder the further up the chain of authority you climb.

I've also never known a professor to lowball on the first offer. Chances are, that first offer is going to be awfully close to the best offer. You'll never hear your instructor say, for instance, "An A? I don't know. I'll have to check with my manager to see if I can do that." So don't consider an offer of a compromise the beginning of a negotiation. You can probably get away with a bit of haggling right on the spot—but not much more.

Getting a Grade Changed

Grades are the most common source of conflict between students and professors. This makes sense: Good grades are one of the principal pursuits of college. At least they're supposed to be. Of course for most of us, they're incredibly important on the day they're handed out and easily forgotten during the prior four months. Loads of things take precedence earlier in the semester: members of the opposite sex, alcoholic indulgence, *The Simple Life*, alcoholic indulgence while watching *The Simple Life* with a member of the opposite sex . . .

Unfortunately, getting a professor to change a grade is incredibly difficult to do. For starters, the assignment of grades is an area where professors are given almost total control. This is in part due to the concept of academic freedom (which we'll discuss later in the chapter) and in part due to the fact that you and your professor are the only two people who really know what happened all semester. Second-guessing by a disinterested third party like a dean or department chair is impractical. Professors know this and will be steadfast in their grading decisions. In fact, without really good evidence that your grade was unfair, it's nearly impossible to frighten, guilt, bully, or coerce a professor to change a grade. So, if the reason your grade is lower than you'd like is due to too much time with Paris and Nicole, it's probably not worth it to even try.

Your Lawyer Says:

PROOF FOR YOUR PROF IS KEY

Don't ever walk into a professor's office and try to get a grade changed off the cuff. Do your homework, so to speak, and craft a fully developed argument with supporting proof. Unplanned pleas get very calculated "nos" from professors.

STEP ONE: DETERMINE THE PROFESSOR'S METHODOLOGY

The first thing you're going to have to do is figure out exactly how the grade was calculated. There are really only two places to get this information: the syllabus or straight from the professor's mouth.

Most of the time, the syllabus that your instructor handed out at the beginning of the semester will have some discussion of how grades will be computed. It can be anything from a simple breakdown of the grading process—40 percent for papers, 10 percent for class participation, 20 percent for the midterm, and 30 percent for the final—to a meticulous point-by-point, class-by-class accounting.

If you can't track down a copy of your syllabus (be sure to check online), you might have to go ask your professor in person how the grade was calculated. He'll probably know what's going on and may try to confront you right then and there about your grade. It's not wise to engage at this point— you're not prepared yet. Just say that you wanted to check something, that it's not a big deal, but you'd really appreciate the information.

While we're on the subject, it bears mentioning that the proper time to examine and evaluate the way your grade will be computed is sometime *before* you get your report card. Make it a habit to carefully inspect the grading policy as soon as the semester starts. If it's not in the syllabus, ask about it and write down what you hear. Not only will it help in the course of study, it will make your life a lot easier later on if you've got a problem with your grade.

Grading Policy Gray Areas   Smart professors intentionally leave vagaries in their stated grading policies. Hell, if you were the master of your own universe, you would, too. It's always best to leave yourself some leeway. If you're confronted with such a policy—one with undefined terms, hazy delineations, or CYA phrases, like "the instructor reserves the right to change the grading policy without notice," do your best to pin your professor down as to their exact meanings. Again, this is the type of thing that is much better dealt with at the term's opening rather than after you've gotten a D. But no matter when you launch your fact-finding mission, be delicate about it: at the semester's start, you don't want to establish yourself as the class asshole. In the face of a grading grievance, you don't want to annoy the person to whom you'll be appealing in a few days.

For Whom the Bell Curve Tolls   If the policy mentions anything about grading on a "bell curve," or if curves come up at all in relation to your grade, pay close attention. Bell curves are almost always unfair. They assume there will be a "normal" distribution of achievement (and therefore grades) among the students in a class—a small percentage will excel and score in the absolute top echelons, the majority will be clumped in the middle, and the remaining students, a number equal to the high achievers, will fail miserably.

Why exactly this distribution is considered "normal" has always escaped me. Maybe, *maybe*, the range of knowledge in a classroom at the *beginning* of the semester would fall into the bell curve mold. But by the end of the semester, if the teacher's done anything at all, the averages should be shifted to the right side of the equation. The students should all know far more than they did when they started.

So why, after taking all the trouble to instruct you, would a professor force you into some mold that probably didn't even really apply before the class started? It's a good question, and, if your class is going to be graded on a bell curve, one I think you should ask your professor as soon as possible.

STEP TWO: CALCULATE YOUR GRADE ON YOUR OWN

This part is pretty self-explanatory. Gather all the graded materials you received during the course of the semester and run the numbers yourself. *Do not* simply glance at your work and make an estimate. Calculate the averages exactly as delineated in the grading policy. Make estimations (honest ones) in subjective areas like class participation.

If you're dealing with letter grades, be sure that you're using the correct numeric conversions for the grades. Most schools use the standard 4.0 conversion, but many use a 4.3 or other scale. The wrong scale will result in an incorrect calculation. Check your student handbook or ask the registrar's office if you don't know what the scale is.

Now just see where you come out. Maybe it seemed like you were pulling a solid A all semester when you were actually barely making a B. If your calculation comes within a few decimal points of the grade your professor awarded, then you've probably already reached the end of the road. The small discrepancy is probably due to something that you didn't estimate correctly or a factor you didn't account for. If you really want to push the issue, go ahead and make an appointment with your professor and ask about it. But don't get your hopes up—there's very little chance that you're going to be able to get the grade changed at all.

STEP THREE: ASSESS YOUR NEXT STEP

Most schools have formal grade challenge procedures in place. They spell out steps that need to be taken to lodge a formal complaint. Usually the process ends with a hearing—either in front of a student or faculty board—or a departmental review of the grade. The actual steps and procedures vary significantly from school to school, but almost all require that the student consult with the professor as the first step.

If you've gotten to this point and still think that there's something fishy going on with your marks, you certainly have the option to begin the formal grievance procedures. I absolutely think that you should find out what they are—there may be a statute of limitations and other rules that you'll need to be aware of as you continue your quest. But in most situations filing a formal complaint this early on is foolhardy.

Even if your school's policy doesn't require that you try to work the conflict out with your instructor, you should give it a shot. Once you play the grievance card your professor is going to dig her heels in hard. What could have been between you and your professor will now be between you, your professor, and all of her peers. No teacher wants to look like a pushover in front of her colleagues. In fact no one employed in any profession wants that.

Second, you don't want to get a reputation among the faculty members as a complainer. Filing a formal complaint will guarantee that your other (present and future) professors will know about the affair, which could tarnish your name as a student and hurt you in the future.

So at this point, keep the whole matter between you and your instructor. Have your discussions behind closed doors and don't talk to anyone else about what's going on. Keeping the deal as quiet as possible will only help you.

STEP FOUR: PREPARE AND APPROACH

The next step is to talk to your professor and state your case. As you've probably gathered from the many explicit statements that appear earlier in this chapter, the meeting between you and your professor is probably *the best chance you'll ever have to get your grade changed*. So don't blow it by going in unprepared.

Take the meeting very seriously. Prepare for it as if it were an oral presentation for class. Make an outline of the key points. Plan carefully what you're going to say and, most importantly, be able to back up your points with cold, hard facts. You might even want to practice in front of a friend.

If there are any written materials that back up your position, make copies to hand over to your instructor at the appropriate times. Putting something in writing makes things seem more real. This is a trick used by trial attorneys—a written document is always more believable than someone's oral statement. Juries love to hold things, to examine them, to see facts in black and white. Your prof is probably a little more savvy than the average juror, but the theory still applies.

STEP FIVE: MORE SERIOUS ACTIONS

If after meeting with your professor, you're still stuck with the sucky grade and think you've been railroaded, your only option is to move up the chain.

If your school has a formal grievance procedure, now is the time to avail yourself of it. You've already done all the hard work, so you shouldn't have any trouble crafting a well-written statement or making a case in front of a board. You might want to give your prof one more chance before you start the ball rolling, though. Stop by his office and say, "I just wanted to let you know that I'm going to start formal grade grievance proceedings today and wanted to make sure that there isn't any way we could work this out on our own." Who knows? Given the choice between a pain-in-the-ass hearing and changing your B- to a B+, he may just opt for the latter.

If your school doesn't have any formal procedures in place, your next step is the department chair. Make the same presentation you made to

Holy Shit! I Got a C in Philosophy!
A Decision Tree to Help You Challenge a Low Grade

START HERE

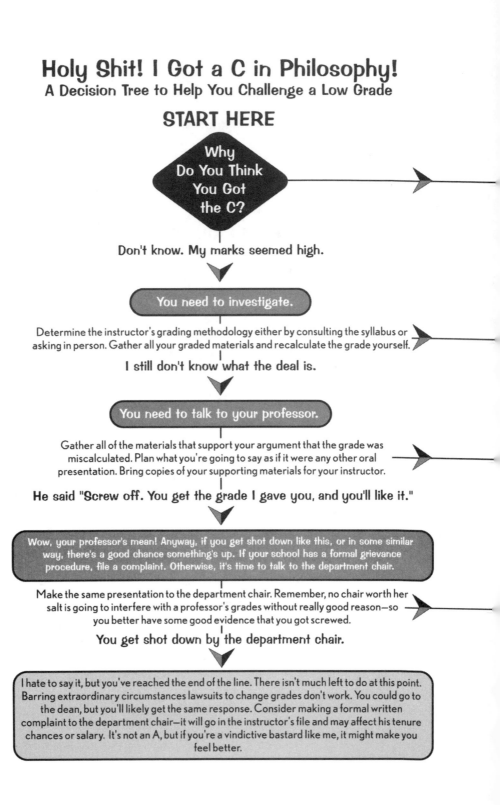

Why Do You Think You Got the C?

Don't know. My marks seemed high.

You need to investigate.

Determine the instructor's grading methodology either by consulting the syllabus or asking in person. Gather all your graded materials and recalculate the grade yourself.

I still don't know what the deal is.

You need to talk to your professor.

Gather all of the materials that support your argument that the grade was miscalculated. Plan what you're going to say as if it were any other oral presentation. Bring copies of your supporting materials for your instructor.

He said "Screw off. You get the grade I gave you, and you'll like it."

Wow, your professor's mean! Anyway, if you get shot down like this, or in some similar way, there's a good chance something's up. If your school has a formal grievance procedure, file a complaint. Otherwise, it's time to talk to the department chair.

Make the same presentation to the department chair. Remember, no chair worth her salt is going to interfere with a professor's grades without really good reason—so you better have some good evidence that you got screwed.

You get shot down by the department chair.

I hate to say it, but you've reached the end of the line. There isn't much left to do at this point. Barring extraordinary circumstances lawsuits to change grades don't work. You could go to the dean, but you'll likely get the same response. Consider making a formal written complaint to the department chair—it will go in the instructor's file and may affect his tenure chances or salary. It's not an A, but if you're a vindictive bastard like me, it might make you feel better.

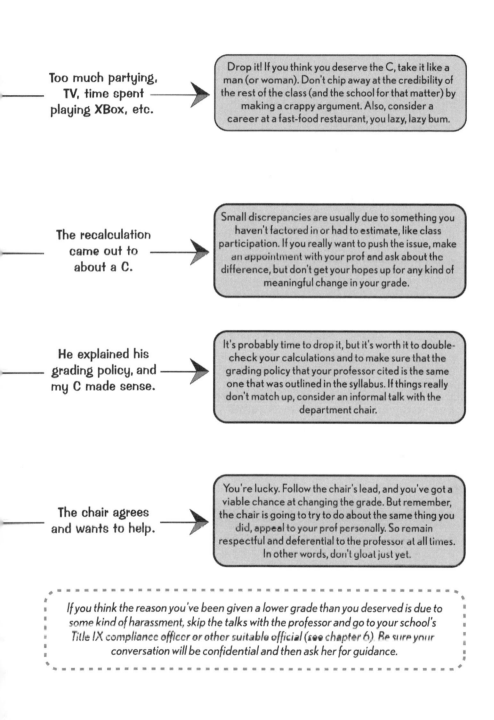

Too much partying, TV, time spent playing XBox, etc. → Drop it! If you think you deserve the C, take it like a man (or woman). Don't chip away at the credibility of the rest of the class (and the school for that matter) by making a crappy argument. Also, consider a career at a fast-food restaurant, you lazy, lazy bum.

The recalculation came out to about a C. → Small discrepancies are usually due to something you haven't factored in or had to estimate, like class participation. If you really want to push the issue, make an appointment with your prof and ask about the difference, but don't get your hopes up for any kind of meaningful change in your grade.

He explained his grading policy, and my C made sense. → It's probably time to drop it, but it's worth it to double-check your calculations and to make sure that the grading policy that your professor cited is the same one that was outlined in the syllabus. If things really don't match up, consider an informal talk with the department chair.

The chair agrees and wants to help. → You're lucky. Follow the chair's lead, and you've got a viable chance at changing the grade. But remember, the chair is going to try to do about the same thing you did, appeal to your prof personally. So remain respectful and deferential to the professor at all times. In other words, don't gloat just yet.

If you think the reason you've been given a lower grade than you deserved is due to some kind of harassment, skip the talks with the professor and go to your school's Title IX compliance officer or other suitable official (see chapter 6). Be sure your conversation will be confidential and then ask her for guidance.

your professor and see what she has to say about it. If she decides to be your ally, follow her lead; she's probably got a good chance of getting you where you want to be.

If she blows you off, you can move up to the next level, the dean of students. Go through the same steps and see what happens. To be honest, at this point your chances of getting the grade changed are even lower, but the dean may be able to work out some other kind of deal—such as offering you the option to take the class over with a different professor. Keep an open mind to these more creative solutions.

ENDGAME

Eventually, either your grade will be changed or you'll run out of administrative options. Unfortunately, if you had your say in front of the school's upper echelon and received no satisfaction, the game's pretty much over.

It's tempting to consider suing the school and letting the courts decide what's fair. But put that thought out of your head right now. It simply won't work. Barring extreme circumstances, no one has ever successfully sued a school to get a grade raised. Yes, you read correctly: There is not a single instance in our entire court system's history where a court has sided with a student in a commonplace grading grievance. Certainly, countless grades have been changed through other methods, but the courts stay out of academic matters.

Unless your parents have loads of money and are willing to donate a new science building or field house to the school, you're probably just going to have to suck it up and accept the grade. If you really do think you were treated unfairly, take the time to write a formal letter of complaint and ask that it be placed in the professor's file. It won't do anything to get your grade changed, but if the instructor is a junior professor, it will be reviewed when he or she is up for tenure, and even for tenured professors a negative letter like that could affect future promotions or salary increases. It's no A, but it's something, right?

Curriculum and Classroom Behaviors
INADEQUATE COVERAGE OF THE COURSE MATERIAL

Most of the time a lame professor is a welcome break from the usual rigors of classwork. But every once in a while you'll actually want to learn something—something specific. What if you come to find that it's not going to be covered in the class you've signed up for? Can you force your professor to change his plans to include what you want?

Unfortunately course coverage, like grading, is an area that falls squarely into the realm of professorial privilege. They're the experts on the subject, so they're the ones who get to decide what's important and what's not so important. And often, lesson outlines are developed by the entire department—especially in lower-level courses. Asking for an overhaul of a survey course usually means taking on not only your personal professor, but a majority of the department as well.

So unless your professor's gone somewhat off the deep end, you probably can't make much more than a general complaint. For example: If your physics instructor decides to shorten the discussion of Avogadro's hypothesis to one day so that more time can be spent on translational kinetic energy, it's probably well within his rights. But if he spends roughly half of every class talking about Jackie O's hat collection, you've probably got grounds to get things changed.

Exactly where the line of acceptable divergence lies is hard to determine. Instructors might come at a subject matter in an unorthodox way using seemingly unrelated materials. This is especially true in the liberal arts. A literature professor could, justifiably, have you read works that fall outside the pertinent period to show you the foundations of what you're studying. Still, if you signed up for a course in the modern novel and there's nothing more recent than Hawthorne on the reading list, you should speak up—first to your professor, then to the department chair if your complaints aren't addressed.

Of course, it's a little different if the syllabus and your actual class experience bear little resemblance to one another. Technically, your syllabus creates a contract between the students and the professor and, in turn, between the students and the school. This is especially true when the syllabi are available before the beginning of the semester. If you can point to significant discrepancies between how the course was "advertised" and how it's actually being taught, the school should make amends. They may not force the professor to rework his teaching mid-semester, but you may be offered the option of a directed study or a second chance to take the course with a different professor.

PREPARATORY CLASSES

Test prep classes are a different story altogether. Universities don't often get into the business of out-and-out test preparation—they generally leave it to outside third parties that specialize in standardized tests and certifications. But if you do enroll in a course or program whose purpose is to prepare you for some sort of test, you can hold the school to it. This works much better on the micro, rather than the macro, level. It would be hard to force a law or medical school to change its entire curriculum based on the contents of the bar exam or the medical board, for example. But at the undergraduate and the course level, it works. If there is some sort of standardized test looming in your near future—teaching, engineering, flight certification, or the like—your school probably should be working to get you ready.

43

Of course, this is going to take a bit of legwork on your part. Early on in your academic career take the initiative to find out what kind of test will confront you in the collegiate afterlife. Investigate what's covered and compare it to the education you're getting. If you sincerely think that you're not getting the instruction you'll need to make the grade, complain. This is generally the type of thing that is best brought up with someone who ranks relatively high up in the department.

A WORD ON ACADEMIC FREEDOM

If you're an undergrad, here is the quick and bad news: You don't have any academic freedom. Sorry. Students often cite it as one of the reasons they should be able to say or do something—why they should be able to write a paper about a certain topic or guide the discussion to a certain place. But in actuality, it rarely offers any support for their actions.

These mistakes are totally understandable. Academic freedom is probably the most misused term in higher education because it's an incredibly complex concept. It regularly baffles some of the country's best lawyers and judges.

Unfortunately, academic freedom is something that protects professors, not students. Unfair, maybe, but the real point of academic freedom is to protect researchers and teachers seeking and teaching what they believe to be the truth. This requires that teachers be able to put forth controversial, new, even seemingly ridiculous ideas (remember at one point the idea of a spherical earth was ridiculous) without punishment. And, peripherally, it requires that professors be able to teach those truths in the way they best see fit.

So, undergrads, chances are if you're even considering letting the words "academic freedom" escape your lips in protest, be prepared to be shot down quickly and completely. If you really want to go off on your own and study something funky, there are usually ways to do that—a directed study, senior project, or other nontraditional course. Exercise your intellectual freedom (because that's really what you're talking about) there. Don't even try in a conventional class.

As a graduate student your piece of the academic freedom pie is a bit larger, but not much. You're still under the tutelage of your advisers. This is true both in respect to your research and your in-class actions. Your professors are there to guide you, so if you stray too far beyond the constraints of their guidance, they can refuse to award you a degree—and academic freedom won't be able to save you.

WEIRD CLASSROOM RULES

Professors can be a strange lot. They can also have some very strange and oppressive in-class rules. I've heard hundreds of them over the past few years. Most are pretty mundane—"no gum chewing," "no hats," "no food," and so on. But they can get utterly bizarre: "Perfume or cologne are not allowed in my classroom"; "All hickies and other blemishes must be covered with a Band-Aid"; and, my personal favorite, "If you're more than five minutes late to class, you have to sit on the floor for the remainder of the class period."

Can your professor make and enforce any of these seemingly silly rules? It's a close call, but the technical answer is probably no. Can and should you do anything about it? Well, it depends.

Professors are given a lot of latitude when it comes to the classroom. Of course, their rights aren't absolute. There's a continuum. As we've already discussed, at the most protected end are the central components of instruction—pedagogy, grading, and course coverage. At the other are things that have absolutely nothing to do with teaching.

A request (and that's really what it is) that students not wear hats or too much Brut falls toward the nonteaching side. But it might be close enough to the middle to offer the professor some protection. Maintaining a cap- and fragrance-free classroom isn't paramount to the learning process, but your prof could probably make a passable (albeit antiquated) argument about respect and the learning environment to support her rule.

But the stranger the rule, the less support it will get from the administration. This is especially true if the rule is somehow demeaning to the students—such as being forced to sit on the floor.

No matter how benign the rule is, if push came to shove and your grade was lowered based entirely on headdress, perfume, exposed hickies, or something similarly strange, your professor would probably run into trouble. I doubt any dean would support that kind of action. Of course, since most grading at the college level is subjective, your prof will never have to say that you were penalized for your hat. She could just give you poor marks for class participation, or even grade your papers lower. Then the matter of your grade becomes relatively untouchable. I'm not saying that a professor would do such petty or deceptive things, but why find out?

My point is: Challenging a professor over something small probably isn't worth the risk or the effort. But if the rule is hard to bear, step up and complain. Make an appointment and ask your instructor to support her silly rules with something other than "I don't like hats" or "perfume is smelly." Do it politely, but question the instructor's position and offer your own. If you can make a cogent argument for your side of things, you might be able to sway your prof and get the rule changed. And of course, if you really want to push the issue, you can always work your way up the chain of command if you can't make headway with your instructor.

Romantic Relationships with Professors

It's a cliché practically as old as clichés themselves. From the ancients to today, romance between students and professors has been a standby of the educational world. Socrates himself—the prototypical professor—engaged in sexual relationships with many of his students. Many scholars have theorized that, had Socrates attracted a less virile and politically ambitious group of admirers, he never would have caught the eye of the courts and never would have been sentenced to death.

Today's punishments are far less severe than a cup of hemlock. Most schools have astonishingly lenient policies about student-teacher romances. Firings for infractions are very rare. In fact, most schools have no official policy at all, just an off-the-record warning that such things are "frowned upon."

To find out what your school's policy is, you'll need to check the student handbook. If the school has adopted anything official, it will be included there. There are a few common types of sexual fraternization policies:

1. *Outright Bans*. Some schools simply ban any type of romantic contact between students and professors. These types of policies are very rare.
2. *Supervisory Bans*. This type of policy only bans relationships where the professor is in a position to supervise or evaluate the student. In other words, teachers can't date people they will be grading. Generally, the student and professor are given options about how to remedy the situation, like dropping the class, having another professor grade the work, and so on. Some policies also allow the professor to continue to grade the student if they get the permission of the department chair (weird, I know).
3. *General Discouragement*. A majority of schools aren't even willing to go so far as to ban sex with supervisory professors. Many simply have a general statement that the school looks poorly upon these types of things.
4. *No Policy*. This is probably the most common—simply no written policy at all. Chances are the school doesn't really want teachers shagging their students, but they're not willing to put it down in writing.

Why are schools so relaxed about this? I don't know. As a lawyer it makes me nervous for the schools. They're open to all sorts of trouble if (or more likely when) one of these relationships goes sour. But, as I've said before, I don't draft college policies—I just teach kids how to get around them.

That said: This isn't one of the loopholes that I would recommend taking advantage of. Dating is difficult to begin with. When a relationship involves a power differential as significant as the student-teacher dynamic, it's nearly impossible. Anyone who's been around colleges enough can also tell you that these types of affairs generally end badly. Sure, every academic department has one or two stories of the freshman and professor who fell in love, dated secretly for four years, and are still happily married today. But those are by far the exceptions, not the rule.

CHAPTER 4

Academic Dishonesty

Handing in the same (or almost the same) paper for two classes is a form of academic dishonesty called "dovetailing." It's not quite as bad as buying your thesis from some guy on eBay, but it's still unethical. So when a professor asks you to write a paper, write one.

Chapter Contents

According to every recent study, college students cheat big time. A 1999 survey taken by Duke University's Center for Academic Integrity (www.academicintegrity.org) found that 75 percent of college students participate in some sort of cheating during their time at school. A full third of the students surveyed admitted to "serious" cheating on a test, and about half said that they participated in significant dishonesty in written assignments.

And that poll only measured acts of intentional (and self-reported) cheating. A lot of the incidents of academic dishonesty are unintended—due to carelessness or ignorance of the rules. My point: You guys are deep into this crap. So read on and read carefully because, more than any other chapter in the book, this stuff is probably going to come up in your academic career.

What Exactly Is Academic Dishonesty?

The best way to avoid an accusation of academic dishonesty is to steer clear of even the appearance of impropriety. So you need to truly understand what constitutes each type of infraction. Every school's policy is different. Wording and coverage vary. And some schools have less comprehensive policies that may not specifically discuss a few of the less in-your-face types of violations. But the following, all-inclusive list should still act as your guide no matter how lax your school's policy is. Everything discussed below is, at its base, dishonest.

CHEATING

Often, cheating is used as a catch-all word for any act of academic dishonesty. I use it that way throughout this chapter. But in the vernacular it's a more concise type of infraction. Cheating is the *use of unauthorized materials in an academic exercise*. This includes

- ✓ *Using a crib sheet on a test*. Whether it's old school—a tiny scrap of paper with microscopic writing—or employs some new technology like a Palm Pilot or Blackberry, it's cheating.
- ✓ *Out-and-out copying*. Either during an examination or for homework, with or without the original author's permission, if all you're doing is writing down someone else's answers, you're cheating.

✓ *Using prepared answers or work.* Things like looking up the answers in the teacher's manual or reading CliffsNotes instead of the assigned work are prohibited.

✓ *Looking at old tests.* Some teachers allow this, but most don't. And, really, who asks permission before they rifle through the old test file at their fraternity?

✓ *Unauthorized collaboration.* There's a line somewhere between working together, which is usually acceptable, and splitting up the assignment so that everyone does a fraction of the work. It's hard to define exactly, but your conscience will tell you when you've crossed over.

PLAGIARISM

In its simplest terms, plagiarism is using someone else's ideas, words, or line of thought without giving them credit. In ethical terms it's intellectual theft—taking the work of someone else and pretending it's your own. As you can imagine, this broad definition encompasses a variety of specific behaviors:

Complete Plagiarism   The most obvious instances of plagiarism are when an entire piece is used. Students simply take a paper that someone else wrote, put their name and the applicable course number on the cover, and hand it in. I can't imagine that anyone wouldn't know that this is a form of plagiarism, but this list is, as I said, all-inclusive. So here's the most obvious entry.

At the college level students usually use papers from friends or siblings. But some are dumb enough to buy them from "professional" sources. When I was a student, you could always find advertisements in the back of *Rolling Stone* magazine selling term papers (they're still there). Today much of the industry has moved online. Do a quick search on Yahoo, and you'll get a few million results.

Two kinds of purchased papers are available: file papers and custom research. File papers are boilerplate works that are sold and resold countless times. Because they get so much use, they're generally pretty cheap. Some sites even offer a bunch of these papers for free. Custom research is work that is, theoretically, written specifically at a student's request. In practice they're about the same thing. New "custom" papers are almost always immediately added to the files. So your very special essay, written just for you, will probably be hitting other campuses (and maybe your own) faster than you can say "rip-off."

Needless to say, it's a very bad idea to buy a paper from one of these services. First, the papers are often very poorly written. These companies aren't looking to build a long-term, loyal clientele. They want to sell you one paper, make a quick buck, and never deal with you again.

Second, a lot of those file papers have made the rounds many, many times before (especially the free ones). Your professor may have seen that *exact* paper before. Or worse yet, another copy of it may have been handed in with yours. The chances of getting caught are dangerously high.

Finally, why would you ever give your credit card number to one of these places? It's not uncommon for these companies to grossly overcharge their customers. Then, when the students complain, the company threatens to notify the school about the purchased paper.

Paragraph, Phrase, or Word Theft You don't have to steal a whole paper to be guilty of plagiarism. In fact, sometimes the use of a single word is enough.

The use of any *identifiable words or phrases* without giving the original author credit is plagiarism. This microversion is also called apt-phrase plagiarism. Obviously there are certain things that can't be broken down any further or stated in any other way, but in almost any piece of writing there will be key phrases and words that sort of belong to the original author. For example if your source said:

    New images of Jupiter's moon Europa show an icy sur-
    face riddled with cracks and fissures. These breaks
    in the ice are a clue that water may exist there.

And you wrote in your paper:

    Recent photos taken of Europa's surface show that the
    ice is **riddled** with fractures, a good clue that water
    may be present.
    Source, *Dull Book About Planets*, by . . .

. . . you'd have plagiarized. Even though a source is cited, the word *riddled* should be in quotation marks because it's the work of the original author. This is an extreme example, to be sure. It's just one word in an otherwise well paraphrased and properly cited passage. Most professors would probably let it slide even if they did notice it. But anytime you take a part of someone else's writing, a part that has personality, so to speak, it's technically plagiarism.

Mosaic Plagiarism Mosaic plagiarism is actually an offshoot of word theft. Here the student steals words or phrases, then embeds them in their own writing without using quotation marks. It creates the literary equivalent of a mosaic: little pieces of someone else's writing strung together to create a whole.

Suppose the following (very accurate) paragraph is your source material:

    C. L. Lindsay, the author of this book, is without a
    doubt one of the sexiest men in the world. True, he

has yet to appear in *People* magazine's 50 Most
Beautiful People issue, but this is due to their unfair bias toward people who are "famous" and "good-
looking." Lindsay's attractiveness transcends those
silly societal constraints. To fully understand
C. L.'s sexual prowess one needs to think outside of
the box and take into account his dazzling intellect,
his razor-sharp wit, and his enduring modesty.

The following paragraph shows what mosaic plagiarism taken from the source above might look like.

C. L. Lindsay is truly an attractive man. His appeal
transcends **those silly societal constraints** that affect most. He has a **dazzling intellect**, a **razor-sharp
wit**, and **enduring modesty**.
Source, *C. L. Lindsay: A Man among Men*, by . . .

The phrases in bold should be in quotation marks because, again, they are the original author's words. It's the same as word or phrase theft, just with a concentration of infractions that form a mosaic of the original work.

False Paraphrasing   False paraphrasing is a direct quote masquerading as a paraphrased passage. It occurs when you quote material directly from a source, cite the source, but don't put the materials in quotation marks. It appears to whoever is reading the piece that you've paraphrased the origi-nal author's work, but in actuality you've used their exact words.

Here's an example using the same source material:

To fully understand C. L.'s sexual prowess one
needs to think outside of the box and take into account his dazzling intellect, his razor-sharp wit,
and his enduring modesty.
Source, *C. L. Lindsay: A Man among Men*, by . . .

If this appeared in your paper, it would be an instance of false paraphras-ing. The work is cited correctly, but this is a direct quote. The absence of quotation marks makes it academically dishonest.

Footnote Theft   You don't have to take actual words from an author to plagiarize. Taking other products of their work, including their research, is also plagiarism.

Footnote theft is using the footnotes or material quoted in a source as if they were the results of your own research. We've all been there. You find a perfect article in an academic journal that discusses a lot of the things that your paper covers. The article includes passages, properly cited pas-sages, from a number of other works. If you simply copy the quotes or

Academic Dishonesty

paraphrased materials—citations and all—from the article and incorporate them in your own paper, you're stealing the original author's work.

You can certainly use the author's research to further your own—track down copies of what he cited, read them, and pull your own quotes from them. But just appropriating his work and including it in your paper is plagiarism.

I know, the distinction is a bit, um, academic. You're thinking, "All I'm going to do is get the source, then take the same quotes that he did. It's a lot of maneuvering to just confirm what he already did." Well, it's the "already did" part that's the problem. That research is the original author's work and claiming it as your own is dishonest.

Idea Theft   If you include an idea that you read or heard elsewhere in a written assignment and don't cite the source, it's plagiarism. You don't have to copy actual words to steal. The idea itself belongs to someone else and they deserve credit. This rule operates on both micro and macro levels: Whether you use someone else's idea as only a tiny part of an argument or base your entire thesis on someone else's thoughts, you need to cite your source.

Structural Plagiarism   Structural plagiarism is probably the most esoteric of all the types. It's also one of the least talked about. Personally, I didn't even know it existed until I got to college. If you base the structure of a paper, or a part of a paper, on someone else's work, you are plagiarizing. So, for example, if you were to write a paper on the types of academic dishonesty and you followed the organizational structure of this chapter, you would be plagiarizing me. This would be true even if every other aspect of your essay was on the up-and-up—well paraphrased, correctly cited, and so on. The simple use of the organizational scheme, without acknowledgment, is academic theft.

Dovetailing   Believe it or not, you can actually plagiarize yourself. Combining assignments for two courses is a form of plagiarism. It's commonly referred to as dovetailing, and if it's done without permission, it's considered to be a form of academic dishonesty.

There are ways that you can combine assignments without breaking any institutional or ethical rules. For example, a form of dovetailing is employed fairly regularly by graduate students. They'll be assigned a lengthy research project in two different courses and ask both professors if they can combine the two projects. If they're allowed to, usually the scope or length of the paper is increased, so that the overall amount of work stays the same.

The key component in those instances is the getting permission part, which needs to be done beforehand. Dovetailing as plagiarism is a shortcut. A student will simply hand in an old paper a second time for a different course. Why is this academically dishonest? You wrote it. Because the professor asked you to *write* a paper, not just rummage through your closet to find an old one, it's plagiarism.

FABRICATION

This is, to be blunt, making shit up—fabricating lab results, making up sources for a bibliography, a faked interview. Any time you intentionally invent information or citations for an assignment, you are guilty of fabrication.

AIDING AND ABETTING

If you facilitate someone else's academic dishonesty, you're guilty of academic dishonesty too. So if you lend your homework out or let someone copy off of you in a test you've aided and abetted a cheater, and you're guilty, too.

FALSE WITNESS

It's one of the Ten Commandments, *and* it's against the rules in most schools. "Thou shalt not bear false witness against thy professor." In contemporary terms: It's academically dishonest to manufacture an excuse about an assignment or exercise. Most commonly this comes up in relation to homework: "Um, my dog ate it." But any type of fictional excuse counts—a made-up explanation for missing a test, telling your prof that you handed a paper in when you didn't, even a fib about why you were late to class (although I doubt even a school with the strictest honor code would take much notice of something that trivial).

While almost everyone did this kind of thing in high school without much trouble, at the postsecondary level it can be quite serious business. Take the case of Scott Doree, a former graduate student from Michigan State University, as an example. Doree was working toward a degree in microbiology and was, supposedly, working on a vaccine to prevent pneumonia in pigs. But he hadn't actually done any research in years. To cover his lack of progress he told his professors that his notebooks, computer disks, and samples had been stolen.

In this day and age stolen viruses are serious business. So the FBI, the Joint Terrorism Task Force, and the USDA got involved and spent hundreds of thousands of dollars investigating the crime. When it finally came out that there had been no theft—that Doree had made the whole thing up—no one was amused. He was brought up on criminal charges for mail fraud and making false statements to FBI agents. He was sentenced to ten months in prison and was ordered to repay $70,000 in federal research grants.

Now, there probably won't be a criminal investigation the next time you tell an instructor that your dog, or pig, ate your homework. But making up excuses is academically dishonest, and if it's serious enough, it could easily get you a seat in front of the school's judicial board.

FREELOADING

If you're assigned a group project and don't contribute your fair share (or at all), you're committing a form of academic dishonesty. Handing in that group project with your name on it is, just like plagiarism, taking credit for the work of other people.

This isn't the type of thing that's adjudicated very often. But technically it's an infraction.

SABOTAGE

Academic sabotage is just what you'd think: taking action that makes it harder for others to do well. It can take many forms and can be directed toward a specific person or the whole class. In law school, for example, people would tear out important pages of reserved materials in the library so that no one else could read them. That's the most common type of sabotage, but its forms are only limited by students' creativity— people tamper with other students' experiments so that the research is flawed or change the posted assignments so that others will do the wrong work. I've even heard of instances where disabling computer viruses have been planted on classmates' computers for the purpose of impeding their work.

Unbelievable. Absolutely disgusting. But true.

How You'll Get Caught

Chances are you won't. Three out of every four students cheat at least once during college. Only a tiny fraction— probably less than 1 percent—are convicted or even accused of academic dishonesty. Most professors are hesitant to do anything anyway, even when they catch their pupils in the act. A recent survey by the Center for Academic Integrity showed that nearly a third of college professors that had detected cheating ultimately did nothing about it.

Your Lawyer Says:

JUST BECAUSE YOU CAN CHEAT, DOESN'T MEAN YOU SHOULD!

Sure, you'll probably get away with it. But the possiblility of getting caught isn't the only reason you shouldn't cheat. First off, intellectual laziness is habit-forming. Someday you're going to have a real job and you're going to need the skills you're supposed to be honing in college. If that's not enough of a reason to fly right, then think of your classmates. When you cheat you artificially lower their grades—either by raising the curve or through comparisons to your "superior" work. Either way, your shortcut hurts everyone else in the class. Is that really how you want to treat your friends?

But college administrators and professors are starting to take note of the epidemic proportions of the cheating problem and are doing something about it. They're starting to turn the same technologies that make cheating easier against the cheaters themselves. And, of course, they're still using the low-tech strategies that have existed for centuries. Here are some of the methods professors will employ to nab your lying, cheating, low-down, dirty, double-dealing asses:

CHEATING

Examinations   The ways to sneak information into an exam have come a long way from writing the answers on a chewing gum wrapper. Blackberries, handheld computers, wireless phones, and a million other technological advances can be used to convey answers. But the main defenses are still pretty low-tech.

Active proctoring is still the primary protection against in-test cheating. It works equally well against everything from crib sheets to cellular technologies. Teachers simply look for suspicious behaviors, roving eyes, and unnecessarily nervous students. Most professors say that if they suspect something they'll hover nearby, both in attempt to gather evidence and as a warning to the student to stop whatever they're doing. So if you seem to be getting the evil eye from a proctor, it's probably time to eat the evidence.

There are also time-honored test-drafting strategies used by teachers to trip up cheaters. The primary deterrent is handing out different copies of the same test that vary the order of the questions or the arrangement of multiple-choice answers. Some teachers go so far as to give completely different tests. When employing the test change-up, professors will mark where each student sits during the examination period. If a student has a number of incorrect answers that coincide with the correct answers on a test that was at an adjacent desk, it's a good sign there was cheating.

Written Assignments   The main way to detect cheating in written assignments is through comparison. Teachers will compare students' papers to each other, to materials available on the Internet, or to the answers in the teaching manual. Remember, if you can find the answers somewhere, it's likely that your instructor can, too. This method can also detect the use of work from previous semesters. Did you ever wonder why some of your instructors ask for two copies of everything you hand in? They keep a copy on file. If something seems strangely familiar, they'll look through their archive of old work to see if they can find the original source and confirm the copying. It's a cumbersome and imprecise system, to be sure. But they don't just hand out Ph.D.s from Harvard, you know. Professors are smart people with sharp minds. Maybe smart enough to catch you up.

Simple common sense is often enough to catch some students red-handed. If you, for example, never actually show up for a lab but manage to turn in A+ lab reports, your instructor is going to get suspicious. Likewise if your work takes a sudden jump in quality.

Academic Dishonesty

Your Lawyer Says:

BE CAREFUL!

A lot of people accused of plagiarism commit their sins unintentionally. Carelessness is one of the main reasons this happens. So take specific steps to ensure that negligence doesn't trip you up:

- ✓ Document everything. At the earliest stages of your research make photocopies of source materials or careful notes about where you found things.
- ✓ Do everything you can to make it as easy as possible to go back and check your sources, if you need to, later on.
- ✓ When in doubt, line your paper up next to the source and do a side-by-side comparison to make sure you didn't subconsciously lift words or phrases.

PLAGIARISM

Many of the techniques used to catch cheaters in written assignments are also employed to ferret out plagiarizers. Primarily teachers will look for sudden, inexplicable changes in the quality or style of a student's work. This can operate on the level of a whole paper or can be evident in a single phrase or paragraph that stands out as different than the rest of the paper. We each have a distinct writing style—your instructor has got some sense of yours. If your work strays too far from that style, it will raise suspicions.

And believe it or not, a professor might actually go through the effort of checking your sources. It takes about ten seconds online to find out if a book was published or not. Remember, the whole point of using citations is to make it easy for readers to track down original works. For honest scholars this is fine. But if you've plagiarized, you're forced to leave behind a succinct set of clues that could be used to find you out.

Comparison also figures largely into the plagiarism detection scheme. Again, if you can find it, so can your professor. And many keep files of old papers to prevent cross-class sharing.

Electronic Plagiarism Detection Services Computers and the Internet have made cut-and-paste plagiarism a three-keystroke process (back in my day we actually had to type out the stuff we were going to steal). But the same technological advances have also been employed to catch plagiarizers in a new, high-tech way.

There are a number of commercial services that electronically check students' work against databases of published work and cheat-site file papers. They seek to find similar phrases and structures. Most of them check the student papers against a database of published works and don't keep copies. But the leading company in the business, Turnitin.com, keeps a copy of every paper submitted, constantly building a database of student-written papers.

Clearly this makes the service much more effective. But it does raise a legal question or two. Everything that you write, from critical analyses to creative works, is your property and is protected by copyright laws (you own the copyright in something the moment you create it—no paperwork necessary). Copying your work for a commercial purpose is probably an infringement.

These practices may also violate the Family Educational Right and Privacy Act (FERPA), which prohibits schools from releasing student records without permission. (See chapter 7, "Student Records," for a thorough discussion of FERPA.) Under FERPA your work could be submitted and checked but not retained or used for any purpose.

These issues are relatively new, so there is no hard law on the subject. But, based on the law in similar areas, I would say that it's highly likely that such practices are illegal. I'm not a fan of plagiarism, but I'm also not in favor of eschewing the law. If one of my professors was infringing on my rights in order to catch potential cheaters, I'd complain loudly.

FABRICATION

Lying is always harder than telling the truth. As soon as you create a fiction, you have to work to keep it from being discovered. It can be hard simply to remember the details of the lie, let alone steer clear of inconsistencies or impossibilities.

These types of discrepancies are the biggest potential pitfall for fabricators. Numbers that simply don't look right—or look too right—on a lab report, contradictory facts, a hole in a story, or any other type of incongruity could betray the lie.

It's certainly not foolproof, but just like anywhere else in life, if you tell enough lies, sooner or later one of them is going to trip you up.

AIDING AND ABETTING

Comparison is really the only way to detect someone who's allowed copying. Remember, to the teacher who is correcting the work, it won't be clear that your work was the source material. Your assignment will simply be one of the identical papers. You may wind up defending yourself against an accusation of outright cheating, not just helping others.

FALSE WITNESS, FREELOADING, AND SABOTAGE

Aside from getting caught in a bad lie, there aren't really ways to detect people who participate in these last three categories of academic dishonesty. The heavy lifting of these offenses takes place far out of the range of professorial oversight.

The biggest risk is being turned in by a fellow student. This is actually a possibility in any type of academic dishonesty. Wouldn't you consider ratting out a classmate if you gave up fun for six straight weekends to pull a B+ while he cheated and got an A? Yeah, me too.

A WORD ON HONOR CODES

While we're on the subject of ratting on each other, it makes sense to talk about honor codes. Almost every college has an academic integrity policy. But only a handful—fewer than 100—have traditional honor codes. Under these traditional codes students pledge at the beginning of school (and sometimes at the end of each test) that they will not cheat and will report others who do. This is one of the hallmarks of the traditional honor code. Students are bound to report each other. Failure to do so is, in and of itself, a violation.

Students also play a larger role in the adjudication of infractions at these schools. The hearings are generally held behind closed doors. And, almost always, the punishments for cheating of any sort are much more severe. At the University of Virginia, for example, there is one, and only one, punishment for an incident of academic dishonesty—immediate expulsion. This isn't uncommon.

There's a lot of statistical evidence that honor codes reduce cheating. When surveyed about cheating, students at schools with honor codes usually admit to doing less of it. But, really, if you were at a school with a draconian policy where a bunch of your peers could conduct a secret trial and expel you, would you answer questions about your cheating habits honestly? Probably not, no matter how many assurances you got that the survey was confidential.

In theory I believe in honor codes. But lots of things that work in theory fail miserably in real life—communism, online dating, and the Nielsen ratings come to mind. Honor codes follow suit. In practice, I'd rather be tried in Pakistan than in front of an honor court. They're often badly managed by power-seeking students who administer justice inconsistently. And they very often convict a disproportionate number of minority students, a good sign that they are racially biased.

If you're at a school that lives by one of these codes, I strongly urge you to take a good hard look at it, both its rules and regulations and its actual administration. Maybe it's working well. But I'll bet it isn't. If you see something that you think should change, get involved and do it soon. The time to initiate change is before, rather than after, you've been accused.

What To Do If You're Accused

THE LAW OF THE LAND

If you're accused of cheating, you are 100 percent stuck with your school's academic integrity policy. No federal, state, or city law is going to affect the outcome of your situation. The law set forth by your school is the law of the land.

So go get a copy of the student handbook and read the section on academic integrity. Get familiar with it. What's the process like? What are the potential punishments? Who's in charge of proceedings? In short, if you think there's any chance you'll ever be accused of academic dishonesty, you need to read the policy carefully. And do it soon. As you'll see in a bit, you may be required to make some quick decisions, and you'll want to have as much information as possible.

VENUE SHOPPING

Okay. Someone suspects you've cheated. What next? Unfortunately the first, and most important, decision will probably be made for you: the venue. There are two courses an accusation can take at this very early stage. The teacher can informally deal with the problem one-on-one—ask for an explanation, look at the situation, and dole out the punishment herself. Or she can dump it directly into the school's disciplinary system. In this chapter we'll only deal with the informal route. Information about how to navigate a more formal hearing, either in front of administrators or a judicial board, can be found in chapter 10, "Disciplinary Proceedings."

THE ONE-ON-ONE SOLUTION

There's a good chance that an instance of suspected dishonesty will begin informally, with the teacher approaching the student one-on-one. Teachers, even those at schools with traditional honor codes, generally prefer to deal with suspected infractions this way. A hearing is a pain in the ass for both parties, not just the accused. And a one-on-one solution allows for some learning to come out of the process—both about ethics and about the academic processes that were violated.

An informal resolution will probably net the best result for you, the accused, too. Dealing with any kind of undesirable accusation is always best kept in private. And the punishments doled out by professors, rather than adjudicators, are significantly less severe. A professor

Your Lawyer Says:

IGNORE THE RULES (IF YOU CAN)

Many academic integrity policies don't allow for an informal resolution. They mandate that all instances of suspected academic dishonesty be tried in the school's judicial system. Savvy students ignore that rule. Professors are always more lenient than judicial boards. So do what you can to deal directly with your prof, even if there is such a rule at your school.

doesn't have the power to expel a student. Most are reluctant to even fail one.

So if you're lucky enough to start out in an informal setting, do everything you can to stay there. It's almost always best to work things out with your professor rather than involve others. Nowhere is that more true than in instances of academic dishonesty.

Your First Job: Delay   Of course, there's a downside to an informal resolution. You won't have a chance to prepare. Your instructor will ask you to stay after class or drop by his office. Then, unless you have an incredibly guilty conscience, you'll be blindsided by an accusation.

At this point, you'll be faced with an age-old question: fight or flight? Choose flight. An accusation of academic dishonesty is difficult to deal with given all the time in the world to prepare. Off the cuff it will be nearly impossible. Do whatever's necessary to postpone the meeting. Throw up, wet your pants, start crying, tell your prof you've got to be somewhere. I don't care. But try to get yourself a day to gather your composure, your thoughts, and your evidence. It will be worth it.

But before you fake a seizure, you need to get two critical pieces of information out of your instructor: One, what he thinks you did and two, in which assignment or test he thinks you did it. Without knowing those two things, you won't really be able to prepare much.

And try not to give up any information yourself at this point. Opening up your pie-hole at this early stage will only work against you.

If you can't buy yourself a day, ask to go to the bathroom and take five minutes to calm yourself. Splash some water on your face and get your thoughts together. It's not a night's sleep, but it will be helpful.

By the way, this is why I said earlier that it was critical to have a working knowledge of your school's policy. You may get caught in just this type of situation—an impromptu meeting about academic dishonesty. The more you know at this point, the better. At the very least you should be aware of the potential punishments and the type of hearing you could face. So if you haven't gone and read the policy yet, go do it now. And listen to me next time I tell you to do something. I'm not just making this stuff up, you know.

Preparations   If you manage to get a day or two to prepare, take full advantage. Track down all the information that is remotely pertinent. If you were with anyone when you did the assignment or near someone during a test, talk to them and see if they saw anything or have any input. As with any trial—and don't kid yourself, even at this informal level that's what it is—written evidence is the most convincing. So if you have an outline you made while you studied or notes on scratch paper you made while preparing the assignment, make copies to give to your professor.

As with grading grievances, you should treat the meeting like an oral project for a class. Have a thesis, outline your arguments, and polish your presentation. This is important, so do the prep work as well as you can. You're only going to get one shot at this, so make it count.

For some more detailed information and tips on how to prepare, see the sections about getting a grade changed included in chapter 3, "Your Professor." It's probably also worth your time to read, or reread, the sections on how to talk to your professor. They apply here, too.

The Meeting At some point you're going to actually have to have the dreaded meeting. Hopefully you'll have bought yourself some time and will have done some preparation. Maybe all you'll have had is a few seconds to reel yourself in. Either way, you'll need to step carefully for the next few minutes. So focus.

BE SILENT. BE STILL. At the beginning keep your mouth shut and let your professor do all of the talking. This may be hard to do. You're going to have nearly irresistible urges to interrupt, to interject your point of view, to defend yourself. Fight them. These first few minutes are your best chance to gather as much information as possible about your professor's take on the situation. The longer you keep quiet, the more he'll talk and the more information you'll get.

Teachers use this technique in class on their students. They know that no one likes silence. It's uncomfortable. They'll just ask a question and shut up. Sooner or later someone will venture a guess just to stop the noiselessness. Turn this technique back on your prof. Let him wallow in the quiet a bit and see where it gets you. Make eye contact, but don't speak unless you're specifically asked a question.

By letting your professor have his say, you'll probably get all of the basic information you'll need to assess your next

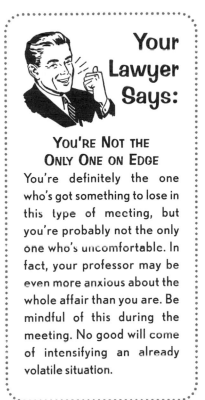

Your Lawyer Says:

YOU'RE NOT THE ONLY ONE ON EDGE

You're definitely the one who's got something to lose in this type of meeting, but you're probably not the only one who's uncomfortable. In fact, your professor may be even more anxious about the whole affair than you are. Be mindful of this during the meeting. No good will come of intensifying an already volatile situation.

step. If you're lucky, he may even go so far as to tell you what he plans to do about the situation. Then you'll have what you need to decide whether or not to cut a deal.

Academic Dishonesty

CROSS-EXAMINATION   But sometimes the silent treatment simply doesn't work. Unfortunately, before you can make any kind of decision about what to do, you need a few pieces of pertinent information. So you'll have to ask. You need to find out:

- ✓ *The exact nature of the accusation.* What type of dishonesty are you being accused of and on which assignment. And remember, it's possible that the meeting is about more than one infraction.
- ✓ *The evidence your professor has that incriminates you.* Is there written evidence, the oral testimony of another student, or just a feeling in your prof's gut that you're a cheater?
- ✓ *His plan.* Is he fed up with all the cheating and is just giving you a courtesy heads-up before turning you in, or does he want to work it out?

Phrase all of your questions in a "what if" manner. For example, don't ask "So what are you going to do to me?" That makes you sound guilty. Instead say, "What if I did do this, what would the punishment be?" You'll still sound a little cagey, but at least your questions won't be confused for confessions of guilt.

CONFESSIONS OF A DANGEROUS MIND   The most critical decision you're going to have to make at this meeting is whether or not to confess to your crime. I wish I could give you a formula that would tell you what to do, but it's just not that simple. It's a judgment call of the most delicate sort.

In most instances it's better to cop to it and ask forgiveness rather than fight tooth and nail. But it all depends on what you've found out. You certainly don't want to confess in this informal setting only to have that used as evidence against you in a formal hearing. So weigh your options carefully. Think about what you've found out so far—evidence, potential punishments, and so forth. If you've been accused or caught at cheating before, take that into account as well. Then make your decision.

And by all means, if you choose confession, be respectful about it. And act like you're truly sorry for what you've done, even if you aren't.

THE INNOCENTS   Of course if you're innocent, don't confess. Instead, have your say. Be clear, concise, and respectful. In short, follow all the rules covered in chapter 3, "Your Professor."

Chances are, if you truly are innocent, things will work themselves out quickly and easily. There are subtle things an innocent person does when falsely accused—attitudes, body language, speech patterns. Your professor will pick up on these, and they'll work in your favor. Plus, absolutely nothing is more convincing than the truth.

That doesn't mean that those who are innocent should take this informal opportunity to resolve the situation lightly. Quite the opposite. No matter how innocent you are, there's still a chance that the incident could get bumped to a formal proceeding. So make a real effort. But do it with confidence because, more likely than not, the truth will set you free.

Academic Dishonesty

CHAPTER 5

Animal Rights

According to U.S. laws, your four-legged (or otherwise inhuman) friends have no inherent rights. So if you really want to free Willy from the university aquarium, you'll have to couch your claims in terms of your rights, not his. You'll also need a really big baggie.

Chapter Contents

There are few instances on campus where beliefs and practice collide in such a tangible way as they do with lab animals. You may have strong views about abortion or the death penalty. But the closest you're ever going to come to those issues is a heated discussion in a philosophy class. You're certainly not going to have to actually pull Old Sparky's 2,000-volt switch in Criminal Justice 101.

But in the lab, it's all right there in front of you. You may be asked to actually hurt or even kill a living creature. That may not be something you're willing to do. Or, even if you support the use of animals in research, you may want to be sure that they're treated as well as possible. Wherever you fall on the animal rights spectrum, staring at that Pamela Anderson PETA poster isn't going to help you move your platform forward (ahem). Understanding the laws and issues involved will.

The Philosophy of Animal Rights

There are almost as many theories that support the rights of animals as there are species to protect. People base their views on moral, ethical, religious, and personal reasoning. There are, however, a few major, nonreligious theories that are credited with being the foundations for the entire movement. Anyone interested in protecting animals should be familiar with them.

UTILITARIAN THEORY

Most point to Peter Singer as the founder of the modern animal rights movement. His book, *Animal Liberation* (which, by the way, is worth reading if you really want to be the Pied Piper of lab mice), jump-started the animal rights movement when it was published in 1975.

Singer argues that the distinction of species is arbitrary—as useless as race, gender, or religious affiliation in determining the relative rights of living things. The ability to feel pain is what he says should be used to evaluate an animal's standing. After that it's a simple balancing: If the benefit to humans outweighs the cost of the pain to the animal, it's a justifiable act. If not, it shouldn't be done. As you've probably deduced, this theory allows for most uses of animals from food to scientific research, so long as the processes are humane.

TRUE RIGHTS THEORY

Thomas Regan's work *The Case for Animal Rights* (also worth reading) is the foundation of the movement arguing for the out-and-out rights of animals. He argues that each creature has independent rights and importance, regardless of what its use to others entails.

He concedes the benefits of scientific research, but argues that those gains are unjust, no matter the overall benefits to humans. He calls, in fact, for an abolition of most normal uses of animals such as hunting, agriculture, and experimentation. This is because, if we recognize that all animals have rights, there is simply no justification for harming them. Killing a rat becomes the moral equivalent of killing another human—no matter the benefit, it's unjust.

Your Lawyer Says:

KNOW THYSELF

Think of animal rights as a continuum. At one extreme would be human dominion (kill 'em). In the middle would be animal welfare (kill 'em . . . but be nice about it), and at the other end would be true rights (please please please don't kill 'em). It's important to know where you fall on this scale because it will help you define your ideas and determine exactly how far you're willing to go for them.

HUMAN DOMINION THEORY

The final theory of animal rights—although it's better termed a theory of "no rights"—is often called the "human dominion" theory. It was first advocated by John Locke, who based his theory on Genesis. It basically argues that we are the masters and animals are our servants. According to this school of thought, humans can do anything they want with the little critters, from scientific research to staging cockfights.

THE LEGAL BASIS OF ANIMAL PROTECTION

Here's the short, stunning truth: The law of the United States recognizes no rights in animals.

As a human, the inherent nature of your rights is practically unquestioned. Our entire government is based on that assumption—all men "are endowed by their Creator with certain unalienable rights" among which are "life, liberty, and the pursuit of happiness."

Great, if you're human. But our four-legged brethren aren't so lucky. There's no similar assumption about animal rights. The laws and statutes that do exist have been pushed through by activists and lobbying groups based on the desires of people, not the rights of animals. In other words, their justification is "lots of people like

Animal Rights

animals and don't want to see them unnecessarily hurt" instead of "animals have a right not to be hurt." It's a fairly strange distinction but, so far as the law goes, a very important one. It means that if you want to move forward legally in this arena, you have to couch your claims in terms of human, not animal, rights.

Vivisection and Dissection of Animals

One of the most prevalent uses of animals in education is as subjects for either dissection (analysis of a corpse) or vivisection (analysis of a living animal). Biology and science courses as early as middle school require students to euthanize and dissect insects, frogs, and smaller animals. At higher levels of instruction animals are often given anesthesia and operated on while alive so that students can see organs and biological processes in action.

A HUMAN RIGHTS CLAIM TO STOP ANIMAL HARM

The First Amendment of the U.S. Constitution states that "Congress shall make no law respecting the establishment of religion or prohibiting the free exercise thereof." For a student looking to avoid performing dissections, it's the "free exercise" part that matters. In plain language this guarantees that we're all allowed to act in accordance with our religious beliefs without intrusion from the government. This can take the form of an action, like smoking peyote. Or it could translate into a right to abstain from something, like dissection.

I know. This is a pretty narrow basis—many animal rights activists have no religious basis for their beliefs. But if you want to get out of cutting up Mr. Whiskers, it's your only legal route.

THE ELEMENTS OF A FIRST AMENDMENT CLAIM

Of course, it's a little more complex than telling your teacher that God doesn't want you to hurt animals. In order for your First Amendment claim to succeed you'll have to prove five things:

State Action   As you know, the Constitution only applies to the government. So, in order for a student to be able to make a claim under the First Amendment, the school must have enough of a relationship to the federal, state, or local government so that it's as if the state itself is taking the action (i.e., asking you to dissect an animal). At a public school this is pretty much a no-brainer—it's state action. But at private schools it can be a difficult question. Each instance will be looked at on a case-by-case basis. Courts look to the connections between the school and the government, such as financial support, direct regulation by the government, or any other relationship that would show that the two are working as one.

Religious Belief   A moral or ethical belief isn't enough. Your reasons for wanting to abstain have to stem from your religion (unfortunately, there's

no free expression of morals clause in the Constitution). Thankfully, religion is defined fairly broadly for First Amendment purposes. First of all, you aren't limited to the mainstream beliefs of your chosen church. So, if you subscribe to a traditional, organized religion—like Judaism or Christianity—you aren't bound by what its leadership says. Even if the church you belong to has an official stance on animals allowing for dissection, your personal religious beliefs are still valid. Second, you don't even have to belong to an organized church, or even believe in a god or gods for that matter, for your beliefs to be considered "religious." Really, all it has to be is a belief system that you honestly hold to be your religion.

Sincerity   The belief must be sincere. Obviously this requirement goes hand-in-hand with establishing that the belief is a part of a religion. For those who subscribe to a nontraditional religion, it's really the same question. It becomes slightly more important for people who are part of an organized religion but hold more comprehensive views about animals than are reflected by the official party line of the established church.

Burden   Next, it must be shown that the action that the school (really the state) is taking is a burden on your religious beliefs. In the case of dissection and vivisection, this is a pretty easy question to answer. If your beliefs prohibit you from hurting animals and the school is asking you to either kill or use animals killed by someone else, then it's a burden.

Compelling Government Interest   Finally, if you show that all of the things above are present, the government has one more way to compel you to comply. If the government can show that forcing the dissection on you serves a "compelling government interest," they may be able to stop your First Amendment claim. In practice, it's hard to show a compelling government interest that supports forcing students to perform dissections or vivisections. There may be an argument at the graduate and professional school levels—that the government needs to make sure that all doctors are competent, for example—but the availability of nonanimal alternatives makes that argument a bit difficult to use.

POSSIBLE OTHER SOURCES OF LEGAL SUPPORT

Federal constitutional claims are the most popular and usually provide the strongest legal basis for abstention, but there are some other areas of law that might also be of help to an animal activist student.

State Constitutions   Each state has its own Constitution. Most have their own language pertaining to the free exercise of religion. Sometimes these state-level guarantees are broader than the federal version. Generally you'll have to jump through a very similar set of hurdles to prove the claim under the state law. But there may be some distinct advantages to working under state law. For example, some states define state action much more broadly than the federal courts do, which can be critical if you attend a private school.

Animal Rights

At any rate, it may be worth it to take the time to track down your state's Constitution and see what it says about religious freedoms. If you want to be especially enterprising, do a quick Internet search to see if there have been any animal rights cases brought under it.

Specific State Statutes   A handful of states have statutes that specifically grant students the right to refuse to participate in vivisections and dissections. At the time of writing, Florida, California, Maine, Pennsylvania, Louisiana, New York, Rhode Island, and Illinois had such laws in place. Lobbying groups are pushing for similar laws in other states. But, unfortunately, these laws apply only to students in primary and secondary school. So they're not much use to a college or graduate student. Still, they're worth knowing about—if you live in a covered state, the law may be of some argumentative value.

State Religious Discrimination in Education Laws   Most states, in addition to the broad protections against religious discrimination included in their constitutions, have specific laws that prohibit religious discrimination in educa-

Your Lawyer Says:

USE FINDLAW TO FIND LAWS

Findlaw (www.findlaw.com) is probably the largest compendium of legal information on the web. It's almost always a good place to start if you're doing any kind of research. Because of its size, it can be a little overwhelming at first (and because it's a commercial enterprise, you'll get inundated with advertisements for lawyers while there), but it's entirely searchable and has almost all of the relevant source materials in its databases.

tion. Often these statutes require that the school receive some type of state funding for the law to apply. But these requirements are often much more inclusive than the state actor tests that a First Amendment analysis would use. For example, California's educational discrimination law applies to "all educational institutions located in California which receive or benefit from state financial assistance or enroll students who receive state financial aid." So if your school has students who receive state aid, then they're covered. Needless to say, many private schools that would be outside of the scope of the federal Constitution can be reached by laws like this one.

I can't take the time to discuss each state's laws, but you can find out for yourself pretty easily. A quick online search will tell you if your state has one of these laws and how comprehensive it is. FindLaw and your state's official website are good places to start.

College Rules and Regulations   A growing number of schools have drafted their own dissection policies. Often these guarantee a student the right to refuse to participate and require that the instructor offer an alternative.

Here's a typical policy, from Sarah Lawrence College:

> In most cases, Sarah Lawrence College does not require students with ethical objections to participate in dissection. Students who choose to refrain from such activity will be given alternatives that provide similar experiences. Those who choose such alternatives will not be penalized, although they will be responsible for the material presented in dissection exercises. If appropriate, separate evaluations of their learning experiences may be designed. In courses where dissection is considered essential to understanding the biological principles at hand (such as advanced biology courses) students should discuss concerns with the instructor during interviews prior to registration.
>
> Students who feel that undue pressure to dissect has been placed upon them, or question the designation of a course as requiring mandatory dissection, may file a complaint with the Dean of the College.

This is a well-drafted policy. It states the general stance of the school, which is that most students won't be forced to dissect or vivisect animals. But it recognizes that, in certain high-level courses, the professor may deem that participation is necessary (remember our old friend academic freedom—teachers have fairly broad latitude when it comes to their curriculum). But, even under one of those circumstances, it gives students a venue to voice a concern or complaint.

Check your student handbook to see if your school has a policy like this one. As always, the college's own rules and regulations are the strongest possible foothold. So if you find one, rejoice.

WHAT TO DO

It makes no sense to jump right into a lawsuit. Even at a public school, making a constitutional claim stick is hard to do. On a private campus, it's even tougher. At both it would take months and tens of thousands of dollars (and those are conservative estimates). So why did I spend all of that time explaining the laws? Because no matter how you proceed, it's always smart to understand the laws that will, or won't, support you if push comes to shove. Try to work things out using other methods first. When you've exhausted all of those options, then, and only then, think about filing in federal court.

Animal Rights

Some General Principles for Objecting

TIMING If you've already been handed a cat's corpse, it's probably too late. Talk to your professor as soon as possible about your concerns—certainly no later than the drop/add deadline for the semester. That will give him time to consider your request and will give you the chance to bail if you can't reach an agreement. This will take some vigilance on your part. You're going to have to find out ahead of time if the class involves animal experimentation.

STANCE Remember the general rules for dealing with professors (see chapter 3, "Your Professor"). They're people, too. And they often have big egos and limited free time. So be wary and respectful of both. Be firm, but concise and polite.

PRIVACY This is an issue of your personal views and beliefs, so make it a private matter between you and the instructor. Don't simply raise your hand in class and complain. Make an appointment. Talk about it behind closed doors. Not only is this respectful to the rest of the class, but taking the time to make an appointment outside of class tends to show that your concerns are genuine.

FORM ALLIANCES That said, don't be afraid to team up with other like-minded classmates. There is power in numbers, and the concerns of a group of students might get a more willing ear than the opinion of one. But there are downsides to teaming up. First, if you recruit others, make sure that they really are similarly minded. The last thing you want is to include a bunch of insincere slackers in your campaign. And even if the whole class is sincerely opposed to dissection, avoid ganging up. Don't trot twenty students into your instructor's office and expect things to go smoothly. Choose a few representatives to go and speak for the group.

Step One: Research Alternatives Do your homework and find out what alternatives are available. Advances in technology have invaded the educational market, and there are now lots of ways to virtually kill frogs and mice.

Many major scholastic publishers and equipment suppliers offer some alternative products. In addition to the traditional plastic models, there are now many software programs that allow students to perform procedures on very realistic computer-generated animals. Neotek (www.neotek.com), Scienceclass (www.scienceclass.com), Ward Science Supplies (www.wardsci.com), and Ventura Educational Systems (www.venturaes.com) are a few of the leaders in the field. Get them to send you brochures, endorsements, specs, and any other relevant information.

Step Two: Research Institutional Practice Of course, check to see if your school has a written policy concerning dissection and vivisection. If there's a policy that guarantees you an out, avail yourself of it. If there isn't, sniff around and see if you can find out whether any other students have been allowed to use alternative learning tools. Ask upper-classmen in the specific major, teaching assistants, or a trusted professor if they know of any instances of this type of thing.

Step Three: Approach Your Teacher It's best to make your first request in writing. Send a (typed, signed, and dated) note to your teacher. State that you understand that there will be some form of dissection involved in the class you will be taking and explain your objection. Even though we're not at the lawsuit level yet, it's important to couch your objection in terms of religious belief because that will hold the most weight. Say something like "I won't be able to participate in the dissection because I have a strong religious belief in the sanctity of all life." Ask to use an alternative and include copies of the materials you've gathered. Also reference the school policy and past instances of allowing alternatives if there are any.

Your Lawyer Says:

CONSIDER AN ALTERNATE SOLUTION; ENROLL WISELY
I'm not a big fan of avoiding issues. In almost every instance, fighting for what you believe is the best thing to do. That's how things get changed. But if you're truly committed to animal rights and want to pursue an academic career in the sciences, it might be wise to factor that in when choosing a school. Many excellent undergraduate schools and several graduate and professional schools are animal-free. You have to decide how far you're willing to go on this issue, but transferring to one of those universities might be worth considering.

Be sure to ask for a quick response. If you haven't heard anything in a week or so, make a follow-up appointment to see where you stand.

Step Four: Work Your Way Up If your professor won't budge, work your way up the academic food chain. Talk to the department chair, the dean, the provost, and the president. Someone along the way may help you find a way to both get an education and maintain your belief system.

Lab Animal Treatment

Universities also use and house large numbers of live animals. Many students worry about their standard of care. This may seem somewhat paradoxical—keep the rats happy while you inject them with cancer—but maintaining palatable living conditions does seem to be the least we could do. The little guys are literally donating their lives to science.

Animal Rights

Concerned students will be happy to learn that there are a number of regulatory schemes that govern exactly how animals must be treated. But, as you'll see later, there are large exceptions and some major holes in their applicability.

THE ANIMAL WELFARE ACT

The Animal Welfare Act (AWA) is the most comprehensive regulation regarding the treatment of animals in the United States. It's administered and enforced by the Animal and Plant Health Inspection Service, an arm of the USDA. This federal law requires minimum standards of care for all animals bred for commercial sale, exhibited to the public (it specifically prohibits raccoon baiting, by the way—which is totally irrelevant here, but sort of fun to know), transported for commercial use, and *used in research*.

Its scope is broad, but it specifically excludes mice, rats, birds, cold-blooded animals, and invertebrates from coverage, leaving the most common lab animals without AWA protection. Still, if your school uses any other type of warm-blooded animals, they will be covered by the AWA.

It's a very detailed and complex law. But here are the high points:

✓ *Housing.* The act establishes minimum housing standards with a level of minutia that baffles the mind. For example, it includes a table titled "Additional Space Required for Each Sea Otter When More Than Two Are Kept in a Primary Enclosure." The act delineates acceptable standards for indoor, outdoor, sheltered, shared, and mobile shelter facilities for most every species on the planet, usually by defining minimum space requirements and temperature standards.

✓ *Feeding and watering.* The act requires that adequate, palatable food be provided to each animal in amounts that will sustain it. It gives specific instructions for each species. Rabbits, for example, must be fed at least once a day and must have their water receptacles sanitized every two weeks.

✓ *Sanitation.* Schedules are set for each species's enclosure. How often waste should be removed, when apparatus should be replaced, acceptable absorbent bedding practices, and other similar things are covered. Monkey cages, for instance, need to be cleaned at least daily, and their climbing bars need to be replaced when visibly worn.

✓ *Veterinary care.* Under the act, each facility is required to have an attending veterinarian that oversees the well-being of the animals. The vet need not be a full-time employee, but there must be a formal agreement between the research facility and the vet. And there must be an adequate schedule of regular visits.

✓ *Protection from extreme weather and temperatures.* All animals must be protected from extreme conditions that would be hazardous to their health.

✓ *Minimization of pain and suffering.* The act requires that suffering be minimized. Procedures and research cannot unnecessarily duplicate prior experiments. Humane methods of euthanasia are to be employed. Animals are to be given the proper drugs for the relief of pain and distress. No paralytics are allowed to be used without anesthesia. And so on.

As you can see, the AWA is a very comprehensive and very detailed law. The examples above are just that, examples. They should give you an idea of what types of things are included. If you have a concern about a specific type of animal, go to the U.S. Department of Agriculture's Animal Care website (www.aphis.usda.gov/ac). The full text of the AWA is online. It's long but searchable and comprehensible.

PUBLIC HEALTH SERVICE POLICY

If your school receives aid from the Public Health Service (PHS), it must also comply with the Public Health Service Policy on Humane Care and Use of Laboratory Animals. There's actually a good chance your school falls under PHS coverage. Each year hundreds of research institutions receive funding either directly from the PHS or from one of its subagencies—the Agency for Health Care Policy Research, the Agency for Toxic Substances and Disease Registry, the Centers for Disease Control and Prevention, the Food and Drug Administration, the Health Resources and Services Administration, the Indian Health Service, the National Institutes of Health, and the Substance Abuse and Mental Health Services Administration.

The significant difference between this set of regulations and the AWA is that the PHS policy includes *all live, vertebrate animals*—warm- or cold-blooded.

Other than that, the policy operates in much the same way as the AWA. It's a very different type of document, written in much broader strokes. But the end results are about the same. For example, the PHS policy requires that animal enclosures "allow for the normal physiologic and behavioral needs of the animals" and gives some limited direction as to what that means. The AWA, on the other hand, gives mathematical formulas for each species that determine the minimum amount of floor space required. At the end of the day, they mean about the same thing.

In its more general way, the PHS policy requires pretty much everything the AWA does—vet care, adequate housing and nutrition, the minimization of pain, and protection from the elements. The full text is available online at grants.nih.gov/grants/olaw/olaw.htm.

Animal Rights

INSTITUTIONAL ANIMAL CARE AND USE COMMITTEES

Both sets of regulations require that each research facility appoint an Institutional Animal Care and Use Committee (IACUC) to oversee the treatment of the animals. Each committee must have three members—one has to be unaffiliated with the university and one has to be a vet. The committee must review and inspect the facilities at least once every six months. They also respond to, and investigate, complaints of mistreatment.

VOLUNTARY ACCREDITATION

A number of schools and research institutions have voluntarily sought accreditation from the Association for Assessment and Accreditation of Laboratory Animal Care (AAALAC).

In order to become an accredited institution, the school must submit itself to an extensive internal review of its policies, procedures, and records. Those that "exhibit excellence in animal care and use" are awarded accreditation. After that, the school's got to submit to a reevaluation every three years.

Of course, the AAALAC uses yet another set of standards to evaluate care. They rely on the *Guide for the Care and Use of Laboratory Animals*, published by the National Research Council (NRC). This is one of many third-party policies that are published by organizations involved in animal research. The NRC's guide is probably the most widely used.

You can read about the AAALAC ad infinitum at their website, www.aaalac.org, and order a free copy of the guidelines from them.

APPROACHING YOUR SPECIFIC CONCERNS

So you think that Mr. Fluffy is getting the shaft. Here's how to proceed:

Step One: Determine Regulatory Coverage First, figure out which, if any, of these regulatory schemes apply to your school. This shouldn't be that hard. If you're dealing with anything that's warm-blooded and not a rat, mouse, or bird, then the AWA applies. If not, go to the departmental office that oversees the lab and ask to see a list of grants that support the research. If there's a PHS agency on the list, then their guidelines apply. Finally go to the AAALAC's website and see if your school is accredited (there's a searchable database of accredited institutions).

Step Two: Get Specific If your school does fall under one of those schemes, get yourself a copy. If it doesn't, pick one. I suggest the AWA; it's the most specific. But choose whichever you want. Or use all three. Your school might not be legally bound to the regulations, but they'll still be good tools to assess whether the treatment you are concerned about is humane.

Then see if what you're worried about meets the standards. Run the numbers or see if the practices conform to what is deemed acceptable. And document as you go along. If you get a chance, take a photo of the offending action or make copies of the records that support the deficiency. This may require a bit of undercover work, but you should be able to pull it off without getting in trouble.

Step Three: Make a Complaint   Start with the professor who's in charge of the experiment or the lab. He may not even know that there are deficiencies in standard of care. So start at that level.

Your Lawyer Says:

DON'T WRITE OFF YOUR PROF AS CRUEL

It's easy to think of a researcher that participates in animal experimentation as cruel and unfeeling simply because of her job. But chances are she cares about the well-being of the animals as much as you do. And even if she is the academic equivalent of Cruella DeVille, treating her as such won't help you get the results you want.

If you don't get the results you want, it's time to go to higher authorities. If your school has an IACUC, that's the place to go. If they're accredited, call the AAALAC. If neither applies, you know the drill: Go to the dean or department chair. Make your complaint in writing and be sure to include copies of all of the documentation you've gathered.

Step Four: Leverage the Media
Even if you make all the right complaints to all the right people, you may still not see a change in the way animals are treated. First of all, what you see as abhorrent behavior may be within the acceptable limits. Or the lab's activities may fall outside the scope of any of these regulatory schemes.

But remember, all of these rules represent the *minimum* standards of care. There's no reason your school can't, or shouldn't, exceed these minimums. So if you've reached the end of the procedural line and haven't gotten what you want, don't be afraid to involve the school or local newspaper. Animal rights are a very sexy issue—especially among college-age readers. Make an appointment with the news editor and hand over your findings. There's a good chance that you'll get some coverage. And nothing motivates a college to change faster than bad press.

Animal Rights

Part Two
THE LAW ON CAMPUS

CHAPTER 6

Harassment & Discrimination

Discriminatory motives for treating someone badly: race, gender, disability, and (in certain locations) sexual orientation. Nondiscriminatory ones: pretty much everything else. As long as you avoid the big four, you can be a jerk all the time, for any reason you want. You won't make many friends, but it's legal.

Chapter Contents

Somewhere between "you look nice today" and "you've got a really great ass" there lies a line. On one side are compliments, comments, or any other benign behavior related to someone's gender. On the other is harassment. This line is difficult to figure out, and it's often hard to even see. Tone, context, personal experiences, and a million other intangible things blur it. Simply put, the whole concept of "offensive" is incredibly subjective. What's appropriate to one person may be completely insulting to another.

Similarly, it's nearly impossible to determine, with any kind of certainty, the motivations of another person. While we can clearly see their actions— he fired me, she gave me a bad grade, he's always asking me the hardest questions in class—we can only guess at what's causing them. Bad treatment by a professor *could* be due to some sort of bias your professor holds. But it could just as easily be because he's going through a bad divorce or is having money troubles or is just plain mean-spirited. Unless you can get inside your teacher's head (which you can't), you just won't know.

But these are the types of questions that need to be answered in instances of harassment and discrimination. In the context of interpersonal relations, navigating these kinds of ambiguities can be difficult enough. Legislating around them is nearly impossible. As you'll see, trying to articulate a fair and effective set of regulations that prohibit these kinds of behaviors is a complex task. Even the definitions of *harassment* and *discrimination* themselves require multiple tests and factors.

This chapter will walk you through the law in relation to race, gender, disability, and be sexual orientation. You'll learn how the standards work and be shown how to apply them to your own experiences. Understanding those legal frameworks is important. But your first test, especially in instances of harassment, should always be your gut. You'll know, better than any set of rules could ever teach you, when someone's crossing the line.

Sexual Harassment and Discrimination

GENDER-BASED HARASSMENT

Incidents of sexual harassment on campus are astonishingly commonplace. Between 20 and 30 percent of undergraduate women report that they were harassed in some manner by a professor, administrator, or other authority figure during their four years at school. At the graduate level things get even worse: between 30 and 40 percent say that they've been victimized. And, although the vast majority of those who are harassed are women, men aren't immune. Harassment against male students, usually perpetrated by a male teacher, isn't unknown. Studies show that it's on the rise.

Sex Harassment Defined   Most of us associate sexual harassment only with physical acts—the touchy, grabby types of incidents. But the legal definition is far more comprehensive than that: Any instance of unwelcome sexual behavior is sexual harassment. If you read that carefully you'll see that there are two parts to the definition. First the behavior needs to be *unwelcome*. If you're open to whatever is happening, it's not harassment. Courts have defined this more specifically, stating that unwelcome means that the victim did not solicit or incite the behavior and regarded the conduct as undesirable or offensive. As courts are prone to do, they've made a fairly simple concept a bit of a mess.

Second, the acts need to be *sexual* in nature. For these purposes *sexual* is about as inclusive as it can be. It's the exact opposite of Bill Clinton's famous definition of sex, which apparently only included coitus. Here sexual behavior means virtually any conduct that includes or refers to sex. Aside from the obvious touching, grabbing, and out-and-out asking for sex, this can include profane language that has sexual connotations, sexually charged jokes and humor, comments about a person's body or physical attractiveness, and even leering looks.

Beyond this general definition, sexual harassment is broken into two subsets: **quid pro quo** harassment and **hostile environment** harassment.

QUID PRO QUO HARASSMENT   The Latin phrase *quid pro quo* translates to "something for something." In the sex harassment arena, quid pro quo means *sex* for something. An authority figure will offer a higher grade, a chance to retake a test, admittance to a special course, or some other reward in return for sexual favors. Any kind of sexual favors count, from a hug all the way up to a full-out ride on the undergrad-go-round. Quid pro quo can also work in reverse, where a professor threatens a lower grade if sexual favors are withheld.

A related infraction is called sexual favoritism—preferential treatment based on romantic involvement. A teacher will give a student higher marks or other benefits based on the fact that the two of them are sexually involved. The victims are the other students in the class. Their grades, by comparison, are unfairly lower. Successful cases have been brought under this theory in the workplace (where a supervisor grants raises and promotions based on a romance). It hasn't yet been tested in a student and professor situation, but based on the outcome in the workplace cases, it's likely that the theory can be applied on campus.

Discrimination

HOSTILE ENVIRONMENT   Hostile environment harassment is much more vague and complex. And it's much more common. It's a situation where the presence of sexually charged conduct creates an atmosphere that is intimidating or offensive. While quid pro quo harassment must come from a superior, a hostile environment can be created by anyone—professors, fellow students, really anybody. In fact, it's possible for you as a student to create a hostile environment that affects your professor (so be careful when you're leering at him).

Hostile environment is a legal term so, of course, it has a multifaceted, somewhat confusing definition. Like I said above, pretty much anything unwanted and sexual is harassment, but if you want to legally prove you have been exposed to a hostile environment, you're going to have to show four things:

> **Vocabulary Lesson**
>
> **REASONABLE PERSON—** Many of the elements of a sexual harassment claim are fairly subjective. What one person might find utterly offensive another might think is fun and playful. That's why these types of things are decided on the basis of how a "reasonable person" would react. In other words, legally, the victim's personal perceptions are less important than the more objective reasonable person standard. In the case of sexual harassment, the gender of the victim can also be taken into account—because generally men and women have different standards for acceptable behavior.

1. *That you're a member of a protected class.* Of course, when we're talking about gender harassment, since everyone's either male or female (or a little of both), everyone's a member of a protected class.
2. *That the action or comment was based on your sex.* In other words, if the actions or comments wouldn't have happened but for the fact of your gender, then it's based on sex. "You have a really great body" would probably be gender specific. "You're really dumb" wouldn't. It's mean, but it's gender neutral.
3. *That the action was unwelcome.* Again, you can't have solicited or incited the conduct. In court this element can get rather sticky since flirting is inherently vague and difficult to decipher.
4. *That the action was intended to or actually did interfere with your work or created an intimidating, hostile, or offensive environment.* Generally this means that either whoever was doing this stuff has to admit that yes, they were trying to make you uncomfortable (which they won't) or you have to show that the harassment was so severe and pervasive that it made it difficult to function.

There is one final caveat to proving a legal case. It's called **respondeat superior**. There's absolutely no reason for you to know the Latin name for it (your college administrators probably don't), but it may make you sound smart at some cocktail party. Respondeat superior stands for the proposition that you have to give the school an opportunity to solve the problem themselves, or they can't be held legally responsible. Think about it. Your professor makes several salacious comments to you over the course a month or so. You say nothing, complain to no one, and just go about your business. A month later you file in court claiming hostile-environment harassment. How can your school possibly be held liable when you never said you were having a problem? Simply put, it can't. To successfully bring a case, you have to complain and then the university has to fail to take effective remedial action.

The respondeat superior requirements are also met if the school *should have known* about the harassment. This is called constructive (rather than actual) notice. This can happen in a number of ways. Sometimes the harasser's activities are so well known that knowledge will be imputed to the school itself. Another common scenario involves prior complaints about the harasser's behavior—if there have been ten complaints over the last year about one of your professors, the school's probably on notice and can be held liable.

GENDER DISCRIMINATION

As opposed to harassment, which is unwanted behavior linked to sex, discrimination is unequal treatment based on the victim's gender. For example, if a company pays its female employees less than male employees who perform the same job, that's discrimination. Likewise if a professor consistently gives female students higher grades than their male classmates. In theory it's pretty simple. If there's different treatment because of sex, it's illegal. There are two main types of discrimination: **disparate treatment** and **disparate impact**.

Disparate Treatment Discrimination   This is the straightforward type of discrimination. It's sometimes also called intentional discrimination. It's when a teacher or employer proactively treats someone differently because of gender. It sounds simple enough, but, as always, the law stretches the definition out into something much more complex. For a legal claim of harassment to stick under the disparate treatment theory the following has to happen:

✓ an employee or representative of the school must have treated someone differently in a way that interfered with or limited the ability of a student to participate in or benefit from a school program;

✓ the treatment must have occurred in the course of the official duties of the employee or representative; and

✓ the treatment must have been based on the gender of the victim.

Of course, as simple as disparate treatment discrimination is to describe, it's equally hard to prove. It's really easy for a professor to say, "She got a C because she's a poor student, not because she's a female." And very few professors, when confronted with an accusation of discrimination, simply say, "Yep, that's it. You got me. I don't think women should be mathematicians, so I always give them bad grades."

Because of this, the vast majority of harassment claims prove discriminatory intent through inference. Most commonly this is shown through statistics. Figures, such as grading trends, or stats proving that it takes females twice as long to get a promotion than it does men, are offered to show intent. Plaintiffs also often use something called comparative evidence— proof that similarly situated students or employees, who are not in the protected class, have been treated more favorably.

Disparate Impact Discrimination   Disparate impact discrimination is the more complex of the two types. It occurs when a school or company policy inadvertently excludes members of a protected class from some benefit. On its face, the offending policy may look completely neutral. In fact the people who made the policy may have had the best possible intentions. But if the policy discriminates in operation, it's illegal.

In the real world, disparate impact discrimination often comes up when an employer sets physical requirements for their employees. For example, fire companies used to subject potential firefighters to grueling physical endurance tests as a part of the hiring process. Some of the skills measured were absolutely necessary for the demands of the job. But much of what was required was more than what was needed to fight fires. The result: Many qualified women were unfairly excluded.

In the educational arena, the SATs are often criticized as having disparate impact on women (and minorities) as they score lower on average. The Department of Education's Office of Civil Rights took on the issue late in the Clinton administration, threatening that colleges that relied too heavily on the SATs could be guilty of discrimination. In the face of resounding resistance from the higher education and educational testing industries, the administration significantly softened its position. When Bush (II) took office, the issue was "archived." It hasn't seen the light of day since.

THE LEGAL BASES FOR SEXUAL HARASSMENT AND DISCRIMINATION CLAIMS (AND SOME STUFF YOU SHOULD KNOW ABOUT THEM)

As far as the statutes go, it doesn't matter whether your claim is for harassment or discrimination. At the federal level (and in most states), a single statute prohibits both. So, the legal basis for your suit and, more importantly, the procedures you have to follow are identical.

Title VII of the Civil Rights Act of 1964   If you're a graduate student, or any kind of student-employee, the actions of the university are actually the actions of your employer. So if the offending acts happen during the course of your employment, the legal basis for your claim will be the same federal law that covers all employees—Title VII of the Civil Rights Act.

Title VII is administered and enforced by a federal agency called the Equal Employment Opportunity Commission (EEOC). Before bringing a lawsuit under Title VII, a plaintiff is required to first file a complaint with the EEOC. This can be done in writing, by phone, or in person at a local field office. If there's a state or local law that also offers some sort of remedy (see below), the victim must file a complaint with that agency before complaining to the EEOC. All complaints must be filed within 180 days of the act of harassment or, in jurisdictions where there is local protection, within 300 days of the acts or within 30 days of notice from the state or local agency that it has terminated its processing of the charge—whichever is earlier.

The EEOC will then conduct its own investigation of the incident—conducting interviews, looking at records, and so on. If they find no evidence that there has been discrimination, they will release the case. At this point, if the victim wants to, she can proceed to the federal court system for a trial.

Your Lawyer Says:

WHEN IN DOUBT, CALL THE EEOC

If you're having trouble figuring out when to file a complaint with the EEOC, just ring them up. The worst that can happen is they'll tell you that it's not time yet, which is way better than letting the statute of limitations slip by.

If the EEOC does find evidence that harassment occurred, they will work with the university to try to remedy the problem. Essentially they attempt to broker a fair settlement between the victim and the school. The settlement could include a monetary award, employment changes for the offender, or other compensation. If the settlement fails, the EEOC may bring a federal suit on behalf of the victim. Or the victim can bring one himself or herself.

State and Local Anti-Harassment Laws   Most states, and many localities, have their own anti-harassment statutes. Many are modeled after the federal laws, but often they are more inclusive and offer broader remedies. Laws differ from state to state; contact your state's Equal Employment Agency for specific information about local procedures and statutes.

Discrimination

Title IX of the Education Amendments of 1972   Students who aren't employed by their school aren't covered by Title VII. They have to rely on Title IX. If this law sounds familiar, it's probably because you've heard it discussed in relation to college athletics. It's the law that mandates gender equality and, therefore, equal sports programs for men and women.

But Title IX is much more than a sports law. It is, simply put, one of the most sweeping anti-discrimination laws ever drafted. The heart of it is short, only 35 words: "No person in the U.S. shall, on the basis of sex be excluded from participation in, or denied the benefits of, or be subjected to discrimination under any educational program or activity receiving federal aid." But its effects are far-reaching.

Practically every school in the country, public or private, from elementary schools through graduate and professional schools, receives some form of federal aid. So chances are, as a student, you are afforded the protections of Title IX.

Courts and federal agencies look to Title VII when they're interpreting Title IX. So the theories of the laws operate almost identically. But there are some significant procedural and administrative differences between the two.

Title IX is administered by a different federal agency—the Office for Civil Rights (OCR). But the process is very similar. A complaint must be filed within 180 days of the harassment. The OCR will then investigate. If they find evidence of harassment, they will attempt to mediate between the school and the student. If those efforts fail, they may bring a case in federal court on the student's behalf.

But, unlike claims under Title VII, students have no obligation to either exhaust state remedies or file with the OCR before going to court. This means that a victim need not even deal with the OCR and their investigation before going off and filing a full-out lawsuit. And, if a suit is brought in federal court, the statute of limitations will be governed by state law. Most give claimants a year to file, many two. Because of this, and the fact that there is no monetary limit placed on Title IX awards, many lawyers chose to proceed under Title IX rather than Title VII.

Internal Grievance Procedures   Title IX also requires that each school have its own policy and process to deal with complaints of sexual harassment or discrimination. The details of the procedures are left open to the school, but most policies will, at least, include a method of filing a complaint, an investigation process, and some sort of hearing. Finding your school's policy shouldn't be difficult. Title IX also requires that students be notified of the policy—it's usually included in the student handbook or catalog.

And the law requires that each campus have a designated employee who is in charge of all Title IX compliance and complaints. The name and contact information of this person needs to be published in the same way the procedures are.

Racial Harassment and Discrimination

RACE-BASED HARASSMENT

Comprehensive national statistics about racial harassment on college campuses aren't available. The Clery Act (a law that requires schools to report crimes to the U.S. Department of Education; see chapter 12, "Campus Safety & Security," for a full discussion) and most other studies measure only hate crimes, not all racially motivated incidents.

Those hate crime statistics are certainly harrowing. A 1998 study conducted by the FBI found that of the 450 colleges and universities surveyed, 222 had at least one hate crime on campus during the previous year. Similarly, the Department of Education's statistics show that, in the year 2000 alone, 1,994 hate-motivated assaults took place on college campuses. Most recently, a 2001 report by the U.S. Department of Justice concluded that hate crimes "occur at virtually every type of college and university and in every part of the nation."

Although this chapter deals only with noncriminal incidents of harassment, I think the hate crime statistics clearly show that racial prejudice, and really all forms of intolerance, are still prevalent on America's campuses. Sadly, today's minority students will likely encounter some form of bigotry during their time at school.

Racial Harassment Defined

Obviously, racial incidents of quid pro quo harassment aren't possible. So the only theory under which racial harassment can be shown is **hostile environment**. Hostile environment harassment in the racial arena operates almost exactly the same way it does with gender harassment. It's a racially charged atmosphere that intimidates or interferes with school or employment. The high points of how the law operates follow:

✓ It can be perpetrated by anyone, not just an authority figure.
✓ The racist acts can be verbal, physical, written, or communicated in any way.

Vocabulary Lesson ?

RACE—Although most lawyers refer to this area of law simply as "racial" harassment and discrimination, the law also includes discrimination and harassment based on color, religion, or national origin. While racial discrimination is the most common of the four, problems with the others do occur. For example, someone may treat a person badly simply because their skin and features are dark. The discriminator may not even know the person's race, but will treat them poorly because he "looks like an Arab." To make things simple here, I'll refer to the whole lot as "racial." But as you read, understand that the laws and advice cover all four.

Discrimination

✓ They need not be directed at the victim for the atmosphere to be hostile. So long as the victim can see or hear them, it doesn't matter who they are intended for.

✓ They need not be based on the race of the victim. They could be based on the race of a friend, a spouse, a colleague.

✓ The harassment has to be sufficiently severe or pervasive enough to limit or interfere with the ability of the victim to participate or benefit from a university activity.

✓ Finally, our old friend respondeat superior applies, so the university has to have had actual or constructive notice of the behaviors and failed to take action to remedy the situation.

RACE-BASED DISCRIMINATION

Racial discrimination also operates as the parallel to gender discrimination—the critical difference being that the disparities are, obviously, based on the race rather than gender of the victim. Just as in gender discrimination, it's possible to prove racial discrimination under either the *disparate treatment* or *disparate impact* theory. See above for a full discussion.

THE LEGAL BASES FOR RACIAL HARASSMENT AND DISCRIMINATION CLAIMS

Again, as in gender discrimination, the law doesn't differentiate between claims for racial harassment and discrimination. So the laws under which you'll bring a claim, and the procedures you'll have to follow, are the same whether you've been discriminated against or harassed.

Title VII of the Civil Rights Act of 1964 Title VII prohibits racial discrimination as well as sex and gender discrimination. So if you're a graduate student or any kind of student-employee Title VII protects you. As detailed in the section on gender issues, the EEOC administers the law. After exhausting state and local avenues, students can file complaints directly with the EEOC, who will investigate and try to broker a settlement. Remember, the time limit to file is within 180 days of the act of harassment or discrimination. Or, if local remedies are available, the limit is within 300 days of the acts or 30 days of notice from the state or local agency that it has terminated its processing of the charge—whichever is earlier.

State and Local Anti-Discrimination Laws Most states, and many localities, have their own employment anti-discrimination and harassment statutes. They may be more inclusive and favorable than the federal statute. And if you want to file a complaint with the EEOC, you'll need to avail yourself of those laws anyway. So check them out.

Title VI of the Civil Rights Act of 1964 Title VI is the sibling of Title IX. It prohibits discrimination based on race, color, or national origin at any institution that receives federal financial support. Almost every college in the nation receives some amount of federal money, so for nonemployee students, Title VI is the basis of any racial harassment or discrimination claims. Title VI is, like Title IX, administered by the OCR. And the rules and procedures operate in almost the same way, with a few notable exceptions:

- ✓ The school is not required to adopt a specific grievance procedure. They are, however, required to adopt an anti-discrimination policy and notify their students and employees of it. These usually amount to little more than "The University does not discriminate on the basis of race, color, or national origin."
- ✓ The school is also not required to designate a program coordinator. So there may not be an obvious place to go to lodge your complaint.

The rest, including the time limits and the overall process, is the same. In practice, these regulatory variations don't make much difference in the way schools work with Title IX and Title VI. Most colleges and universities use the same internal grievance process for both racial and sexual harassment. And, usually, the university official responsible for Title IX compliance also deals with Title VI problems. So if you're at a loss about who to talk to at your school, go see the Title IX designee. Even if she doesn't handle race issues at your school, she'll certainly be able to point you in the right direction.

What to Do about Race- or Gender-Based Problems

If you think you've been the victim of racial or sexual harassment or discrimination, you have some decisions to make. Foremost, should you take action or take the abuse? I'd love to be able to give you a piece of advice that could simplify your decision, but I can't. The fact of the matter is: Bringing a claim, even an informal one, can be extremely hard on the victim. Even in the idealized world of a college campus, you may encounter all sorts of negative side effects if you proceed.

I don't want to scare you off. Those who harass and discriminate should be flushed out and punished. But bringing these types of claims is a very serious business. I wouldn't want anyone to go into the process lightly. So, if you think you've been harassed in some way, your first order of business should be to think. Take a deep breath, step back from the situation, and

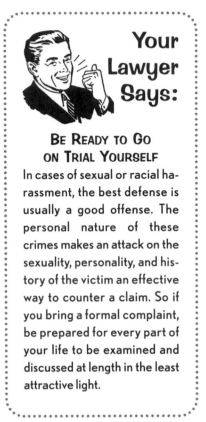

Your Lawyer Says:

BE READY TO GO ON TRIAL YOURSELF

In cases of sexual or racial harassment, the best defense is usually a good offense. The personal nature of these crimes makes an attack on the sexuality, personality, and history of the victim an effective way to counter a claim. So if you bring a formal complaint, be prepared for every part of your life to be examined and discussed at length in the least attractive light.

try to evaluate it as objectively as possible. Think about the two paths ahead of you: bringing a claim or not. And choose the one that's best for you.

UNIVERSITY FIRST

If you do decide to proceed, it's almost always best to begin with the university's internal procedure first, rather than jumping straight into an agency complaint or a court case. And, because of the respondeat superior requirements, if you wanted to bring a hostile environment complaint, you'd probably have to show that you made some sort of complaint anyway. More importantly, navigating the school's system is going to be infinitely simpler and quicker than the other avenues available to you.

So make an appointment with the school's Title IX compliance officer and have an informal talk about what happened and what your options are. You'll be able to get a lot of good information. But make sure that the conversation will be confidential before you talk. It should be, but just as a precaution ask before you spill the beans. And stay true to your agenda, not his or hers. At all times make decisions based on what's best for you, not what's best for other people.

Keep your eye on the clock as you work through this. Remember there are time limits for filing complaints, so be wary of them. If the 180 days is creeping up on you and you're getting nowhere with the internal process, it may be worth it to contact a lawyer and discuss your options.

If the incidents were of the more serious variety—quid pro quo, severe harassment, or blatant discrimination, it's probably a good idea to talk to an attorney at the outset. I generally think that the internal procedures are the best way to deal with on-campus harassment. But sometimes in severe cases there may be some merit in considering a private lawsuit.

Disability Discrimination

More students with disabilities are enrolled in colleges and universities today than ever before. In 1978 less than 3 percent of college freshmen were disabled. But in just over twenty years, this figure has almost tripled. In 1994 it had risen to more than 8 percent. By 2000, 9.3 percent of all college students reported having some sort of disability—that's more than one and a half million people.

This dramatic shift is probably due to two factors. First, there are more opportunities for disabled people today. Over the past few decades, colleges have made their facilities and programs more accessible to those who have disabilities. Some of these changes have come out of the goodness of administrators' hearts, but many have come about because of increased legal protections for those with disabilities.

The second cause of this rise is an increasingly inclusive definition of disability. The introduction of conditions such as ADD, ADHD, dyslexia, social anxiety disorder, and many other disabilities—ones that were unknown not long ago—has increased the population of the disabled. This expansion underscores an important conceptual distinction between disability discrimination and other types: the concept of disabled is malleable.

THE LEGAL DEFINITION OF DISABLED

Either you're a boy or a girl. And, in most cases, there's little interpretation required to determine someone's race. But disability, really, works on a sliding scale. *None of us* is perfect. *I* could certainly be smarter or a faster runner or have better eyesight. There's also something wrong with one of my shoulders. It hurts when I type for too long. But I certainly don't have a disability. So where does the line between able-bodied and disabled lie?

It's a difficult question. And, unfortunately, the deeper into the law you get, the more convoluted it becomes. All of the laws that offer protections to those with disabilities operate under, basically, the same, oblique definition. They say you're disabled if you

1. have a physical or mental impairment that substantially limits a major life activity,
2. have a record of such an impairment, or
3. are regarded as having such an impairment.

Clearly, the first of the three is the most straightforward. It's also full of terms that are fairly hard to define. For starters, what's a "major life activity"? And how bad does your condition have to be for it to be considered "substantially limited"? The regulations written by the various governmental organizations meant to offer guidance on these questions are pretty ambiguous. They generally offer examples: "Major life activities means functions such as caring for oneself, performing manual tasks, walking, seeing, hearing, speaking, breathing, learning, and working." Not much help, huh?

Discrimination

So it's largely been left up to the courts to decide just how inclusive the definition of disability should be. They vary in their decisions. Generally, lower courts favor a broader definition, while the federal courts tend to restrict it. Some of the higher court judges have even gone so far as to read the regulations literally and only include conditions specifically mentioned.

There's even an ongoing debate about the standard of comparison for the "substantiality limits" part of the definition. Let's say you're in medical school and you have a learning disability, one that makes it difficult for you to concentrate for long periods of time in examinations. Clearly, taking tests is a major life (or school) activity. And your problem makes it more difficult for you to take the tests than the other students. But are your fellow med students the people you should be compared to when evaluating the substantiality of your condition? If so, then you're probably disabled. But what if the standard was the general population? Hell, you've gotten into medical school. You're probably *way* better at taking tests than most people. So maybe your learning disability isn't, legally, a disability. Or what if the standard is, as some courts have decided, between your inherent capacity and your actual performance? I suppose anyone who didn't always "work up to their potential" could potentially be disabled.

My point: There's no simple definition of "disabled." Certainly there are clear-cut conditions that no one would deny qualify. But at the limits of the term, there is a substantial grey area. In those instances it really is for the courts to decide on a case-by-case basis.

Otherwise Qualified At the postsecondary level, the laws require that the disabled student be otherwise qualified to participate in the programs. If you think about this, it makes perfect sense.

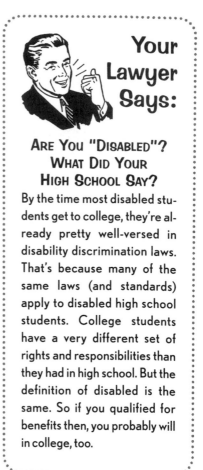

Your Lawyer Says:

ARE YOU "DISABLED"? WHAT DID YOUR HIGH SCHOOL SAY?

By the time most disabled students get to college, they're already pretty well-versed in disability discrimination laws. That's because many of the same laws (and standards) apply to disabled high school students. College students have a very different set of rights and responsibilities than they had in high school. But the definition of disabled is the same. So if you qualified for benefits then, you probably will in college, too.

First off, regardless of the student's, or potential student's, disability, the school can still maintain academic standards. So if the disabled person can't meet the essential requirements set by the school, either with or without accommodations, then the school can refuse them admission.

The courts, generally, defer to the judgment of the schools in these types of instances. The second circuit court explained this position well in a 1981 case that involved a disabled student who was denied admission to New York University based on the fact that he was not otherwise qualified:

> [C]ourts are particularly ill-equipped to evaluate academic performance. . . . For this reason, although the Act requires us rather than the institution to make the final determination of whether a handicapped individual is otherwise qualified . . . considerable judicial deference must be paid to the evaluation made by the institution itself, absent proof that its standards and its application of them serve no purpose other than to deny an education to handicapped persons.

Still, courts aren't beyond overturning a decision if the facts support it. A good example of this is *Pushkin v. Regents of the University of Colorado*. There, an M.D. with multiple sclerosis was denied admission to a psychiatric residency program. The admissions committee based its decision on their opinion that, given his condition, the program would be too stressful for him and that he would require too much ongoing medical attention himself to be able to satisfy the requirements of the job. They were also concerned about how psychiatric patients might react to his disability. They gleaned all of this, evidently, in a single forty-five-minute interview.

The court sided with Pushkin, pointing out that the denial was based, in large part, on assumptions of inability and presupposed disabilities. They ordered he be admitted to the program.

DISABILITY LAWS AND COVERAGE

No matter what kind of school you go to, there's probably a law that protects your rights as a disabled person. Not so long ago this wasn't the case. Before 1973 the only potential source for legal satisfaction was the Fourteenth Amendment, which provided protection in, really, the most general of terms. It guarantees equal protection under the laws and due process where life, liberty, or property is at stake. Certainly this could be interpreted to include protections for the disabled, but it's a bit of a stretch.

But in the last thirty years, the legal landscape has changed significantly. Congress enacted a comprehensive scheme of disability laws. There are two components to it: the Rehabilitation Act, passed in 1973, and the Americans with Disabilities Act (ADA), enacted in 1990. Between the two, almost every sphere of public and private life is covered.

In Employment   Title I of the ADA prohibits private employers with more than fifteen employees, state and local governments, employment agencies, and labor unions from discriminating against otherwise qualified employees

Discrimination

based on disability. A parallel law, Section 501 of the Rehabilitation Act, prohibits disability discrimination by the federal government.

These laws are the disability equivalents of Title VII. So if you're a graduate student or any other type of school employee, at either a public or private school, and the discrimination occurs in the course of your employment, these laws will be the basis of your claim.

In Public Schools   Title II of the ADA prohibits public entities from denying disabled persons the right to participate in the programs and services they provide and from otherwise discriminating based on disability. For disabled students at public schools, this is one of the legal sources of protection.

At Schools Receiving Federal Assistance   Section 504 of the Rehabilitation Act says that no otherwise qualified person with a disability may be denied the right to participate in or benefit from, or may be subjected to discrimination under, any program that receives federal financial assistance. In practice, pretty much every school in the country receives some form of financial assistance, so the reach of Section 504 is far-ranging. It probably applies to 99 percent of the students in college or at universities in America.

Catch-All   Finally, colleges that aren't under the purview of any of the above laws (meaning private schools that receive no federal assistance) still have to afford disabled students rights based on the fact that the school operates *places of public accommodation*. Title III of the ADA prohibits disability discrimination by private entities that operate areas of public accommodation. Most parts of the average college fall under the Department of Justice's definition of public accommodation. Dorms, cafeterias, concert halls and auditoriums, stores, laundry facilities, health service facilities, and gyms are all included. And the law specifically names undergraduate and graduate schools as being covered.

REASONABLE ACCOMMODATIONS

One of the most significant differences between disability law and other types of discrimination law is the concept of making reasonable accommodations. With race and gender discrimination, there's no affirmative arm to the school's responsibilities. They can't treat you differently based on your status, plain and simple. But under disability laws, the school has to make the necessary adjustments (within reason) to accommodate the special needs of their disabled students. And they can't charge the disabled student for them. For example, if your school offers housing to its students, then it needs to offer similar, accessible dormitory facilities for disabled students. Or, if a student with impaired vision enrolls at a college, the school may have to provide special, large-format texts or offer the services of a reader to help with assignments.

The types of accommodations a school might offer are determined based on the specific disability and needs of the student. They could be almost anything: modified academic requirements, a reduced course load, the substitution of one course for another, sign language interpreters, extended time for testing, note-takers, computers with voice recognition or other adaptive equipment, or anything else.

But, as mentioned earlier in the discussion of the otherwise qualified requirements, the school has no obligation to provide an accommodation that would lower the standards or have a substantial effect on the content of the education.

How to Request an Accommodation Of course, a school isn't required to psychically intuit which students are disabled, then offer up the appropriate accommodations. Most of the burden for ensuring that the proper accommodations are made falls on the disabled student.

The student has to inform the school that he's disabled and will need some sort of accommodation. Today most schools have at least one staff member that specifically deals with disabled students. Often they're called the Section 504 or ADA Coordinator. This is whom you'll need to talk to about your situation.

DOCUMENTATION Your school will most likely require some sort of documentation to prove that you are, indeed, disabled. What's required varies from school to school, but expect to be asked for, at the very least, documentation from an appropriate medical professional (a doctor or psychologist) that includes the credentials of the professional, a diagnosis of your condition, the date of diagnosis, and a description of how your disability affects you and your academic performance.

Some schools require that the diagnosis be relatively recent. So you may need to get a new evaluation. Unfortunately, the school is not required to pay for the new evaluation if they require it. So those costs will probably fall on you.

REVIEW AND DETERMINATION After you've submitted all of the documentation, the school will review your request and offer the accommodations

> **Your Lawyer Says:**
>
> **REQUEST ACCOMMODATIONS ASAP**
> You can request an accommodation at any time during (or before) the school year. But the process of evaluating a situation and arranging for an accommodation can take a lot of time. Expect it to be, at the very least, six weeks. So don't hesitate. Talk to your school's ADA coordinator about your situation as soon as possible.

Discrimination

they feel are adequate. If you've requested a specific adjustment, they may agree to it or they may offer an alternative they feel will be more effective. If they believe it's necessary, the school may also perform their own evaluation of your condition (this time they're responsible for the costs).

BE PROACTIVE AND INTERACTIVE Smart students will try to make this whole process as cooperative as possible. Approach it as a progression where you and your school will work together to find the best solution. But keep a critical eye on your school's dealings with you. Although they're required to help you, they may not do it in the quickest or friendliest manner. And, more importantly, they may be more attuned to their needs than yours. I know of a school in the Southwest that, until very recently, had elevators in only two of its academic buildings—those that housed the engineering and the accounting departments. When students with mobility issues enrolled, the administration did everything they could to get them to major in one of those two areas. Can you imagine the ridiculous conversations that must have occurred every time a student in a wheelchair was interested in the humanities? "I was thinking about majoring in French literature." "Hmm, that's an interesting idea, but what about engineering instead?" "Umm, no, I hate math." "Okay, then, how about accounting?"

That's an extreme example, to be sure. But it's good to be aware of the fact that disability discrimination may manifest itself in more understated ways than outright denial. Your school may try to subtly move you to a place that suits their agenda rather than yours. Be on the lookout for moves like this.

Also, take ownership and responsibility for the entire course of action. If you want things to proceed at a reasonable pace, it will probably be up to you to move the process along. And if you get stuck, don't be afraid to think creatively. Sometimes the best resolutions come way out of left field. It may be up to you to think of what you need.

Maintain this stance *after* you've been granted an accommodation, too. Adopt a plan of constant reevaluation. Is the accommodation working? Is there a way it can be modified that will help you or the school? Are there components that aren't necessary? Don't be afraid to request modifications along the way if something isn't working.

And remember, sometimes an accommodation can bring added responsibilities with it. I knew a hearing-impaired student who was assigned a notetaker to help him with his classes. The arrangement worked out well, for the most part. But in his physics class (a required course that he had absolutely no aptitude for, and no interest in), he tended to zone out. His notetaker had an eagle eye, though, and would give him an elbow in the side every time he started to nod off. Needless to say, my hearing-impaired friend wasn't really pleased with this value-added service. He would have much rather slept than listened to a lecture about adiabatic change. But because he had a note-taker, it meant he also had a chaperone of sorts. And if the note-taker had to be awake and paying attention to the class, then he was damned well going to make sure that the person he was taking notes for was, too.

Always keep in mind that, even though you may be legally entitled to a given accommodation, the people who are accommodating you are still making an effort, sometimes a big effort, on your behalf. Do what you can to show that you appreciate them and that you respect their time and hard work. Remember, you may need new or modified accommodations in the future. Reports from your note-taker that you always slept during, or rarely showed up for, your classes will work against you.

BRINGING A CLAIM FOR DISABILITY DISCRIMINATION

Disability discrimination also has the more conventional, reactive component—a lawsuit. If you feel you've been treated unfairly based on your disability, you can bring a claim for discrimination. Section 504 (which is what most college disability claims are brought under) is, like Title VI and Title IX, administered by the Office of Civil Rights. So most of the procedures described earlier apply. You're not required to exhaust state or institutional remedies before filing, but you must file within 180 days of the discriminatory act or within 60 days of the completion of the school's grievance procedure.

Internal Procedures   Also like Title VI, Section 504 requires that schools develop and implement an internal procedure for dealing with claims of disability discrimination. And it requires that they have a designated employee who deals with these issues. Information about all of this is generally included in the student handbook. Again, aggrieved students aren't required to use the school's process before filing with the OCR, but the school's system will, most likely, result in a faster solution. I recommend giving it a try first.

Sexual Orientation Discrimination

As unbelievable as it seems, there are no federal laws that protect the rights of gays, lesbians, and bisexuals—not in employment, not in education, not even in government employment. Stunning, isn't it? A few states, and some local governments, have laws that prohibit sexual orientation discrimination, but that's it. So far as the federal government is concerned, those with so-called alternative lifestyles are on their own.

Discrimination

STATES WITH LAWS THAT PROHIBIT SEXUAL ORIENTATION DISCRIMINATION IN EDUCATION

✓ California

✓ Connecticut

✓ District of Columbia

✓ Massachusetts

✓ Minnesota

✓ New Jersey

✓ New York

✓ Vermont

✓ Wisconsin

Thankfully, this is one of the areas where colleges have, for the most part, stepped up to bat and adopted their own policies. Today, the vast majority of schools have designated sexual orientation as a protected class. The Human Rights Campaign did a broad study of schools' anti-discrimination policies and documented more than 300 schools that offered some sort of protection for orientation discrimination. Their list isn't, in any sense, all-inclusive. It's just a sampling of what's out there. In my experience I see that schools today, much more often than not, have a policy that protects against sexual orientation harassment and discrimination.

Colleges generally employ one of two kinds of policies: an actual *anti-discrimination policy* or a *conduct code*. Anti-discrimination policies are more common and offer stronger protections. They're typically drafted as a declarative statement that covers all types of potential discrimination: "The university is committed to a policy of nondiscrimination and equal opportunity for all persons regardless of race, sex, color, religion, creed, national origin, disability, or sexual orientation."

Conduct codes, as you've probably guessed, set forth appropriate behavior for their students. Some schools, rather than having a blanket anti-discrimination policy, simply list acts motivated by anti-gay bias as something that's not allowed: "The school prohibits . . . harassment of any member of the university community including harassment on the basis of race, sexual orientation, age, gender, religion, and physical disability." Since this type of policy is limited to the specific acts it mentions, their coverage is sometimes less broad than that of a proper policy.

WHAT TO DO

Research the "Laws"   If you feel you've been the victim of some form of sexual orientation harassment or discrimination, your first step should be a thorough search for laws or rules that might protect you. Since we already know there's no federal statute in place, it's best in this case to start at the bottom of the hierarchy and work your way up. So first see what kind of policy your school has in place. Check the student handbook. Chances are any anti-discrimination policies will be included there. But even if you don't find anything there, it's probably a good idea to go to the office of student life and make a verbal inquiry. They'll know what kind of rules are in place.

Next, move to the municipal and state level. As mentioned above, a few states and many local municipalities (thank God for those open-minded municipalities!) have adopted sexual orientation policies. Lambda Legal (www.lambdalegal.org) keeps an updated, state-by-state list online. Check there to see what's in place in your area. In fact, it's probably worth your time to give them a call no matter what you find online. They are a great organization and are the absolute experts in this area.

Approach an Official   It's possible that you'll entirely strike out in your legal research. There may be no state or municipal statute, and your school might not have an inclusive policy. No matter what you find, I would suggest approaching a school official to discuss your problem. Go to the school's designated Title IX coordinator (since she deals with other types of discrimination, she'll likely know what to do) or even an adviser or trusted professor and lay out the situation. Obviously these talks will be easier if there is some policy or law in place that protects you. But even in their absence, there's a good chance you'll get some sort of resolution. Most colleges want no part of intolerance based on any kind of bias. Sure, they may not have codified their views about sexual orientation just yet, but that doesn't mean they want it to happen on their campus. So approach an official and see what comes of it.

Consider Some Activism   Hopefully you'll be able to resolve your situation using internal avenues. But if you can't, maybe it's time to effect some much-needed change at your school. Start asking questions about why your school doesn't have a policy. And work toward getting them to adopt one. I'm betting you'll find an abundance of support among the

Discrimination

school's faculty (professors tend to be a liberal, open-minded lot). It's probably also good to contact Lambda Legal at this point; they've worked nationally to help college students and faculty persuade their schools to adopt sexual orientation policies. They'll be a great deal of help.

And don't forget the media. Colleges *hate* bad press, especially the kind that portrays the school as an intolerant and bigoted place. Consider telling your story to the school newspaper, the local media, or even some selected national outlets. It's never bad to have the press on your side.

CHAPTER 7

Student Records

"Anonymous" grade postings using social security numbers violate student privacy laws. And having to check your marks in front of a crowd of ogling spectators is downright demeaning. If one of your professors posts scores this way, tell her you'd like your grades communicated to you in a legal (and humane) manner.

Chapter Contents

Although most of us think of educational records in terms of grades and transcripts, your college has a wealth of other data at their fingertips. Some of it is mundane—payment schedules, housing forms, and so forth. But student files do contain some sensitive materials. And even seemingly benign information needs to be guarded carefully. Identity thieves don't need much—a social security number, for example—to make off with your persona.

There is a federal statute in place that guarantees students a certain level of privacy in such matters. But, as you'll see, it's far from perfect. There are large holes in and exceptions to the regulations. And despite the guidelines, professors and schools sometimes ignore their obligations. So, as always, you'll need to understand your rights and guard them carefully.

The Family Educational Rights and Privacy Act

The Family Educational Rights and Privacy Act (FERPA), sometimes called the Buckley Amendment, is the law that governs student records. It's not a particularly well-written statute. In fact, the act is notorious for its shortcomings. Just after it was passed one Yale University lawyer called it "a masterpiece of wretched draftsmanship." I tend to agree. Even after a quarter of a century of amendments and department guidance, it is still vague and cumbersome. And it is more often used by schools to cover up their mistakes than to protect their students.

But at its base, FERPA isn't complex. It gives students the right to

1. inspect and review their records,
2. contest and amend inaccurate records, and
3. control the disclosure of information about them.

We'll look at each of these areas in turn and explain the exceptions and caveats that accompany them.

EDUCATIONAL RECORDS DEFINED

FERPA doesn't protect every piece of paper the school has; it only applies to "educational records" as defined in the act. The rule of thumb: If it personally identifies a specific student, then it's an educational record. This includes transcripts, financial aid records, class schedules, letters of recommendation, and most other things that have a student's name attached to them. The records don't have to be printed on paper. E-mail, electronic records, and even audio recordings count. And they don't have to include the student's actual name. Any mark that identifies the student is good enough. The most common offending collegiate example is the practice of "anonymously" postings grades, where professors list final grades by social security number and tack them to a wall. Since the lists identify the students, they fall under FERPA's purview.

EXEMPTED RECORDS

A few types of records are specifically exempted from FERPA protection. Most significant is *directory information*. This is your "phone book" type of data—name, address, home and local telephone numbers, dates of attendance, major extracurricular activities, and date and place of birth. For student athletes the concept of directory info is a bit expanded. Height, weight, and performance statistics are considered part of their listing. Schools are allowed to disclose all of this information to anyone they please.

Your Lawyer Says:

KEEP YOUR LISTING ON THE QT

Your directory information is specifically exempted from FERPA, so your school can give it out to anyone they please—*unless* you ask them not to. All you have to do is give a written request to the registrar. Then, only campus officials will be able to get the 411 on you.

Campus law enforcement records are also exempted from the act. So if your name is included in an incident report or some other type of enforcement-related record, it's public. Actual police records are always publicly available, so if your campus security is a commissioned force (or if you get arrested on campus by real cops), the records aren't private.

FERPA also excludes *records that are kept in the sole possession of the maker for personal use*. For example, if one of your professors commits some comments to paper so that she can grade you later, those notes wouldn't be covered by FERPA. You have no right to inspect or amend them. However, this is only true if she's the only one who ever sees them. If they're ever included in any permanent file or given to any other person, they become bona fide educational records and FERPA applies.

Treatment records kept by a campus doctor, counselor, psychiatrist, or any other recognized professional aren't covered by FERPA either. This may seem like a big loophole, but health-related records are covered by the Privacy Rule under the Health Insurance Portability and Accountability Act of 1996 (HIPAA). Much like FERPA, HIPAA guarantees patients the right to inspect and amend their medical records and limits their disclosure.

Finally, *information the school gathers about former students* isn't covered. So any records created by the school after you graduate fall outside FERPA coverage. "Why would the college keep records about me *after* I've left?" you might ask. Well, the day after you graduate your school's focus will shift immediately from educating you to trying to squeeze donations out of you. They'll gather all sorts of information to help them gauge how much money you have and how much they can get you to fork over. Even though these files would make for some interesting reading, you have no right to access or amend them. And the school can disclose the information without your consent.

WHICH SCHOOLS AND STUDENTS?

Like Title IX, FERPA applies to all schools that receive any kind of federal aid, so pretty much every school in the country, private or public, must live by FERPA's rules. FERPA rights only vest in students who have actually enrolled in a school—if you've applied to a college but never actually got in or attended, you have no FERPA rights regarding the school's info. And FERPA rights terminate at death. If a student or former student dies, the school can do whatever they please with the remaining records.

YOUR RIGHT TO INSPECT AND AMEND UNDER FERPA

You have the right to inspect all of your educational records—with two exceptions. First, your parents' financial records are off-limits. The forms they've filled out for financial aid and other payment purposes are their business, not yours. Second, you don't have the right to view any confidential letters of recommendation. You've probably already run into this once or twice in your academic career. Recommendation forms usually have a confidentiality statement on them. They say something along the lines of "I openly and freely waive my right to view this recommendation" and have a space for your signature. If you sign on that line, you've waived your FERPA rights.

The Process Aside from that, you have the right to review and inspect to your heart's content. The process is simple enough. All you have to do is go to your college's student records office or the student affairs office and ask to see your files. There's no specific requirement that the request be made in writing, but if you are serious about getting your hands on your records, it makes sense to submit your request in a letter.

The school then has forty-five days to accommodate you. They can give you either the originals or copies. If there are documents in your file that name other students, the information about them must be redacted before the files are given over to you (they have FERPA rights, too).

Inaccurate Records If something's amiss, you can request that the record be amended to more accurately reflect the truth. Again, you don't have to do this in writing, but you probably should. At this point, the school may just cave and let you amend the file. But if they refuse, you also have a right to a hearing in front of an impartial board. If you prevail at the hearing, then the school has to make the change. If you lose, you still get to add your own statement to the file contesting the contents.

This amendment process is only meant to remedy clerical errors—not the substance that underlies the records themselves. For example, if you got an A in one of your classes but your transcript says you got a B+, then you'd be able to contest under FERPA. On the other hand, if you were awarded a B+, but you think you really *deserved* an A, you're out of luck—at least as far as your FERPA rights go. You'd have to take that issue up with your professor.

THE SCHOOL'S PROHIBITION ON DISCLOSURE

FERPA prohibits any disclosure of your educational records without your written permission. They can't give any identifiable information to your roommates, prospective employers, other schools, the press, or anyone else without your okay. Of course, there are a number of exceptions.

University Employees The FERPA prohibitions don't apply to disclosure within the campus's professional community. School employees can share student-specific information for educational purposes without prior consent. Without this exception, each professor would have to ask your permission before they reported your final grade to the registrar, your financial aid adviser would have to get consent to discuss your case with a colleague, and so on.

Your Parents Most parents and legal guardians can access their kids' records. The test is one of legal dependency. If your parents claim you as a dependent on their tax return, then they have the same rights as you. Parental FERPA rights don't *replace* student rights. They exist in addition to them. So even if you're a legal dependent, you still have all of your FERPA rights. But so do your parents—this means that, just like you, they can inspect and review all of your educational records and consent to their disclosure. So just forget any fantasies about keeping your grades or other school business a secret from Mom and Dad. If push comes to shove, they probably have a right to see your transcript.

Health or Safety Emergencies If there's a health or safety emergency, FERPA allows colleges and universities to disclose information that's necessary to protect the student in question or others. Personally I can't imagine how this would come up—"There's a flood coming, and the only way to stop it is to release your official transcript." But there it is.

Disciplinary Proceedings If a student is accused of a violent crime or nonforcible sex offense (date rape and the like), the results of the on-campus disciplinary hearing may be disclosed under certain circumstances. First, the school is allowed to disclose the final results of the hearing, whether guilty or innocent, to the alleged victim. Second, if the student is found guilty, then the school can disclose the name of the student, the violation committed, and the sanction imposed by the school. All other records created in disciplinary hearings are educational records and are given full FERPA protection.

Drug and Alcohol Violations   If a student under the age of twenty-one has violated any drug- or alcohol-related law, the school may notify the legal guardians or parents of the offending student. This exception applies regardless of the dependent status described above.

Subpoenas   If the school is served with a lawful subpoena or court order, then they may disclose protected records without the student's permission. Normally, if a university is served with such a subpoena, they'll notify the student before the records are produced. And the court will almost always notify the target of the investigation that a subpoena has been issued. This gives the students a chance to seek an injunctive court order of their own if they wish.

THE USA PATRIOT ACT AND STUDENT RECORDS

While we're talking about the disclosure of student records, it makes sense to touch on the recently passed antiterrorism laws. As I'm sure you know, the USA PATRIOT ("Uniting and Strengthening America by Providing Appropriate Tools Required to Intercept and Obstruct Terrorism") Act of 2001 was passed by Congress shortly after the September 11 attacks. It amended fifteen federal statutes in an attempt to give law enforcement agencies expanded resources to investigate terrorism.

Although the PATRIOT Act's purpose may have been to "unite and strengthen" America, its effect on civil liberties has been quite the opposite. Many basic constitutional rights were seriously compromised by these laws. Student privacy is no exception. The PATRIOT Act gives the government two new ways to get at your records. And, what's worse, it allows them to invade your privacy without any notice to you at all.

First, FERPA was one of the affected statutes. The PATRIOT Act amendments allow the government access to student records through ex parte court orders (ones that are issued without notice to the adverse party) in connection with the investigation or prosecution of terrorism crimes.

Second, the act expanded the government's investigative powers under a law called the Foreign Intelligence Surveillance Act (FISA). Under FISA, government agencies involved in an authorized investigation can get a court order to obtain tangible evidence—including private student records—from colleges and universities. The law mandates that the disclosure be kept a secret.

I hate terrorists as much as the next guy. And I fully understand, and agree, that those investigating terrorism should have access to whatever records and other evidence they need. But to allow them to operate with this kind of secrecy makes oversight impossible. How can abuse of these powers be prevented if the process is kept clandestine? In short, it can't.

There's nothing that the average student can do to protect their privacy from PATRIOT Act invasions. The law simply gives the government the ability to ride roughshod over your rights. Hopefully, these laws won't stay in effect for much longer.

Identity Theft

Identity theft is America's fastest-growing crime. Nearly a million victims fall prey to it each year. With the right piece of information, identity thieves can wreak havoc on your financial life—taking out credit lines or loans, opening wireless phone accounts, buying cars or renting apartments. There have even been instances where adept ID bandits have used assumed identities when they've been arrested.

College students are prime targets for identity thieves. Most are way too cavalier about protecting their personal information. Nearly 50 percent of college students receive credit card applications on a weekly basis and simply throw them out without destroying them. Less than 30 percent regularly, if ever, reconcile their credit card and checking account balances. That combination, in and of itself, is an identity thief's dream come true. But discarded credit card applications are just the beginning. Opportunities for ID theft abound behind the ivied walls.

SOCIAL SECURITY SECURITY

Careless use of social security numbers is a major area of vulnerability on college campuses. It amazes me that, given the potential for abuse, schools still use social security numbers for student identification—printing them on ID cards, including them on correspondence, even posting grades with them. Schools are starting to change their ways. This is due in part to altruism, I suppose. But it probably has more to with the fact that states are starting to pass statutes that restrict the use of SSNs at schools.

For example, Arizona recently passed a law that specifically prohibits schools from assigning social security numbers as student ID numbers. It also prohibits the display of an "individual's social security number, or any four or more consecutive numbers contained in the individual's social security number, on any Internet site maintained by the university or other publicly accessible document for any purpose."

Many other states are considering, or have already passed, similar laws. That said, I wouldn't wait around for the law to catch up to your needs. If your school is using your SSN as your ID number, go to the registrar's office immediately and request different digits. They should, with a little prodding, accommodate you.

And be very careful about your SSN otherwise. Tear up documents that display it before throwing them out, don't give it out to anyone—on the phone or in person—unless they have good reason to need it. Do whatever you can to ensure that no one else knows your number.

SHRED EVERY SHRED OF EVIDENCE

As mentioned above, carelessly discarded credit card applications are practically an invitation to identity thieves. All they have to do is fill in a few blanks, and they've got themselves a brand new credit card—in your name. So think before you throw anything out. If there's anything sensitive on what you're about to discard, destroy it before chucking it. Tear up receipts, checks, bank statements, financial aid forms, credit applications, and anything else that has personal information on it. I suggest investing in a paper shredder—you can get one for $30, and it will spare you thousands of paper cuts.

KEEP CLOSE TABS ON YOUR ACCOUNTS

Pay close attention to your bank accounts and bills. If a bill doesn't arrive on time, it might be an indicator that someone's messing with you. And be sure to examine all bills to check for strange charges or activity.

And take a regular look at your credit reports (see chapter 17, "Money Issues," for more information) to make sure all of the information is accurate. Get reports from each of the big three agencies at least once a year. If anyone has screwed around with your identity, it will show up there.

WHAT TO DO IF YOU'RE A VICTIM

Cleaning up after an identity theft has taken place is no easy task. It can take years to set things right. Acting fast can minimize damage. As soon as you find out that someone has made off with your identity, you should immediately do the following:

1. place fraud alerts with the credit reporting agencies,
2. close any accounts that have been tampered with,
3. file a report with your local police, and
4. file a complaint with the Federal Trade Commission (FTC).

There isn't space in this book to coach you though the entire process, but the FTC is actually an excellent resource for victims of identity theft. Their identity theft website (www.consumer.gov/idtheft/) has pretty much everything you'll need to navigate the aftermath, including form letters, contact information, strategies, and tips for resolving credit issues.

CHAPTER 8

Free Speech

Every time a university speech code has been challenged in the courts, it's been struck down—hard. Still, administrations continue to enact them. Funny, you'd think that with all those Ph.D.s among them, they'd figure out that restricting speech on a college campus is just a bad idea.

Chapter Contents

t's easy to think about campus speech in oversimplified terms. Colleges are sanctuaries for open debate and free expression, aren't they? Places where people can speak their minds without fear of reprisal? Shouldn't speech at these havens be entirely unregulated and unrestricted?

Well, no—on all counts.

Imagine a controversial piece of art as an example—maybe the next Robert Mapplethorpe is a young student at your school and is mounting his first big exhibition. Included are all sorts of erotic, homoerotic, and otherwise sexually charged images. No matter how shocking his subject matter, few would outright deny his right to express himself. But should he be able to display his works in a public place on campus, like the student union? Or even in a gallery nearby? What if the pictures intimidate a female student, a rape victim? Does her right to learn in an environment without traumatizing images trump the political entitlements of our Mapplethorpe-to-be? How about a student who strongly opposes homosexuality on religious grounds? Should he be forced to view homoerotic photos on his way to class?

My point: There's never just one side to a free speech issue. There is always, at the very least, a speaker and a listener (or viewer)—both of whom have rights. As you read the rest of this chapter, try to use this idea of competing rights as an intellectual starting point. Think not only of the entitlement of the speaker but of the impact of the speech on the audience. You'll soon see that the "marketplace of ideas" that colleges attempt to maintain is a delicate thing.

Free Speech and the First Amendment—An Overview

GOVERNMENT ACTORS ONLY

I've said it many times before, and I'm sure I'll point it out again: The rules in the U.S. Constitution only apply to *government actors*. Private entities, and therefore private colleges, don't have to live by them. One notable exception exists in the State of California. There, something called the Leonard Law specifically subjects private schools to First Amendment free speech standards. But otherwise, unless you go to a public college, the First Amendment is more a set of ideals than an enforceable law.

But private school students shouldn't give up just yet—and they certainly shouldn't stop reading. True, the First isn't law. But most private schools are pretty hesitant to make and enforce rules that would be unconstitutional elsewhere. It's bad policy, and it leads to bad publicity. So there are usually ways to get even the most private of schools to respect your "constitutional rights." Pressure from student groups, attention from the media, even an appeal to what's morally right might persuade your school to recognize your rights.

And even if the school ultimately isn't going to grant you your full free speech due, the First Amendment will inevitably be the starting, and reference, point for any negotiations. In other words, you'll still need to understand it.

THE BASICS

What Is Speech?   Although it says "speech" in the amendment, free expression is what was really intended because speech can take a number of different forms. Of course, there's the old reliable spoken and written word. But for the purposes of the Constitution, speech also includes not speaking and symbolic acts. Any action on the part of an individual that is intended to communicate a message is considered to be speech and is protected.

Let's say you refuse to sing the national anthem as a protest against some recent American military action (or maybe you just hate sappy poetry). Technically you're not speaking at all. But your choice to remain silent is, in First Amendment terms, speech. Or maybe you're part of the polka-dot-ribbon campaign, fighting for the proper use of language and grammar on the Internet (I'm not kidding; there really is such a thing). Wearing the ribbon involves no speaking, but it's speech just the same. Controversial works of art are another good example. They might not involve any spoken words, but they convey messages—often quite loudly.

Restricting the Restrictions   Take another look at the First Amendment right now. When I read it two things strike me. The first is how absolute the language is. It says that the government can't make *any* laws that abridge free speech—period. As a lawyer I can't help but wonder if the framers knew how much would have to be extrapolated from those few words. I'm guessing they didn't. Jefferson and his pals lived in a

✳ THE FIRST AMENDMENT ✳

Congress shall make no law respecting an establishment of religion, or prohibiting the free exercise thereof; or abridging the freedom of speech, or of the press; or the right of the people peaceably to assemble, and to petition the Government for a redress of grievances.

simpler time. Speech and communication in general were much more limited propositions in 1787. I also wonder what the same group would write were they faced with the task of drafting the Bill of Rights today. Something along the lines of "Congress shall make no law abridging the freedom of speech, except for the following six thousand exceptions . . ."? Because that's really what 200-plus years of litigation have made the First Amendment. It's a lofty ideal that's been compromised in countless ways. I don't mean to criticize. I'm still a big fan. But I think it's wise to put some intellectual distance between First Amendment law and the First Amendment itself because the two bear little resemblance to one another.

The second thing that I notice—and that I want you to notice—is the structure. "Congress shall make no law . . ." This is a law about making laws. Its point is to make sure the government doesn't overstep its bounds and enact rules that are overly restrictive. Everything that we discuss in this chapter will be framed the same way. In a sense, the First restricts free speech restrictions. Keep that in mind as we go along. This can quickly get confusing if you lose your foothold.

Law Construction One of the more basic ways that governments are kept in check is with guidelines about how actual speech and expression regulations must be drafted. Specifically, they can't

- ✓ *Be too vague.* The rules need to give the affected people specific notice about what's prohibited. Unclear laws often unintentionally affect allowed expression. For example, imagine your school has a problem with drunk students sleeping in the student union. It's certainly within their rights to put a stop to the practice. But if they enacted a rule that prohibited "inappropriate use of the union" they'd probably scare off all sorts of students—not just the drunk, sleepy ones.
- ✓ *Be overbroad.* Similarly, rules need to be concise about what they ban. If they include substantially more than is necessary to meet their end, then they're unconstitutional. In the same example, if the rule outlawed any lying down at all in the union, the rule would be overbroad. All sorts of unintended activities would be outlawed: blood drives, yoga, psychiatry, to name just a few.
- ✓ *Give officials unfettered discretion.* Speech rules can't simply name a person and give them the ability to monitor speech (e.g., the dean will decide what activities are appropriate for the student union). It must include some sort of definitive standards. A dean could have the final call, but there have to be some principles to guide her.

Content vs. Conduct

There are two substantive ways that governments try to curb expression: based on content (what's being said) or based on the time, place, and manner of the speech (how it's being said). The lion's share of free-speech law revolves around those two types of rules.

TIME, PLACE, AND MANNER RESTRICTIONS

All forms of expression involve some sort of physical activity—talking, walking, waving your arms around, chaining yourself to a tree. Sometimes these physical acts of expression conflict with a government interest. Imagine a NORML rally—hundreds and hundreds of stoners gathering together to protest our country's authoritarian marijuana laws. Up front, Woody Harrelson is making a speech. Kids (and over-the-hill hippies) in tie-dye shirts and hemp pants are everywhere. Strains of Phish emanate from dozens of radios. Everyone seems to be jonesing for something sweet to eat.

The potheads at our imaginary protest absolutely have a right to convey their message. And, let's face it, they probably aren't going to make any real trouble—stoners are generally an affable, easygoing group of people. But the government also has an interest in keeping the city moving. So if the rally were, for instance, held in the middle of the street at a busy intersection, the government would have a right to remove them.

Even if Woody and friends protested in a park, where the only thing they'd stop is a game of Frisbee, the government still might have competing interests. They'll probably want to provide for proper crowd control, might have a noise ordinance in place, or may just want to keep the park clean. These are all examples of time, place, and manner restrictions. Within limits, they're legal.

The regulations are different depending on the forum:

In **public forums** the government has the least leeway. They can make and enforce time, place, and manner regulations, but only if the rules

✓ *Are content neutral.* The regulation can't be based in any way on what's being said, and it has to apply evenly to all viewpoints. A law that banned NORML rallies but allowed antidrug activists to assemble would be unconstitutional. So would one that allowed Democrats but not Republicans to collect donations in a certain space.
✓ *Serve a significant government interest.* The rule has to further an important government goal. All of the above examples qualify: keeping traffic moving, keeping noise to a minimum, protecting the safety of citizens through crowd control, litter control, even aesthetics could count.
✓ *Are narrowly tailored.* The rule can't affect more speech than is necessary to achieve that governmental goal. For example, if the point of a rule is to keep traffic moving, a law that bans all protests—even small ones that stay on the sidewalk—would probably be too broad.

Vocabulary Lesson

PUBLIC FORUM—These are the places that we most closely associated with First Amendment rights—sidewalks, parks, streets. The most public of spaces, where anyone is allowed to hang out and everyone is allowed to speak their mind.

NONPUBLIC FORUM—All other government-owned areas are nonpublic forums. This category really comprises most civic land. Places like schools, jails, military bases, courthouses. Sure, they're owned by the government (and technically the taxpayers themselves), but the average citizen doesn't have a right to go and hang out there whenever she wants.

PRIVATE FORUM—This is a private property—your home, a privately owned store or shopping mall, or any other piece of property that a person or a company owns. For those of you at private colleges, your whole campus is, really, a private forum.

✓ *Leave open alternate channels of communication.* The rule can't stop the speech altogether. There has to be some other legitimate way for the speakers to communicate their message, either through a different method of communication or at a different site.

Elsewhere, the government has much more latitude to regulate speech. In **nonpublic** forums, places like military bases and jails, they only have two tests to meet. The rules must be *viewpoint neutral*. And they have to be *reasonably related to a legitimate government purpose*—which probably sounds a lot like the "serving significant government interest" to you, but is in actuality a much lower standard.

In **private forums**, as long as the rules are reasonable, the government can do pretty much what it wants in regard to free speech. There still needs to be content neutrality, but other than that there isn't much of a standard.

That's a lot of legal gibberish, I know. Don't worry if doesn't seem crystal clear—because it's not supposed to be. These are the broad, slippery guidelines that judges use to decide whether or not a free speech law is constitutional. The most important thing to understand is the hierarchy of it all—speech is most protected in public forums, less so in nonpublic places, and hardly at all on private property.

CONTENT RESTRICTIONS

Allowing the government to regulate speech based on its content is, simply put, dangerous. Allowing the state to censor thought is the stuff of Cold War communists and Nazis. It's certainly not what we think of as an American principle.

Still, there are types of speech that need to be curbed. To that end, First Amendment law allows content-based regulations in a few, specific instances. The following are the *only* types of speech that the government is allowed to regulate based on content.

Speech That Creates a Clear and Present Danger of Imminent Lawlessness   Unfortunately this has absolutely nothing to do with bad Harrison Ford movies. The government can forbid speech that is intended to incite lawless action and is likely to actually produce it. In other words, speech that goads people into breaking the law can be prohibited.

Fighting Words   Fighting words are exactly what you'd think they are: statements that are so inflammatory that, when spoken to an ordinary person, they're likely to incite immediate physical retaliation. The First Amendment probably wouldn't protect you if you said something really nasty about some guy's momma, for example. Them's fightin' words.

Obscenities   We all know obscenity when we see it, but it's nearly impossible to legally define. Most often it is discussed in relation to pornography. But not all pornography is obscene (and not all obscenity is pornography, for that matter). In fact, most pornography wouldn't be obscene under the constitutional definition.

What exactly is obscene is determined on a case-by-case basis using the following standards. The material must

1. appeal to a prurient (shameful or morbid) interest in sex,
2. portray sex in a patently offensive way based on the local community standards, and
3. have no serious literary, artistic, political, or scientific value.

Not a particularly definitive standard, eh? As you've probably already guessed, that "local community standard" bit is the most problematic part. It makes it very difficult to forecast what will be considered to be obscene. For starters, everything changes based on geography. What's offensive in Provo, Utah, may be perfectly appropriate in the East Village. There are a few things—like child pornography and snuff—that are almost universally regarded as obscene. But in most cases it's a judgment call.

Defamation   You probably already understand the basic concept of defamation: If you say something that harms another person, they can sue you. In practice it's a bit more exacting than that. In order for a plaintiff to prove they have been defamed, they must show that:

1. *The defendant said something defamatory.* It has to hurt someone's reputation, usually by impeaching the target's honesty, integrity, sanity, virtue, values, or other similar things. It can be a direct statement, a satire, a picture, or anything else that gets the point across.
2. *The statement identified the target clearly enough that a reasonable listener or viewer would know who is being discussed.*

3. *The statement was published to a third party.* This isn't publishing in the common sense (you don't need to include it in a book or magazine article). Something has been "published" when it's communicated to anyone other than the speaker.
4. *The defamation actually caused damage.* In most cases the plaintiff won't have to show actual loss of dollars; if you hurt someone's reputation, it will be presumed that they have been damaged.

Commercial Speech—A Special Case While advertisements and other types of commercial speech aren't outright prohibitable (like defamation, obscenity, and fighting words are), they are treated a bit differently than other types of expression. First, false advertising and advertisements for illegal activities (We Sell Beer to Underage Drinkers! Only $50 a Case!) are offered no protection at all.

Otherwise, the government can regulate commercial expression, as long as the regulations are narrowly tailored to promote a substantial government interest. This is why, for example, billboards can be restricted for aesthetic reasons or businesses can be prohibited from handing out flyers in certain areas.

I know this brings us to—yet another—murky free-speech test, the crux of which is two additional ambiguous terms: narrowly tailored and substantial. I can actually make this one pretty simple, at least as far as the application to on-campus speech goes. *A policy that prohibits all commercial uses of university space is narrowly tailored and serves a substantial government interest.* In other words, it's legal.

> **Your Lawyer Says:**
>
> **PUBLIC FIGURES ARE TREATED DIFFERENTLY**
> These defamation standards only apply to private citizens. If the target of the speech is a public figure—anyone who's famous or infamous—the standards get stricter. It varies depending on the type of public figure, but generally the target will also have to show that the statements were false and in some instances that the speaker knew they were false before publishing them.

Specific On-Campus Applications

You now know the basic framework—the broad structure that's used by courts to decide whether or not a speech law is constitutional. Theoretically you could take these rules and apply them to any situation. But there are a lot of subjective components. It's entirely possible for two people—or more importantly, two judges—to come out with entirely different results.

The best way to determine whether or not any given practice is constitutional is to look at how the courts have applied the law in similar, previous cases. The rest of this chapter analyzes some of the most common campus speech issues in exactly that way.

SPEECH CODES

Campus speech codes had their heyday in the late eighties and early nineties. They were the flagships of the "politically correct" movement. The drafters had their hearts in the right place. They were looking to combat discrimination and harassment. But the codes were generally unconstitutionally vague and overbroad.

One of the more famous and well-documented codes was enacted by the University of Michigan in 1988. The U of M is probably best known for producing the smartest and best-looking lawyers in the county (myself included), but in the late eighties it was getting a reputation for being an intolerant place. Racist incidents were becoming commonplace.

Justifiably, the administration wanted to put a stop to this trend. So they enacted a speech code, an incredibly inclusive one. It subjected students to discipline for "any behavior, verbal or physical, that stigmatizes or victimizes an individual on the basis of race, ethnicity, religion, sex, sexual orientation, creed, national origin, ancestry, age, marital status, handicap, or Vietnam-era veteran status."

The policy included a guide for students that gave examples of behaviors that violated it. Some of the prohibited activities were

- ✓ displaying a Confederate flag in your dorm room,
- ✓ excluding someone from a study group because they're a different race, sex, or ethnic origin,
- ✓ laughing at a joke about someone who stutters,
- ✓ commenting in a derogatory way about someone's physical appearance.

In short, it was a pretty ridiculous set of rules. I don't think laughing at people who stutter is a good thing either. But come on. You just can't get away with this kind of oppressive regulation.

And that's what the courts said. In 1989 a graduate student challenged the speech code on the grounds that it was vague and overbroad. He pointed out that in his field of study, psychology, differences in personality or mental abilities were often discussed in class. Under the existing code, those lectures would be unlawful.

The court struck the code down, saying, "While the court is sympathetic to the University's obligation to ensure the equal educational opportunities for all of its students, such efforts must not be at the expense of free speech."

Your Lawyer Says:

LOOK TO NONPROFITS FOR HELP

If you have any kind of issue with (or even a question about) free speech on your campus, don't be afraid to reach out to one of the many public interest organizations that specialize in this type of thing. The ACLU, the Foundation for Individual Rights in Education (F.I.R.E.), and my organization, the Coalition for Student & Academic Rights (CO-STAR), are all good places to call.

Free Speech

The Michigan code is an extreme case, to be sure. But much more limited speech codes have been held unconstitutional. In fact, in almost every instance where a university speech code has been challenged in court, it's been struck down. Many scholars, myself included, are of the opinion that the idea of a speech code is outright wrong.

Still, they exist on many campuses. In fact they've seen a bit of a renaissance in the past few years. They're much more carefully written than those of the early nineties—and some are even disguised as anti-harassment policies—but most of them still violate the First Amendment.

If free speech is something you care about (and if you've read this far, it probably is), then I suggest you find out about the rules at your school. Read the anti-harassment policy and anything else similar (they'll be in the student handbook) and use what you know about the First Amendment to analyze them. If you think they're the least bit suspicious, do something about it.

FREE SPEECH ZONES

Free speech zones are the time, place, and manner cousins of speech codes. Their purpose is to restrict student protests and activism and, well, speech to specific places on campus. They first appeared in the sixties, when protests and rallies were everyday occurrences on college campuses. The administrators, and the students, recognized that having huge crowds of students milling around all the time could get in the way of classes and other educational activities. So schools enacted rules about where and when rallies could be held. They didn't create much of a problem back then, mostly because the rules themselves were fairly innocuous.

But free speech zones have also seen a resurgence over the past decade. And the new versions are much more restrictive than their predecessors. Often they limit free speech to a minute amount of space. One that was recently rescinded at West Virginia University allowed free speech on less than 5 percent of its campus.

The schools that have these types of rules argue that they're simply content-neutral conduct restrictions and are, therefore, constitutional. Opponents point to the concept of the public forum (see above) and state that there's no way that such codes could meet the constitutional standards.

As of this writing, no court has considered the issue. A few students have sued their schools over the speech zone rules, but the colleges have—without exception—backed down before their cases ever saw the inside of a courtroom.

In my opinion the entire concept of a free speech zone is moronic. The establishment of a special place where speech is free implies that it isn't elsewhere. That kind of message has no place on a college campus. But until a court decides a free speech zone case on its merits, what I think is little more than that—my opinion. A well-reasoned and correct one, but an opinion just the same.

Still, if you go to a college that has one of these strange rules, I wouldn't hesitate to challenge it. Every school that's been called on its free speech zone policy in the past few years has backed down rather quickly. Chances are your school will, too.

ARTISTIC EXPRESSION

Surprisingly, the question of artistic censorship on college campuses hasn't come up all that often in the courts. The parties involved are usually able to work things out on their own. And the opinions in the few cases that did make it all the way to trial left a lot of open questions. So it takes a bit of deduction (and some guessing) to figure out what exactly a college can or cannot do in regards to censoring provocative art.

That said, there are some generalizations that can safely be made:

As is the case with many First Amendment issues, the forum where the art is being displayed is usually the critical issue. If the art is being shown in a place where the school has invited others to speak or show art (if it's a public forum), then as long as the art isn't legally obscene (in which case the art gets no First Amendment protection), the university can't censor it.

Of course there's a big exception. If the art has racial or sexual content, the university does have some right to relocate the work. Consider our young Mapplethorpe example again. The school is probably allowed to move work like that to a more private gallery where children or squeamish adults won't stumble onto it. The theory is that people should be able to choose whether or not to view extremely provocative art. If something very sexual is in a main hallway, then it will be thrust upon a number of potentially unwilling viewers. But the audience that walks into a gallery—even one that is unmonitored—knows that they might see some unsettling things.

A case much like this one actually went to trial in the early eighties. At issue were a series of eight stained-glass windows designed by an art professor at Prairie State College. Five of the windows were abstract, but the other three contained provocative sexual, and potentially racist, images.

All of the human figures in the work were made of amber-colored glass. Although the artist himself stated that he didn't intend them to be taken as African American, he used darker glass in some (especially two of the women) to create contrast. By most accounts they looked like they were black or, maybe, Polynesian.

The first window showed the naked buttocks of a dark woman with a white stream of gas shooting out of it. The second depicted the full body of another brown woman, naked except for a pair of stockings. The view was from the rear and the woman was, evidently, masturbating. The final window, titled *The Adoration of the Penis*, showed a third, brown woman squatting before a white man in a robe. The woman, also shown from the rear, was embracing the man's enormous, erect manhood.

These windows were originally installed in a prominent place—a ground floor hall in the center of campus—and were clearly visible to people outside on the main quad. After receiving complaints from just about every group on campus, the school moved them to a more secluded spot on the fourth floor of the same building. The artist sued, saying that the school had violated his First Amendment rights.

The court sided with the school. They conceded that the images were not, in a constitutional sense, obscene. As the court stated, they are "not very realistic; seem not intended to arouse, titillate, or disgust; and are not wholly devoid of artistic merit, or at least artistic intention." Still, the court said the school had the right to move the panels.

But this type of relocation is only allowed in cases where the art includes racial or sexual content. If a work is merely provocative due to its political content, then the school probably can't move it, especially if the original venue is a public forum.

Another solution that comes up with some regularity is the use of warnings. The school doesn't move the paintings, but posts signs at the entrances to the gallery areas that state the exhibit

Your Lawyer Says:

DON'T BACK DOWN

Of course, the school can do whatever they want if you succumb to their demands. So don't. Be flexible as to the conditions, but assert your right to show your work. And don't be afraid to use the situation to your advantage. Think about what censorship has done for other artists—every time Madonna had a video banned her record sales doubled.

contains potentially offensive materials. Courts have held that it's within a university's right to do this.

These theories really only apply to static works of visual art—pictures, paintings, sculpture, and the like. Plays and movies, which are usually held in private theaters for audiences, are usually immune from censorship. Again, this is because the audience has shown its willingness to participate by entering the theater.

GUEST SPEAKERS

Michael Moore and Ward Churchill are two recent examples of speaker censorship. Both were invited to speak on campus, then later disinvited. In the Moore example, his exorbitant fee was offered as an excuse. The administrators who cancelled Churchill cited safety as their motivation (they had received death and bomb threats in relation to Churchill's appearance). But the real reason behind both cancelations was controversy and the administration's desire to avoid it.

Today the clear state of the law is this: If a recognized student group invites a speaker, the school has to allow it. Still, this doesn't mean that your college won't use creative methods to ban someone, citing safety or budget to defend their actions.

And it doesn't mean that they can't (and shouldn't) impose a few requirements on the guest speaker process. The primary one is that of sponsorship. You'll note that in the above paragraphs I referred to the lecturer as an invited speaker. Not every joker who wants to give a lecture gets to come to campus. They need to be invited—sponsored—by a recognized university group or by the school itself through the administration. And it may be the group's responsibility to foot the bill for the visit—paying the speaker's fee or other associated costs.

Imagine a college where this wasn't the case. Every time Carrot Top showed up with nothing better to do, he'd get to put a show on—a harrowing thought, no? This is why schools have these kinds of policies. As long as they're evenly administered and aren't used to ban speakers on the basis of their message, they're fine.

Ironically, today it's not interference from the university, but from students that poses the biggest threat to the First Amendment rights of guest lecturers. There have been countless incidents of students, in protest of a controversial (and generally politically incorrect) speaker, interfering. They pack the audience and chant to keep the speaker from being heard. Or play music on loudspeakers in an adjacent area to drown out voices.

If you're planning on participating in this kind of citizen's censorship, please don't. I admire your conviction and your enthusiasm, but doing that kind of thing is flat-out wrong. Even those with the most abhorrent views— the Grand Wizard of the Ku Klux Klan or a convicted rapist—have a right to speak. That's both the beauty, and the burden, of the First Amendment.

CHAPTER 9

Dormitories & On-Campus Housing

Under certain circumstances, school officials can walk into your dorm room and conduct a search without a warrant or any reasonable suspicion that a rule or law has been broken. If you thought Mom and Dad were the only people allowed to spot-check your sock drawer for contraband, think again.

Chapter Contents

When the first universities were being formed in medieval Europe, thousands of students flocked to these small towns, swelling the streets and pushing the limits of their housing. In the late 1200s, for example, over 20,000 students were enrolled at the Université Paris—more than double the population of the City of Light itself. Left without other options, students lived in tents, slept in open fields, and sought shelter wherever they could. There are even accounts of undergraduates burrowing into the sides of hills to sleep.

Gradually things improved. Students began to rent rooms—first from professors and townspeople. Later large tenements were built. And eventually the universities took control and exerted authority. By the 1400s most schools regulated the minute details of their students' living conditions.

This, then, was the birth of the college dormitory. Believe it or not, these strange beginnings still affect students today. Colleges and courts have yet to totally abandon the dictatorial and paternal relationship that once existed between school and dorm resident. When it comes to housing, schools are often able to justify the most blatant intrusions of privacy and violations of due process with little more justification than "We thought it was in the student's best interest." This leaves students in a somewhat strange legal place—one that offers little consistency and no guarantee that their constitutional rights will be recognized.

Dorm Room Searches

The Fourth Amendment to the U.S. Constitution prevents the cops or any other government official from busting into your house and rifling through your stuff. It explicitly states that the "right of the people to be secure in their persons, houses, papers, and effects, against unreasonable searches and seizures, shall not be violated."

The law of search and seizure as it pertains specifically to the police is discussed in detail in chapter 13, "The Police." Wherever you live, you should read that section carefully. Many of the same principles apply in the dorms, and you never know when the cops will come a-knocking. But for those of you too lazy to flip forward a few pages, here are the basics:

DON'T CONSENT

The number-one rule about searches is: never, ever consent. There are all sorts of laws and rules that govern when and how you can be searched.

But if you agree to let the police or anyone else search your dorm room, your rights begin to disappear.

So if anyone—a cop, your RA, a professor, an administrator, or anyone else—asks in any way to conduct any kind of search in your dorm room, tell them no. Say loudly, clearly, and slowly, "I do not consent to any search of any kind." Depending on who they are and what kind of school you go to, the searchers may not be bound by the Constitution. And even if they are, they may still have a right to go into your room. But it can't possibly hurt to object, and often it works. So as a matter of course, tell them you'd prefer it if they stayed out.

Roommate or RA Consent If the authorities arrive while you're not around, don't worry—your privacy is fairly safe. Government officials need an OK from the person who "owns" an area for the consent to count. So your RA can't let the cops or anyone else in to look around. The same goes for your roommate. If the two of you share a room, he can authorize entry into the room. But he can't grant permission for a search of your private belongings. The police won't be able to search the spaces that are yours alone, like personal drawers and closets.

WARRANTS

A warrant is a document issued by a judge that gives the authorities permission to conduct a search. If an authority figure shows up at your door with a warrant, you have to let them in. But that doesn't mean that you should just step aside if they flash a document. You should check to make sure that everything's on the up-and-up.

First, always read the warrant. Take it, tell them to wait outside, close the door, clear your head, and take a look. Make sure it's legitimate, that it's for your room, with your name and your address, and signed by a judge or magistrate. Also, check its scope. Warrants don't simply name a place and give the officer free reign. It will only authorize a search for specific objects at a specified time and place.

If anything is amiss—if it's unsigned, not for your room, for a different time—point this out and ask them to leave. If they refuse, make it clear that you do not consent.

> **Your Lawyer Says:**
>
> **WALK THE LINE**
> Search-and-seizure law actually does recognize the imaginary line you and your roomie drew down the middle of your dorm room. Your roommate can only authorize searches of common areas. No matter what she says, the cops have to stay out of your private stuff. So be sure to leave anything you don't want discovered safely in *your* closet or under *your* bed.

If everything checks out, let them in. Stay out of the way during the search, but keep an eye on what's going on. You've read the warrant, so you know if there are any restrictions. If they go out of bounds, call them on it. And remember, just because the authorities have a warrant to search your room, it doesn't mean they can interrogate you. So keep your mouth shut if the questions start.

WARRANTLESS SEARCHES

There are a few ways potential searchers can legally come into your room without a warrant or your permission.

Emergency   If the authorities enter your room in response to what they believe is an emergency, then the search is constitutional. If the building is on fire and an officer sweeps in to save you, whatever he sees while there is fair game.

Emergencies don't have to be that dire for the exception to apply. Consider *People v. Lanthier* as an example. A noxious odor had filled a section of the library at Stanford University. Worried that the odor was dangerous, the school searched for the source. What they found, inside a student's private locker, were thirty-eight packets of marijuana that had, evidently, been treated with a very fragrant preservative. The student contested the charges based on the fact that the search was conducted without a warrant and was unconstitutional. The court sided with the school, citing the fact that the toxic smell presented a potential health hazard as justification.

There doesn't have to be an earthquake or a cyclone for the emergency exception to kick in. So long as the authorities see, hear, or smell something that signifies potential danger, they can commence a search.

Hot Pursuit   If the authorities enter a home, or dorm room, in the immediate or continuous pursuit from the scene of a crime, the search will be valid. A house doesn't work like home base in a game of tag. If the cops are chasing a criminal, they don't have to go get a warrant if he runs inside. They're allowed to follow him in. And if they see anything suspicious while they're in there, they can grab it.

Diminishing Evidence   As explained in chapter 13, "The Police," if delaying a search will create an imminent danger of the loss, removal, destruction, or disappearance of evidence, then the authorities are allowed to perform an on-the-spot warrantless search. Certain types of evidence are too easy to get rid of. Some simply disappear on their own. Most drugs, for example, are very simple to dispose of quickly (flush). And blood alcohol levels return to zero after only a few hours. If the police were required to go to court and obtain a warrant in these types of cases, they would never be able to catch anyone.

Plain View   If the authorities see something that's out in the open, they can legally take it. The halls of your dormitory are public space, so police, school security, and every other authority figure can roam them freely. If one of these people goes past your room and sees a bag of drugs through an open door, she can walk in and investigate. She doesn't need a warrant or your permission because the evidence was in plain view. Once she sees it, the privacy game's over and done with.

DORM-SPECIFIC ENTRY PROBLEMS

As stated in the introduction, your dorm room doesn't quite have the same legal standing as a normal apartment. Some remnants of that restrictive medieval system still linger in the operation of modern dormitories. In specific areas your privacy is limited—allowing unauthorized and, often, unannounced entries into your room.

Health, Safety, and Maintenance Inspections Colleges often need to get into dorm rooms for relatively benign reasons—to inventory equipment, to perform health or safety inspections, or to fix something. When the school en-

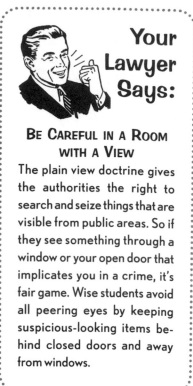

Your Lawyer Says:

BE CAREFUL IN A ROOM WITH A VIEW

The plain view doctrine gives the authorities the right to search and seize things that are visible from public areas. So if they see something through a window or your open door that implicates you in a crime, it's fair game. Wise students avoid all peering eyes by keeping suspicious-looking items behind closed doors and away from windows.

ters your room for reasons like these, it creates a somewhat unique situation. In a normal apartment, these duties would be the responsibility of your landlord. If she came in and saw something illegal, she might call the police, but chances are she'd just look the other way.

But the dormitory setting is different. Your school is both your landlord *and* your disciplinarian. If a school employee comes in and sees something incriminating, there's really no looking the other way—because the guy snaking your toilet *is* the authorities.

The courts are split as to the legality of convicting students based on evidence found this way. To be safe, never leave anything suspicious out in the open when you leave your room. You never know when the water main is going to break, and your school's plumber/evidence gatherer will be poking around in your stuff.

"Maintaining Order" On February 28, 1968, the Dean of Students at Troy State University in Alabama (a public school) and two narcotics officers went on an impromptu hunt for drugs. They searched room after room in two of the school's dormitories. They had no real reason to believe they'd find anything, and they certainly didn't have any warrants. They just busted into the rooms, often over the students' protests, and searched.

In a room belonging to a student named Greg Moore, they hit paydirt. They found a matchbox that contained a very small amount of marijuana.

Moore was charged with possession but protested in court on the grounds that the search of his room was unconstitutional. Despite the outrageous facts, the court sided with the school, stating that there was a special relationship between students and the colleges they attended. This, the court said, afforded the university broad leeway in conducting searches. So long as the university had the slightest reason to believe they'd find anything incriminating, they could search the rooms. They had a right to maintain order and discipline on campus.

This case set a very troubling legal precedent that still haunts dorm residents—the strange notion that schools have some special, vague right to search students' rooms. The issue has been revisited by numerous courts since 1968. Some agree with the *Moore* court case. Others come out in favor of student privacy. But, more than thirty years later, there still hasn't been a definitive ruling.

This confusion on the part of the court system leaves you, the dorm resident, in a strange spot. It's anyone's guess as to whether or not a school official can bust into your room under the guise of "maintaining order." I can tell you what I *think* the law should be (public school officials should be required to get warrants just like everyone else), but I can't predict, with any kind of accuracy, what a court would say if your room was searched in some unconstitutional way. There's always a chance that they'll agree with the Moore ruling and allow school officials to do pretty much what they want.

STATE ACTORS

Dorm room privacy is one of the areas where the public/private school distinction is incredibly important. Since the Constitution only applies to state actors, searches performed by private entities aren't within its reach. In other words, all of the rules detailed above don't mean a damned thing if the person doing the searching isn't a part of the government.

Public Colleges and Universities Students at public schools are pretty well-covered. Public school employees are, almost without exception, considered to be state actors. This means that everyone who works for the school, from the president of the board of trustees all the way down to your hall monitor, has to play by the constitutional rules. Well, for the most part, anyway—see the harrowing exceptions above. If they don't, the search is unlawful. So if anyone that is even remotely related to the school wants to come into your room, treat them as if they're the police because for all intents and purposes they are.

Private Colleges and Universities Private school employees are just that—private. They are no more bound by the Constitution than your parents. They can walk into your room with impunity and search to their hearts' content. And these nonstate actors can take anything they find and

On-Campus Housing

WHO'S BOUND BY THE FOURTH AMENDMENT AT YOUR SCHOOL?

	Public Schools	*Private Schools*
Police	No matter where you are, the police are always state actors and are always bound by the tenets of the Constitution.	
Campus Security	Since your school is public, all employees are bound by the Fourth. Campus security—commissioned or not—are government actors for constitutional purposes.	If your school's security is a commissioned force, then they're just like regular police and have to play by the rules. Otherwise, they're private actors—the Constitution doesn't apply.
Profs, Administrators, & Other Employees	Professors, administrators, and pretty much all other employees of the school are considered state actors at public universities. But (since you've read this book) you probably know more about this stuff than they do—so be prepared to provide an impromptu education.	At a private school these people are normal citizens, just like you and me. That means that they can search away without any worries that the Fourth Amendment will come back to haunt them later on.
Resident Assistants	Even though they're students, resident assistants and other student employees are a part of the system at a public school. The Constitution applies.	Dorks? Maybe. State actors? Definitely not. Private school RAs are free from constitutional restraint.

hand it over to the state actors who can use it against you—regardless of the circumstances of the search. This is an incredibly important point (and an incredibly large loophole). Private schools, and all private actors for that matter, can perform the most abhorrently unreasonable and "unconstitutional" searches, then simply submit the evidence found to the police. It doesn't matter that if the police had performed the same search themselves, it would be entirely illegal. So long as the private actor performs the search, it's good. The police can't call up your school and have the uncovered college employees do their bidding. The school has to act on its own volition. But aside from that, they can pretty much do what they want.

Frightening, isn't it?

THE EXCLUSIONARY RULE

There's one final, devastating caveat to the laws of search and seizure on campus. The penalty for performing an unconstitutional search is, well, underwhelming. Evidence obtained through an unconstitutional search can't be used in a criminal trial. That's it.

Needless to say, this is generally of little use to college students. For starters, on-campus disciplinary hearings aren't criminal trials. So the exclusionary rule has absolutely no effect on what happens within. Every last bit of evidence, no matter how it was obtained, can be used against you there.

THE BOTTOM LINE ON DORM ROOM PRIVACY

Legally, your dorm room is not a particularly private place. The constitutional constraints really only apply to the police and public school employees. But even then, the courts have given broad latitude to schools—allowing for frequent intrusions and warrantless searches under vague theories like maintaining order.

Add to that the fact that the exclusionary rule has absolutely no import in university judicial systems—where most dorm room infractions are tried—and it becomes obvious that dorm rooms are not a good place to store anything that's the least bit incriminating.

Housing Rules

Life in the dorms is, in most ways, less strict than life under your parents' roof. Still, rules abound. Schools often regulate the appliances you can use (no hot plates or refrigerators over a certain size), the ways you can decorate (no candles), and the hobbies you can pursue (no pets).

These rules, and every other facet of your housing situation, are contained in the housing agreement between you and your school. It's a contract that details both parties' rights and responsibilities. In the real

On-Campus Housing

world this agreement would be one document—your lease. But at a college the documentation that governs the relationship is usually spread out over a number of sources.

You should take the time to track down all of the components of the agreement and look at them. There are three common sources for campus housing rules:

OCCUPANCY AGREEMENT

This is usually a multicopy document that establishes the basics of the agreement. It will name the parties, the space to be rented, the term, the rent, and the frequency of the payments. Although it looks like a basic lease, it probably isn't. Most schools use a license agreement rather than a standard lease. This is a critical distinction. A lease creates a property right. A license doesn't. This allows the school to do all sorts of things—most significantly, assign you to a different room if they want. This is because under a license you've rented a certain amount of space, not a specific room or suite.

Your Lawyer Says:

WHEN FILLING OUT THE INVENTORY, BE ANAL

The inventory you complete at check-in will be the only record of the move-in condition of the room. At the end of the year, if something's broken and it isn't on the checklist, you'll pay for it. So be very careful when you fill the thing out. Look for anything that might incur a charge. And, since there's no penalty for being overinclusive, why not include a few things that *might* happen (e.g., tape marks on the walls or stains on the carpets)?

Usually the housing agreement is combined with the housing application—meaning you signed it sometime over the summer. It also means you probably don't have a copy with you. It shouldn't be too hard to track one down. Just go to your housing office and ask for a copy of the standard housing agreement. They'll have stacks and stacks of them there.

CHECK-IN DOCUMENTS

You probably also filled out and signed an inventory and condition report on move-in day. A more concise set of the rules that govern your stay was probably included with those papers. These rules outline the more mundane parts of your dorm life: pets, parking, entry, visitors, cooking, storage, furniture, lockouts, lost keys, and the like.

For day-to-day living, this really is the most important document you'll have. It will spell out fairly specifically what you can, and cannot, do in your dorm room. So be sure to keep this handy. You'll need it if you want to spot-check the rules in a specific area.

STUDENT HANDBOOK

The last source of housing rules is the university or student handbook. Generally the housing agreement itself will have specific language that incorporates the handbook's rules into the housing contract. This means that all of the general rules of the university are also part of the contract you signed with the school's housing authority. A violation of those rules could also be a breach of your contract—which could mean eviction.

YOU'RE ALREADY BOUND

If you're already living in the dorms, then you've already signed all of the appropriate documents and, as a result, have already legally agreed to all of the school's rules. And to be honest, even if you haven't sealed the deal in writing yet, there's not really any way to negotiate a more palatable arrangement. University housing is usually a take-it-or-leave-it proposition.

So, since changing the rules isn't really an option, you should do your best to make sure you don't get caught violating them. And you should do your best to minimize damages if you do. Usually this means smart dealings with your RA.

DEALING WITH STUDENT HOUSING STAFF

They go by different names at different schools—Resident Assistants, Student Assistants, Head Residents. Whatever your school calls them, these student prefects are the front line of dormitory discipline. It's tempting to dismiss them as university stooges and treat them poorly. But before you salt your relationship with your hall's overseer, you should consider a few facts:

- ✓ The vast majority of housing infractions begin and end with student staff.
- ✓ They have incredible latitude to overlook or ignore disciplinary infractions.
- ✓ They are usually much more willing to strike deals than their adult counterparts.

In other words, taking the time to establish and maintain a good relationship with your RA is one of the wisest investments you can make. Sooner or later he's going to catch you in some sort of banned activity and you're going to want to be on his good side.

You'll also want to step carefully when that happens. Even if you are the RA's pet you could still blow things and get written up. If you do:

'Fess Up and Apologize Never try to get away with an obvious lie. Staff members often personalize the behaviors of their residents. They interpret student misconduct as a personal affront. In most cases they're less upset

On-Campus Housing

that you've done something wrong; they're more hurt that you did it to *them*.

Lying about what you've done will only compound the problem (and emotions). So don't do it. It's almost always best to admit that you've broken a rule and—sincerely—apologize.

Plea Bargain Your absolute best chance for reaching a compromise, or to get off scot-free, is to cut some sort of deal with your RA. Keeping things at this level—between you and your student staff member—should be your top priority. Once things progress to professional staff your options will be much more limited. If you're offered a deal that you can live with, take it. Whatever it is will probably be better than the punishment the administration would dole out.

CHAPTER 10

Disciplinary Proceedings

You have no right to an attorney in an on-campus disciplinary hearing. The courts have held that college students are smart and sophisticated enough to represent themselves. Flattering? Yes. Helpful when you're in this kind of bind? Not so much. But you can be your own best advocate if you plot a careful defense.

Chapter Contents

T hink back to the last time you were accused of something at home: staying out past curfew, stealing liquor, wrecking your parents' car. Try to remember how you felt when you were confronted about it. You were probably pretty anxious even though you knew that, ultimately, the worst that could happen was a month without TV.

Now take those emotions and multiply them by fifty. That's what it feels like to stand before a more formal tribunal—one that has no parental interest in your well-being and that has the power to do far more than ground you. At an on-campus disciplinary hearing, the stakes and emotions run high. So if you find yourself facing one, you need to take specific steps to ensure that things go as well as possible.

FORGET WHAT YOU THINK YOU KNOW

The first thing I want you to do is forget everything you learned from the movies about how a trial works. There's not going to be high drama. There aren't going to be exciting plot twists and surprises. And, no matter how talented an orator you are, you're not going to be able to back some key witness into a corner and win the day. Just get all of the images of Tom Cruise yelling "I want the TRUTH!" out of your head. *A Few Good Men* is a great movie. But as an instructional tool, it blows.

A disciplinary hearing is more like an exam than a John Grisham novel. It will be tiring. It will require critical thinking and attention to detail. It could even be boring. Most importantly, success hinges on thorough and careful preparation. The hearing itself is, really, only a tiny part of the job at hand. If you've done things the right way, 99 percent of the work will happen beforehand.

A THREE-STEP PROCESS

Success in the courtroom requires a systematic approach. Focus your pretrial efforts in three main areas:

1. *Understand the process itself.* Without a working knowledge of the rules and procedures (and your specific rights), you won't be able to protect yourself or fully take advantage of all opportunities to prove your innocence.
2. *Find and analyze the evidence, both for and against you.* These are the building blocks of the case. A careful consideration of the evidence that supports both sides is the only way to prevent embarrassing, and costly, surprises at the hearing.

Disciplinary Actions

3. *Develop your case.* Just because you understand how all of the existing evidence lines up to prove your innocence doesn't mean that your judge or jury will see it that way. At the hearing you'll need to connect the dots, and do it in a simple way that everyone will understand.

PUBLIC/PRIVATE SCHOOL DISTINCTION

There's one final caveat that needs to be discussed before we get down to specifics: Most of the legal concepts and requirements in this chapter stem from constitutional law. So, as you well know by now, *only public colleges and universities are fully bound by them.* Private schools have to afford their students some level of due process, but they have much more leeway in how they conduct these hearings.

Still, constitutional standards are important at both types of universities. At public schools you can demand them. At private schools you should push for them in the name of fairness. You may not always win the argument, but "It was important enough to be in the Constitution; why shouldn't it be the standard here, too?" is a pretty compelling argument—especially if made publicly.

Step One: Understanding the Process

The Fifth Amendment to the U.S. Constitution states that "No person shall . . . be deprived of life, liberty, or property, without due process of law." This concept of due process is both very important and very vague. In a word, it means fairness. The government can't put you to death, put you in jail, or take your property without following fair procedures. Your college probably won't try to lock you up or execute you if you break their rules. But they could try to deprive you of property—your diploma. Legally, participation in your school's programs creates a property right on your behalf.

If your school takes any action that gets in the way of your participation, then they're depriving you of property in the constitutional sense. This means that due process rights attach if your school attempts to

✓ *Expel you.* Even though you haven't actually earned it yet, your diploma is your most important possession. Any time your school is contemplating expelling you, you must be afforded due process.

✓ *Suspend you.* Even a suspension is a deprivation of your property right in your education. Colleges generally don't suspend students for short periods of time. Usually it's a full semester or a year. But even a suspension for ten days or less involves a protected interest and therefore requires due process.

✓ *Ban you from extracurricular activities.* Most courts agree that extracurricular programs, sports, clubs, student government, and residence hall posts are an integral part of education. So if you're up on charges that could get you thrown off the team, you must be afforded due process.

Due process rights do not, however, kick in if you are being expelled or suspended for poor grades. The processes in place (grading grievance procedures, etc.) protect your rights well enough.

The exact form the process takes varies depending on the severity of the potential punishment. In the real world you don't, for example, have a right to a full-blown jury trial for a parking ticket with a $25 fine. The same theory applies on campus. The stiffer the penalty, the more process you're owed. But you always get the basics: prior notice, fair procedures, and an unbiased decision maker. Vague standards, I know. I'll do my best to pin them down with some level of clarity over the next few pages.

NOTICE

Without notice the concept of fair procedure is pretty worthless. You've got to be notified that a matter is pending in order to defend yourself. The notice must be in writing, must name the time and place of the hearing, and must specifically outline the charges. Some, but not all, courts have also held that the notice must also include some details about the nature of the evidence and a list of the witnesses that are likely to appear.

WHEN SHOULD THE HEARING TAKE PLACE?

There are no strict requirements about how soon the hearing has to take place. The student has a right to a speedy resolution, but he also needs to be given adequate time to prepare. Unreasonable delays or unnecessarily expedited proceedings aren't allowed.

Due process does specifically require that the hearing take place *before* the discipline. The school can't take any adverse action against you until after you've had your day in court. There is an exception for situations where the school has reasonable cause to believe

Your Lawyer Says:

IF THE LAW'S ON THE LINE, POSTPONE

What you say in a campus disciplinary hearing can be used against you at a subsequent criminal trial. So if there are criminal charges pending, do whatever you can to postpone your hearing until after the trial. You don't have a legal right to delay your school hearing, but many schools will allow it. If they don't, you may want to avail yourself of your right against self-incrimination.

Disciplinary Actions

that allowing the accused to stay on campus will compromise the safety of other students. In those cases, an interim suspension is allowed. But even then, if at all possible, the accused student must be granted a preliminary hearing.

WHAT KIND OF HEARING ARE YOU ENTITLED TO?

The law doesn't spell out many details about how the hearing should be conducted. Still, there are few areas where definitive standards have been set:

Burden of Proof   Just like in the criminal big leagues, those accused of on-campus infractions are *innocent until proven guilty*. Students can't be put in a position of having to prove their innocence. The standard of proof, however, is much lower than in an actual court case. In a real trial the prosecution is required to prove the accused's guilt beyond a reasonable doubt. Universities simply need to present *clear and convincing evidence of guilt*. In theory, this is a big deal. It's a much lower threshold to cross. But in actuality this shift in standard doesn't make much of a difference. Jurors and decision makers aren't really able to distinguish between the two. To be honest, I'd have trouble articulating, in real terms, the difference.

Impartial Decision Maker   None of these rules and procedures mean a damned thing if the person, or people, making the decisions are biased. Therefore, due process requires a decision maker with the ability to be objective in evaluating the evidence and doling out punishment.

If you think that one or more of your judges are biased against you, take steps to remove them. But step carefully. There's always a chance that your efforts will fail. So you don't want to point fingers too aggressively and too openly. Find out who you need to talk to about the matter and have a calm, confidential conversation with them about your concerns.

No Right to Counsel   Unfortunately your due process rights don't include the right to be represented by an attorney at the hearing. But try to get your school to let you lawyer-up anyway. Often schools will allow some sort of advocacy. They may cave and simply let your lawyer do her stuff. Or they might allow her to sit in on the hearing but prohibit her from speaking or questioning witnesses. Sometimes they won't allow you to be represented by a licensed attorney, but they will let you make other arrangements—like having a law student or professor act as your advocate.

Open or Closed Hearings   Schools almost universally honor student requests for private hearings—so much so that the issue has rarely been litigated. In the few court cases that have considered the matter, the right to private proceedings has been upheld. In the unlikely event that you request a closed hearing and the school gives you a hard time, wave the Family Educational Rights and Privacy Act in their faces (see chapter 7,

"Student Records," for a complete discussion of FERPA). The act prohibits the dissemination of student records, either orally or in written form, without the consent of the student. Holding an open hearing against the accused student's wishes violates it.

Open hearings are a stickier issue. Schools sometimes balk at the prospect of a room full of rowdy students. The courts are pretty evenly split on the matter. Some have held that closing a hearing not only violates due process but has serious First Amendment implications. Others have pointed to the chance of disruption an audience could cause and have allowed schools to keep the goings-on under wraps.

I've never been a big fan of closed hearings. Justice almost always operates best out in the open. So I almost always advise accused students to push for a proceeding that's open to the public. With the right nudging most schools will agree to allow at least a few representatives of the student body and student press in.

Evidence Issues Most of the formal rules of evidence don't apply in an on-campus hearing. Lawyers sometimes have trouble wading through the complexities of things like hearsay, the parole evidence rule, and documentary authentication. To impose them on college students and their layperson decision makers doesn't make any sense.

This is, for the most part, a good thing. It means you can offer up pretty much any kind of evidence you want to support your case without concern that it will be excluded on some technicality.

There is, however, one area where the spirit, if not the letter, of the rules of evidence must be followed: **relevance**. Only relevant evidence can be considered at your hearing.

If your opponent tries to use irrelevant evidence (the most common area of abuse is evidence that attacks the defendant's personality), object. Stand up and ask, "What does any of this have to do with what we're here to determine?" If they can't offer an explanation, politely ask that the proceedings be confined to what's relevant.

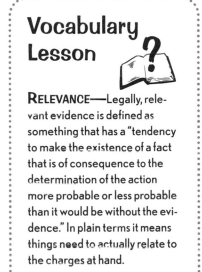

Vocabulary Lesson

RELEVANCE—Legally, relevant evidence is defined as something that has a "tendency to make the existence of a fact that is of consequence to the determination of the action more probable or less probable than it would be without the evidence." In plain terms it means things need to actually relate to the charges at hand.

THE EXCLUSIONARY RULE If evidence is obtained through an unconstitutional search or questioning, it can't be used in a criminal trial. This is called the exclusionary rule. Unfortunately it doesn't apply in college disciplinary hearings. Even if every constitutional right in the book was violated when you were questioned or when your house or room was searched, the evidence found can be used against you at your school hearing. If something that was obtained unfairly is being offered into evidence against you, you should try to get it excluded. But don't expect to win out. The evidence can, and probably will, be allowed.

Witnesses Witnesses play a significant role in most campus hearings. College infractions rarely involve paper trails and forensic clues. So how you deal with the witnesses is of paramount importance. You have a right to confront and cross-examine witnesses who testify against you. The hearing must also implement some form of **compulsory process**.

Your confrontation rights guarantee that anyone who testifies against you will appear at the hearing in person. Their testimony can't be admitted in writing. They've got to look you in the eye when they make their statement. This serves two purposes. One, it gives the fact finders the opportunity to observe the demeanor of the witness. Lies are much more easily detected in person than in writing. Second, it gives you the opportunity to cross-examine any adverse witnesses—meaning you, or your advocate, can ask them questions about their statement.

Compulsory process is what forces witnesses to show up. In the court system it's accomplished through subpoenas and fines if the witnesses fail to appear. Your school doesn't have the power to issue subpoenas, but it should use some of its ample authority to compel witnesses to turn up. Both sides should have access to compulsory process rights—meaning both you and the prosecution should be able to compel people to testify.

Your Case One of the most basic components of due process is the right of the accused to present her side of the story. This means you get to call your own witnesses, speak on your own behalf, offer written documents, or use any other type of evidence to support your case.

You also get to present your case second. The accusing side must present their case before you do. This gives you the ability to respond to the specific charges and evidence against you.

Finally, as someone who's been accused of a crime, you're also afforded the privilege against self-incrimination, meaning that you can't be forced to testify at the hearing. Generally, if you're innocent, staying quiet is a bad idea. Fact finders aren't *supposed* to hold your silence against you, but that doesn't mean they won't. So unless you have very good reason, it makes sense to speak up.

NO RIGHT TO ADMINISTRATIVE APPEAL

An on-campus hearing may be the beginning, the middle, and the end of the process at your school. The law doesn't require that schools have an internal appeal process in place. Often the appeal options that do exist are

minimal—review by an administrator or other person. Your student handbook should outline what posthearing options are available.

If you feel like you've been slighted, it's worth your time to investigate your options. And, even if there are no formal procedures for review in place, you might as well try to get the dean of students or the provost to hear your appeal.

Do what you can to resolve the situation within the campus system because, when that process is over, your only option is the court system. Aside from being expensive and time-consuming, your chances of getting the decision overturned are very low. Courts are extremely hesitant to interfere with this type of school business.

Step Two: Collecting and Analyzing the Evidence

As soon as you're accused you need to embark on a fact-finding mission. Actually you'll need to go on two fact-finding missions—it's just as important to understand and analyze the case against you as it is to build your own case. So work on two fronts. And get in the habit of thinking about things from both sides of the fence as a matter of course.

INVESTIGATING THEIR EVIDENCE

Often the notice itself will include some details about the evidence and witnesses that will be used against you. Other times the notice will simply be a description of the charges. Even if you've been served with the more inclusive type, you shouldn't rely on what's there. Go immediately to the governing body and ask for copies of all the records related to the case and all of the evidence of your guilt. They have to hand it over, so be firm and vocal if they give you a hard time.

Meet with Your Foe It's never a bad idea to sit down with the person that will be bringing the case against you. Take a look at what you've already got and see where the case seems to be going. Then sit face to face with your opponent and

Your Lawyer Says:

ALWAYS ASK FOR MORE
You should never assume that any set of records you're given is complete. Get in the habit of asking, "Is this everything you have?" as a matter of course. You never want to give anyone an opportunity to withhold information simply because you didn't ask for it.

ask for any other evidence he might have. And don't be afraid to ask specific questions about the case he plans on bringing against you.

But be very careful about the information you give up about your case. While you have a right to know all about your opponent's evidence, they have a much more limited right to the workings of yours. So if you're asked a question you don't want to answer, don't.

Go to the Source Track down the prosecution's key witnesses and talk with them before the hearing. Don't rely on what your opponent *says* they'll say. There could be subtle but critical differences between their reported and actual testimony. And, even if you don't uncover any new evidence, it's a good idea to have met the key witnesses ahead of time. That way you'll be more comfortable when you have to talk to them at your hearing.

The same goes for important documents. If there's a piece of paper that's critical to the case, find out where it came from and go there. See if there are any other related documents that might help you. Talk to the people who found or created the documents and find out what you can. You never know, you might be able to diminish their importance or impact with what you uncover.

AMASSING YOUR EVIDENCE

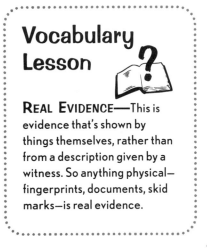

Vocabulary Lesson

REAL EVIDENCE—This is evidence that's shown by things themselves, rather than from a description given by a witness. So anything physical—fingerprints, documents, skid marks—is real evidence.

As you review the opposing side's evidence, the basic form of your defense will begin to reveal itself to you. You'll discover where the weak spots in their theory are and what you'll have to show to prove your innocence.

Use that basic stance as a starting point and investigate everything that's related to your side of the story. Every case is different and every evidentiary expedition works differently. So follow the leads wherever they take you. And always err on the side of overdoing it. There's no downside to following every lead, interviewing every witness, and examining every piece of **real evidence**.

So be as thorough as humanly possible. It increases your chances of success exponentially.

Be sure to think about all of the types of evidence that support your case. Frame your search in the following broad areas:

✓ *Witnesses.* Spoken testimony will probably be the backbone of both sides of the case, so talk to everyone who might know something that can help you. And remember, witnesses can testify to *anything* they've perceived with *any* of their senses. So anything they've heard, felt, smelled, seen, or tasted can be used.

✓ *Documents and other real evidence.* Get copies of any documents that support your case. And take (or take pictures of) any other type of real evidence that's helpful. When using documents or real evidence at the hearing, it's usually best to accompany them with witness testimony that explains them. So when you're gathering this type of evidence, also try to find a witness who will be able to describe what you've found. They don't have to be experts. They just have to be able to say things like, "This is a printout that shows every electronic key that was used to enter the student union last Saturday" or "This picture shows the damage done to the mail room."

✓ *Hearsay.* If a witness doesn't have any direct knowledge of something— if she's been told it by someone else—it's hearsay. At real criminal trials hearsay isn't allowed except under very specific circumstances. You're generally allowed to use it at campus disciplinary hearings. But it's still not wise to rely on hearsay evidence too heavily. "I saw" is way more convincing than "Fred said that he saw."

✓ *Experts.* Forensic and medical experts are fairly common in criminal and civil trials. But few campus trials involve them. Still, if you do need to use some sort of expert, I tender this bit of advice: Be careful about enlisting an unqualified expert. Nothing looks worse than offering someone as an expert who doesn't know what they're talking about. Your whole case could fall down around a mistake like that.

Step Three: Building and Presenting Your Case

Learning to effectively prepare and present a case can take a lifetime. Even among the experts there is disagreement about the best methods to mount an effective defense. Obviously I won't be able to make you into a full-fledged trial lawyer over the next few pages (and to be honest, you probably don't need that level of skill to prevail at a university hearing). I can, however, set you in the right direction by giving you an overall structure to follow.

ENLIST HELP

You may not be allowed a lawyer at the hearing itself. But nothing prevents you from enlisting the help of an attorney, or anyone else, during the preparatory stages of your case. If the charges you are facing are serious enough, and you can afford it, get a lawyer. The insight of an experienced attorney will be invaluable not only in technical areas, but in preparing a cogent and powerful case.

Even if you don't get an attorney, I suggest you recruit a few people to help you. Gather a few of your smartest friends, trusted professors, and anyone else who can be of assistance and ask them to work on your case with you. Obviously, the more people you have on your team, the more ground you'll be able to cover. It's also useful to have more than one person work through the logic of the case itself. Others may make connections, or see problems, you don't.

MAKE A ROAD MAP

After you've rounded up all of the potential evidence, lay it out to see how it fits together. Try to create two complete and distinct outlines: one for their case and one for your defense. These will be your road maps for the hearing.

At this point there may be some holes in one or both of these outlines, places where the evidence that's available doesn't support a logical leap. If the gap is in your defense, you need to go back out and look for more evidence in that area. If it's on the prosecution's side, and it's not too huge, you can probably let it go. As long as you can make out what the main components of the case against you are, you should be fine.

At some point you'll either complete your case or exhaust potential sources of evidence. Your outline will be as complete as it's going to get. You're ready to start putting together your presentation.

DISTILL

Think back to the O. J. trial. Do you remember Johnny Cochran's mantra? "If it doesn't fit, you must acquit." Sure, it's hokey. It may have even been a bit off the point. But in one area it absolutely excels—it's simple. In that respect it is pure genius.

Try to formulate a similar thesis statement for your case. It doesn't have to rhyme (in fact it's probably better if it doesn't). But it should distill the facts and your assertions into an easy-to-comprehend statement. Look at the case the opposition's going to make. Look at the case you've mapped out. And write a thesis statement. Something along the lines of "I couldn't have vandalized the mail room because I was off campus all evening." Or, "It would have been impossible for me to have copied off of her. I was more than fifteen feet away."

This thesis statement should be the guiding star of your case. It should also be the first, last, and most-often-repeated statement during your presentation. You may have spent the better part of the last few weeks dealing with this information. But the judges haven't. They're going to have to comprehend and digest all of the information in the span of an hour or two. If you don't give them a simple theory to guide their thoughts, they may get lost in the mix.

FILL IN THE BLANKS

You've got all of the evidence. You've got a road map. And you've got a thesis statement. Now all you have to do is put it all together.

When planning the presentation of your case, there is one component that merits special attention: the opening statements. It's your first opportunity to communicate the theory of your defense to the decision makers. It's also your chance to make an emotional and personal connection with them. And the decision makers' attention levels will be higher during the opening statements than at any other time. If you want to make an impact, this is the best time to do it. A good opening statement will set you on a trajectory that will carry you for the rest of the trial.

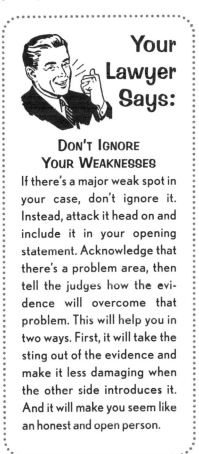

Your Lawyer Says:

DON'T IGNORE
YOUR WEAKNESSES

If there's a major weak spot in your case, don't ignore it. Instead, attack it head on and include it in your opening statement. Acknowledge that there's a problem area, then tell the judges how the evidence will overcome that problem. This will help you in two ways. First, it will take the sting out of the evidence and make it less damaging when the other side introduces it. And it will make you seem like an honest and open person.

There are a few things you should keep in mind when preparing the opening. First, remember to lead with your thesis statement. This is the hook, the framework the rest of the case will fall into. After that, the majority of the opening should be a shortened version of the story of your case. Tell the factual narrative that proves your innocence. You don't need to include every little detail. There will be plenty of time for that later on. Just give the high points. Include all the things that the jury will need to know to reach the right verdict.

Finally, finish your opening with a charge to the decision makers. Tell them what they'll need to do to find the truth (which is: listen carefully to your side of the story). And instill them with confidence, both by assuring them that you have faith in their abilities and by being confident yourself.

Presenting the case itself is as simple as following your road map. Use the narrative that you laid out in the opening as your guide and tell the story that proves your side. Each piece of evidence should correspond to a specific part of the story. As a whole, this should be a broad plan for the presentation of your case.

It's up to you how you prepare for the main part of the case. If you're a comfortable, natural public speaker, probably all you need to do is go over it a few times to work out the gist of it. If you're at the other end of the oratory spectrum, you might want to create a more detailed script for each part of the story and lists of questions you want to ask each witness.

No matter how you approach your preparation, be ready to make at least a few small changes on the fly. Remember, the prosecution's case is going to be presented just before you have your say. You should listen carefully to what your opponent has to say and make any necessary adjustments on the spot.

At the end of the hearing, you'll probably be given the opportunity to make a closing statement. This speech should be the mirror image of the opening. It should include all of the same components: your thesis, a restatement of the narrative, and a charge to the jury. It's also your last chance to diffuse any particularly damaging evidence your opponents introduced.

CHAPTER 11

Cyber Issues on Campus

Your college has a limited right to prohibit you from viewing certain websites in public places. But in private, there's no precedent for them to keep you from looking at whatever the hell you want. So lock the door, and then let your demented little mind take you as far as the Web will go.

Chapter Contents

he Internet is a problem. Yes, e-mail and the World Wide Web are incredible conveniences and unparalleled learning tools. But as far as lawyers and college administrators are concerned, they're a liability. Their beauty is what makes them dangerous—instantaneously and seamlessly, they connect students and professors to the rest of the world.

Student sins and screw-ups used to be limited by physical presence. You actually had to travel someplace to cause trouble there. Not anymore. The laws of numerous countries can now be broken without even leaving your bedroom. It is this possibility—of unlawful actions—that informs many campus computing policies. They don't want the school to get into trouble for the music you download, the pornography you e-mail, or the virus you create. In order to achieve those goals, their practices can be, at times, restrictive and invasive.

HOW TO THINK ABOUT COMPUTING ISSUES

Before we get down to it, I want to suggest a theoretical approach. A lot of legal scholars lose their heads when they think about computing and the law. They think they need to start from scratch, to create an entirely new doctrine in regard to online rights and responsibilities. "It's all too new," they say. "There's no way to possibly predict how laws will play out in cyberspace." In part they're right. This is a very new area of the law, and any aspect of it is subject to change over the next few years.

But to treat the Internet and electronic communications as an absolutely foreign frontier, where existing laws have no application, is not only confusing, it's downright wrong.

So don't get caught in that trap. It's becoming increasingly clear that the same rules and restraints that apply in other media apply in cyberspace. Certainly there are differences in the way that electronic communications function that need to be considered. But aside from those mechanical differences, the basic theories behind the law operate the same way.

When you're thinking about one of these issues, start your assessment of the situation by thinking about the nonvirtual equivalent. For example, before you get pissed off about your inability to view pornographic websites in public computer lounges, think about whether or not you'd be similarly upset if *Hustler* wasn't available in the library's stacks. Or, if you think that punishing a student for posting anti-Semitic messages on the Hillel website is outrageous, consider what the appropriate punishment would be had that same student stormed into an actual meeting spewing racist language.

Exploring the offline version of the infraction will help keep things in perspective and will give you a springboard for analyzing the legal issues. I think you'll find that if you start by imagining the corresponding low-tech situation, you'll discover that your cyber issue is rather familiar. It's just a new version of a problem you've probably already encountered elsewhere.

This chapter, then, is organized via the areas of existing law that affect electronic interactions—*Free Speech*, *Privacy*, and *Copyright and Intellectual Property*. Each section begins with a generalized discussion of the area of law, followed by specific statutes and practical applications to on-campus computing. At the end of the chapter is a final issue that doesn't fit into the overall paradigm—hacking. While this practice could be fairly accurately described as the computing version of vandalism, the laws that deal with computer fraud and abuse have grown up on their own. So they merit their own discussion.

THE PUBLIC AND PRIVATE SCHOOL DISTINCTION

Much of what will be discussed in the following pages is based in constitutional law. So, as you well know by now, it's only applicable to public schools (and because of the Leonard Law, for First Amendment issues, private schools in California). Private school attendees, read on, but keep in mind that the constitutional mandates are guidelines, not the law, on your campus. This means you may have to get more creative if you want to make your school walk the line. You may be forced to shame your school into compliance. Trust me. No administrator wants to publicly answer sticky questions about why their policies deny students' basic rights. So the constitutional concepts discussed here will have a very strong argumentative value.

Your Lawyer Says:

OFF-CAMPUS NETWORKS ARE A DIFFERENT STORY
The laws, issues, and strategies discussed here apply to on-campus networks only. When you access the electronic world through AOL, Verizon, or any other private provider, you are dealing with an entirely different animal. Many of the laws and theories still apply, but often in a different way.

Free Speech and Computing

Most of what you do on a computer network is expressive. Sometimes this is obvious: If you send someone an e-mail, you're speaking to them. Likewise if you've got your own blog. But even the somewhat passive act of looking at someone else's website is constitutionally protected speech. Your ability to read about certain topics or view certain images falls under the purview of the First Amendment.

IS THE COMPUTER NETWORK A PUBLIC FORUM?

As you know from chapter 8, "Free Speech," whether or not a place is considered to be a public forum is critical in any First Amendment analysis (if you haven't read chapter 8 yet, it might be a good idea to review it now). In public areas the government has a very limited ability to regulate speech.

Unfortunately, university-run networks are *not* public forums. Only a few cases have explicitly answered that question, so there's a chance that the status could change. But it's unlikely. When you get down to it, on-campus networks are only open to members of the university community, not the general public. Courts will look to that and continue to hold that the forum is a private one.

This means that the university has much more latitude in regulating the use of the computer system than they would otherwise. They can regulate not only the time, place, and manner of the speech (which is the case in any type of forum), but they may regulate *content* if their rules are "reasonable and are not an effort to suppress expression merely because public officials oppose the view." The key word in that sentence is *reasonable*. In legal terms, that's not a particularly high standard. It gives schools pretty broad power.

UNIVERSALLY PROHIBITED SPEECH

No matter what the forum, there are certain types of speech that aren't protected by the First Amendment. They can always be prohibited. They are fighting words, obscenities, and defamation. They're each described in detail below.

In theory, this is pretty simple—even in the most public forum the government can outlaw speech that falls into these categories. But in practice, that's pretty difficult to do. It's nearly impossible to draft a rule that *only* bans defamation or keeps out *only* obscene materials. The result is often a law that includes many other things. In legal terms, this is called "overbroad," meaning that, although the law's intent is constitutional, it prohibits speech that *does* have First Amendment protection.

Because of this, most university computing policies simply restate the law ("use of university systems to transmit legally obscene materials is prohibited"), rather than wade into the murky waters of constitutional law. But some still do try to build more precise regulations.

If you encounter a rule at your school that addresses one of these areas, take a very close look and see how it actually operates. If it's possible that speech other than the prohibited categories could be constrained by the rule, it's probably overbroad and unconstitutional.

Fighting Words Fighting words are statements so inflammatory that, when spoken to an ordinary person, they're likely to incite immediate physical retaliation. The courts haven't applied this concept to the Internet yet, and they likely won't. The forum just doesn't lend itself to immediate retaliation. Usually those you're communicating with are some distance away. Certainly you could send an inflammatory e-mail to someone. But unless you send it to someone sitting right next to you, the recipient is going to have to see it, get mad, figure out where you are, travel there, *then* kick the crap out of you. It just doesn't work.

Obscene Speech and Child Pornography Obscenity is probably the most discussed Internet topic. It's no wonder. We use the Internet for finding porn more than anything else. (Of course, I *never* use the Internet to look at porn. I only use it to research my favorite scriptures and to find new ways to help the elderly in my community.) In 2003, 12 percent of all websites were porn sites. A quarter of all search engine requests were for pornography, and 8 percent of all e-mails sent included pornographic images—that's roughly five pornographic e-mails being sent to every Internet user every day.

As you know from chapter 8, not all pornography is obscene. In fact, a large portion of what you could find on the Web probably isn't. It's not the type of thing you'd want to look at with your mother, but it's not technically obscene. What exactly is obscene is determined on a case-by-case basis using the following standards. The material must

- ✓ appeal to a prurient (shameful or morbid) interest in sex,
- ✓ portray sex in a patently offensive way based on the local community standards, and
- ✓ have no serious literary, artistic, political, or scientific value.

Although you have no right to express yourself using obscenity, you do have a right to have it in your home for private use. As long as you keep the magazines under your mattress, you can look at whatever you want.

Not so with child pornography. It's a violation of federal law both to distribute or simply possess child pornography. Many states also have their own statutes making possession and distribution illegal. And the standards that define obscene materials that involve children are much less strict. For practical purposes you can simply assume that all visual depictions of minors engaged in sex acts of any nature are obscene.

Defamation The basic concept of defamation is both simple and familiar. If you say something that harms another person, they can sue you. As you learned in chapter 8, in order for a plaintiff to prove they have been defamed, they have to show (1) that the defendant said something defamatory (2) to a third party that (3) identifies the target and (4) damages them.

Cyber Issues

For public figures—anyone who's famous or infamous—the standards get stricter. It varies depending on the type of public figure, but generally the target will have to show that the statements were false and in some instances that the speaker knew they were false before publishing them.

Commercial Speech   Advertisements and commercial speech are treated differently than other types of expression. False advertising and advertisements for illegal activities are offered no protection at all. Otherwise, the government can regulate commercial expression, as long as the regulations are narrowly tailored to promote a substantial government interest.

In the computing realm this test is pretty easy to apply. *A policy that prohibits all commercial uses of the university network is narrowly tailored and serves a substantial government interest.* In other words, it's legal. Most schools have such a policy—they don't want their networks slowed by students' commercial enterprises. These rules are totally legal and enforceable.

FEDERAL LEGISLATION CONCERNING OBSCENE MATERIALS ON THE INTERNET

Congress has been trying for a long time to regulate pornographic materials on the Internet and, so far, has had very little success.

First, in 1996, Congress passed and President Clinton signed into law the Communications Decency Act (CDA). The CDA made it a federal crime, punishable by up to two years in prison, to knowingly transmit obscene materials to a minor. In 1997 just about every rights group in the country filed a lawsuit challenging the constitutionality of the law. The Supreme Court sided with free speech—finding that the law was vague and overbroad—and struck down *most* of the provisions of the CDA.

Then, in October of 1998, Congress gave it another go with the Child Online Protection Act (COPA). This law was narrower in scope, targeting only commercial entities, making it a crime for them to distribute materials that were "harmful to minors." Violation of the act was punishable by a $50,000 fine and up to two years in prison.

COPA was also, very quickly, determined to be unconstitutional—again vague and overbroad.

Finally, in December of 2000, Congress gave up on the idea of a comprehensive law and passed the Children's Internet Protection Act (CIPA). This law requires that schools and libraries that participate in the "E-Rate" program (a government project that provides Internet service at significant discounts) block Internet access to materials that are harmful to minors. The Supreme Court upheld the statute, so it's law. But thankfully for college students, *this law does not apply to colleges.* No postsecondary schools participate in the E-Rate program.

This is the long way of telling you that although Congress has tried a few times to regulate obscenity on the Internet, they've pretty much struck out. There are no special laws that govern Internet obscenity. The normal statutes apply, just like they do to magazines and videos. But that's it.

The Little Gem in the CDA   If you read carefully above, you noticed that I said that *most* of the CDA was struck down. One part of the law did survive. It states that "no provider or user of an interactive computer service shall be treated as the publisher or speaker of any information provided by another information content provider." In plain language it means that ISPs can't be held liable for what the users post.

Since legal liability is often a justification for regulation, it's a very good thing for free speech proponents that this part of the law is still in place. And if your school ever tries to rationalize a restrictive policy based on institutional liability, point to Section 230 of the CDA as your response.

ONLINE FREE SPEECH IN PRACTICE

E-mail   The most often prohibited speech on university e-mail servers is commercial speech. This is probably due to the fact that your school is likely to notice a spike in your usage if you send out thousands of advertisements. Most schools have an outright ban on use of the computer system for commercial purposes. This is within their rights.

This doesn't mean that you're not allowed to sign up to receive offers from commercial entities or otherwise get or send commercially oriented messages. But it does mean that you can't use university resources to further a moneymaking advertising campaign. University-related business that has a monetary component is a different story. Sending out invites to a fraternity or dorm benefit is not "commercial" use of the network. Sending out 200,000 ads for your new herbal Viagra business would be.

Of course, the school can also ban e-mails that fall into any of the other prohibited categories above. Most don't. Drafting language that effectively bans obscenity but allows explicit, but valuable, materials is difficult to do. Congress hasn't figured it out yet. University regulators are wary of the pitfalls and usually don't try.

That said, they may have a catch-all acceptable-use policy that forbids the use of university equipment for unlawful purposes—threats of violence, obscenity, child pornography, and harassing communications. Usually these regulations include the phrase "as defined by law" meaning that the university rules place no further restrictions than the applicable state and federal laws.

But remember, the applicable laws can include lots of things other than the First Amendment. Among other things, e-mail use could violate stalking laws (see chapter 15) or assault statutes (see chapter 12), could be harassing, and could open the school up to liability or violate a university anti-harassment policy (see chapter 6).

Cyber Issues

In other words, your speech in an e-mail is subject to all of the same rules and regulations as other forms of communication. So think before you send something potentially incriminating or inflammatory.

Maintaining a Website Many schools give students a limited amount of space on the university server to maintain personal websites. They can regulate these websites in the same manner they may regulate e-mail. The difference is, since the content is posted out in the open, they'll likely enforce the rules. Assume that some university official will take a look at your site from time to time to make sure that you're not violating any school policy.

Your Lawyer Says:

WHEN IN DOUBT, FIND A HOST ELSEWHERE

If you really feel the need to have a website that includes potentially objectionable materials (or if you just want to be sure your college won't be on your back), avoid the whole issue. Cough up the ten bucks a month it costs to buy space from a commerical, off-campus hosting service.

As in e-mail use, you'll probably be prohibited from using university web space for any commercial enterprise.

The school also has a pretty solid right to prohibit you from using their space to display images that are sexually or racially charged. Title VII of the Civil Rights Act and Title IX of the Educational Amendments of 1972 (see chapter 6, "Harassment & Discrimination," for a full discussion) hold the school legally liable for racially or sexually hostile environments. If your website is provocative enough to make minorities or women uncomfortable, the school could get sued for discrimination.

Accessing the Internet Prohibiting access to objectionable materials was all the rage about ten years ago. Carnegie Mellon University, one of the first truly wired campuses, was also one of the first schools to try to restrict access. In 1994, worried about the large amounts of sexual materials on the Internet and potential university liability, CMU prohibited access to the alt.sex newsgroups. The campus community went, in a word, apeshit.

On the one side were the proponents of unfettered academic freedom who, correctly, pointed out that censoring access to information on a college campus is a miserable thing to do. On the other were those who, also correctly, pointed out that if the university openly allowed illegal acts to take place on their equipment, they could be held liable.

CMU found a clever way out of the conundrum. They declared the computer system a library. Under Pennsylvania law this made it, as all libraries are, immune from criminal and civil liability for the information it stored.

Today Section 203 of the Communications Decency Act shields schools from liability for user-posted information, taking the wind out of the sails of the "we have to regulate or we could get in trouble" argument. Still, the CDA doesn't protect universities from hostile environment discrimination suits. *Some* regulation of sexual or racially charged materials is probably lawful. Prohibiting access in public labs but allowing unfettered access at dorm room terminals would be fine. An outright ban would be unconstitutional.

The Bottom Line   In general, your school doesn't have the right to rein you in any more than the Constitution allows. So the best way to evaluate an on-campus computing policy is to apply the tenets of free speech and see where you come out. You know the limits now: The school can regulate defamatory communications, obscenity (including child porn), fighting words, and, to a great extent, commercial speech. They also have an obligation to avoid racially or sexually hostile environments. So they have fairly broad latitude in those areas.

If you encounter a rule or regulation that you think is a problem, think about it in terms of what you've learned. Is the rule narrowly tailored so that it only regulates a prohibitive type of speech? Does it allow for you to exercise your rights elsewhere, if not everywhere? Will it affect your educational use of the network? If the answer to any of these questions is suspect, it's probably time to take a stand.

Online Privacy Issues

On college campuses e-mail has practically replaced phones, snail mail, and interoffice memos. But unlike their low-tech predecessors, electronic communications are not particularly private forms of communication. If you use a phone or send something through the mail, you are guaranteed a certain level of privacy. Long-held tenets of constitutional law and the Wiretap Act of 1974 assure users that no one will read your letter or listen in.

But the Internet and its trappings are still new technologies. The contours of the laws and how they apply are not yet well-defined. There are two areas of emerging law that govern electronic privacy. Neither affords much protection.

Vocabulary Lesson

EXPECTATION OF PRIVACY—A person's right to be free of unreasonable searches only applies in places where they have a legitimate and reasonable expectation of privacy. There are two parts to this: First, the expectation must *actually* be held. No matter what the reality of the situation is, if the searchee doesn't think that their property is secure, then there's no expectation. Second, that expectation has to be reasonable based on community standards.

Cyber Issues

THE FOURTH AMENDMENT PROHIBITION AGAINST UNREASONABLE SEARCHES

The Fourth Amendment prohibits government actors from performing unreasonable searches of a person's property. Under the terms of the Fourth, if a person has a **reasonable expectation of privacy** with respect to a place, the government may not search there. A lot of legal scholars use the Fourth Amendment to support the concept of e-mail privacy. You should know about it because there may be some theoretical value to the argument. But for a college student, I don't think the Fourth offers much protection. Here's why:

At the outset, the "expectation of privacy" part of the definition is too malleable to have any import in the on-campus electronic setting.

If you look at the vocabulary lesson on the previous page, I think you'll agree that this is a pretty soft set of conditions. It can be easily manipulated by the service provider itself. For instance, your school may have a stated policy that all computer activities are subject to institutional monitoring. Unless you're pretty damned thickheaded, this would directly affect your actual expectation of privacy and could entirely remove the constitutional argument. This might change as societal beliefs solidify on the subject, but for now it's a very difficult place to get a foothold.

And anyway, even if the constitutional prohibitions did stick, their import in an on-campus setting would be limited. In the off-campus world, if a search is found to violate the Fourth Amendment, the only repercussion is that the evidence found in that search wouldn't be admissible in a criminal trial. That's it. Those exclusionary rules simply don't apply to on-campus hearings, where most infractions would be tried.

Add to all of this the fact that the Constitution is in force only at public schools, not private ones, and I've had enough.

Someday the Fourth Amendment may be an important piece of this puzzle. But today, it doesn't offer much help.

THE ELECTRONIC COMMUNICATIONS PRIVACY ACT OF 1986

The ECPA is the other potential source of electronic privacy. It has two significant parts. The first prohibits unauthorized interception of the content of e-mail (and any other computer-to-computer communications, like instant messaging). The second part applies the same rule to messages and communications stored on a system.

So whether or not your e-mail is actually bouncing around cyberspace or simply waiting at a server to be delivered, the ECPA makes it illegal for anyone other than the addressee to read it.

This law applies to state *and* private actors—so both public and private schools are bound by it (as well as any other ISP you might use). Even individuals are covered—your ex who knows your password or an enterprising enemy are also prohibited from getting at your e-mail without your permission.

Of course, there are exceptions. The first is in the construction of the rule itself. You'll notice that the act prohibits interception of or access to the *content* of the e-mail. Log files that report that an e-mail was initiated or completed don't count. So anyone who has the technical ability can look at who you e-mailed and when you did it. They just can't read what you said.

But the real hole applies to service providers themselves—which in your case is your school. Any ISP can intercept or access stored e-mail communications if they do so while "engaged in an activity which is a necessary incident to the rendition of service to the protection of [its] property." And they can forward the message to anyone after they intercept it. What does all this mean in plain terms? A service provider can pretty much intercept and divulge the contents of any e-mail that goes through their system without violating the ECPA.

On top of this, our friend the PATRIOT Act further weakened the ECPA. First, it added a voluntary disclosure clause. If a service provider reasonably believes that an impending emergency that involves imminent physical danger justifies disclosing the contents of electronic communications, it may do so. Second, it granted the federal government much broader means through which it can compel private service providers to disclose information.

UNIVERSITY POLICIES

Most schools have their own published policies on computer privacy. The policy may be included in the student handbook. It's also probably somewhere on the school's website. Find a copy and take a look at it. Your school is bound to that policy, and it may afford you some more protection than the present legislation.

But don't get your hopes up. Chances are the exceptions in the school's policy are bigger than those in the laws. Your school knows better than anyone that their stated policies create a contract between the school and the student, so they draft them very carefully. Sentences like "It is not university policy to monitor student e-mail, but the university reserves the right to do so" are very common.

ONLINE PRIVACY IN PRACTICE

E-mail   You're screwed. If the school wants to read your e-mail, they probably can. The ECPA offers great protection against individuals and other parties, but since your school is also your ISP, they have huge loopholes they can walk through. Similarly, the Fourth Amendment offers almost no protection at all at public universities and none whatsoever at private schools.

Cyber Issues

So treat your e-mail as if it's public. You've probably heard this before, but don't put anything into an electronic message that you don't want other people reading. It's not a bad habit to get into anyway. When you get into the real world and have a job, your employer will have even more of a right to look at your e-mail.

Maintaining a Website   Umm, nothing you post on a website is private. By putting information out there, you remove any expectation of privacy you had. This goes for a site you maintain or even things you post at other sites—like chat rooms. I think it's pretty self-evident, but things that you post are not private and can be viewed by anyone.

Accessing the Internet   Again, you're screwed. Your ISP can pretty readily and pretty legally track the sites you visit. The law simply doesn't require your school to afford you any kind of privacy in this area.

The Bottom Line   There really aren't many legal constraints on your school when it comes to invading your electronic privacy. The real source of law in all applications is the school's own use policy. This is both good and bad news—bad because there's very little federal protection, but good because the school policy is something that students themselves can have an impact on.

Take a good hard look at your school's policy. Read it front to back and make your own assessment. It may be just fine. If so, move on. But if not, take issue with it.

Intellectual Property and Online Copyright Issues

Strange as it may seem, theft is probably the number one crime committed online. We generally think of stealing in terms of tangible items—money, paintings, electronics, your roommate's toothpaste. But intellectual property can be stolen in the same way a CD player or a Picasso can.

You're probably more familiar with intellectual property theft than you think. In fact you've probably committed it. If you've ever snuck into a movie without paying or watched pirated cable, you've stolen an intangible. I'm guessing that pretty much everyone who's reading this page has done something like this at one time or another. I'm also guessing that you knew damn well that what you were doing was wrong. No one had to write a book to tell you about it.

But for some reason, people forget what they know about theft when they log on. "If it's on the Internet, it's fair game" is the prevailing attitude. The best examples of this are file-sharing programs. People who would never steal a CD from Wal-Mart download music with impunity. I'm sure most actually know that this is breaking the law. But they do it anyway because they also know that there's very little chance they'll ever get caught (a nice commentary on the collective ethics of the nation, eh?).

Vocabulary Lesson

PUBLIC DOMAIN—Some creative works aren't protected by copyright laws at all. These works are referred to as being in the public domain, meaning the public has a right to use them. For example, all work created by the U.S. government is in the public domain—so pictures taken by NASA can be used and reproduced by anyone. The copyrights of works by other entities can also expire, usually because a certain period of time has passed or because the author failed to take the procedural steps to protect the copyright. When that happens, the work passes into the public domain.

We'll deal with file sharing and all of its implications at the end of this chapter. But I wanted to point it out now to illustrate the concept of intellectual ownership. Just like those music files you download are owned by Sony or Columbia, much of the other things available on the Internet—pictures, writing, software, even graphics and logos—belong to someone. This section of the chapter deals with just that: who owns what on the Web and what they might do if you steal it.

FEDERAL COPYRIGHT LAWS

Copyright law has existed for a very long time in America—since 1790. It's been updated a few times since then. The Copyright Act of 1976 is the most recent iteration of the laws. And it was amended substantially in 1998 to address computer technologies. But the basic import of the laws remains the same. The act extends copyright protection to "original works of authorship fixed in any tangible medium of expression, now known or later developed, from which they can be perceived, reproduced, or otherwise communicated, either directly or with the aid of a machine or device." Those tangible mediums are

- ✓ literary works,
- ✓ musical works, including any accompanying words,
- ✓ dramatic works, including any accompanying music,
- ✓ pantomimes and choreographic works,
- ✓ pictorial, graphic, and sculptural works,
- ✓ motion pictures and other audiovisual works,
- ✓ sound recordings,
- ✓ architectural works, and
- ✓ computer programs, including the manuals for those programs.

In fact, pretty much any original work is protected by the Copyright Act.

The act only protects the *expression* of the ideas, processes, and concepts, not the ideas themselves. In other words, if you watch *Jaws* on TBS (because, let's face it, *Jaws* is pretty much always on TBS) and decide that you'd like to write a story, or even a screenplay, about a shark terrorizing a town, that's fine. Steven Spielberg and Peter Benchley don't own the idea of stories about sharks. But if you used their script or the general story line or title, then you'd be in trouble.

What an Owner Gets   The owner of the copyright, well, owns the work. In legal terms this means that she has the exclusive right to do, and authorize others to do, the following:

1. *Reproduce* the copyrighted work—simple enough.
2. *Prepare derivative works* based upon the copyrighted work—no *Jaws VII* without permission.
3. *Distribute copies* of copyrighted work to the public by sale or other transfer of ownership, or by rental, lease, or loan—but private use is still okay. In other words, you can listen to the CD you bought in your room or car, but you can't sell, or give away, burned copies of it.
4. *Perform* a copyrighted literary, musical, dramatic, choreographic, pantomime, motion picture, or other audiovisual work—so whenever your college mounts a production of a play, they pay a royalty to the original author or whoever owns the rights.
5. *Display* a literary, musical, dramatic, choreographic, pantomime, pictorial, graphic, or sculptural work.

If you do any of these things without the owner's permission, you're violating copyright law, or as lawyers say, infringing on the owner's copyright. Intent is not a requirement in the copyright realm. In other words, accidental copying or distribution can still get you in trouble (although courts will usually take the accidental nature of the violation into account when punishing the violator).

If caught violating a copyright, the owner can seek a permanent or temporary injunction to stop you from what you're doing, can recover actual damages (the amount you cost them in lost sales or other revenues), or can seek statutory damages (punishment payments) of up to $30,000 in normal cases and, in cases of willful violations, up to $100,000 per violation.

Fair Use   There is a significant limit to the owners' rights. Section 107 of the act states that "fair use" of the copyrighted work for "criticism, comment, news reporting, teaching (including multiple copies for classroom use), scholarship, or research" is *not* an infringement of the copyright.

This pretty much means what it says. You're allowed to use copyrighted works, without permission, so long as it's for one of the reasons listed above. As a college student, clearly, the teaching, research, and scholarship parts are the most pertinent. But it's not as simple as saying that your use was educational. As with all things law, there's a test that's applied on a case-by-case basis. Courts will look at the following:

1. the purpose and character of the use, including if there's any commercial gain for the user,

2. the nature of the work,
3. the amount of the work used in proportion to the whole, and
4. the effect on the potential market for the work by the use.

In court, the fourth part of the test—the economic impact—is usually the most closely examined. Justifiably. Losing money is usually what the copyright owner gets pissed about. So if you're trying to figure out on your own whether or not what you're doing is fair use, think about the economic impact of your actions first. Are you taking away a bunch of potential customers from the owner? If so, your use is probably an infringement.

TRADEMARK LAWS

A trademark is a word, symbol, or other device (or combination thereof) that distinguishes one company's goods from another's. A service mark is the same thing, but refers to a service or set of services rather than a product. They can be almost anything, from a logo to a distinctive combination of colors or packaging to an architectural design. The Playboy bunny, the Nike swoosh, Tony the Tiger, the distinctive look of a McDonald's restaurant, even the three notes in the NBC jingle are trademarks.

In addition to being the property of these companies, as in copyright law, they are inherently associated with their businesses. Owners of servicemarks and trademarks are entitled to exclusive use of the mark and can prohibit others from use if there is a likelihood of confusion, mistake, or deception on the part of the public. In other words, if a consumer could be tricked into thinking that they're dealing with the owner's company based on the mark, then it is infringement.

Trademarks are governed by federal statute, state laws, common law, and by a special law titled the Lanham Act. Often companies register their marks with the Patent and Trademark Office, but doing so isn't required. Continued use in trade is all that's needed to establish ownership.

FEDERAL INTERNET LAWS

In addition to the general copyright laws, Congress has passed a few Internet-specific statutes that protect intellectual property online.

The Digital Millennium Copyright Act The Digital Millennium Copyright Act (DMCA) is an extension of the existing Copyright Act that closes some of the holes in the area of online copyright violations. Among other things, it implemented a number of international copyright treaties that govern how these issues are to be dealt with across national boundaries. It also made some changes that affect the individual American user.

Most significantly, it prohibits the development or sale of devices or services that either provide unauthorized access to copyrighted materials or allow the unauthorized reproduction of authorized materials. In other words, making or selling the programs that allow you to defeat copy

Cyber Issues

protection—cracks, keygens, serial number hacks, and other similar items—is illegal under the DMCA.

The act also limits the liability of service providers for the infringing actions of their users. This doesn't do much for the average student, but it may inform the manner in which your school deals with your use. In order to be immune from liability, an ISP has to meet certain conditions. If notified of an infringement, they must remove or disable access to the offending material and they must have a policy that provides for the termination of the user's accounts for repeat infringers.

The No Electronic Theft Act   The No Electronic Theft or NET Act (clever, huh?) redefines the criminal components of copyright theft in electronic applications. Under offline copyright law, criminal penalties can be imposed if the infringer willfully violates the copyright for the purposes of commercial advantage or personal financial gain. This law works just fine in the real world, but online it isn't much of a deterrent. Most who steal online gain very little from the theft.

So the NET Act imposes criminal liability on those who electronically distribute or reproduce copyrighted works valued at $1,000 or more. To prevent people from distributing works in $999 increments indefinitely, the Act applies to a 180-day period. If a person electronically distributes or reproduces works with a *total* value of $1,000 or more in any six-month period, the NET Act kicks in.

INTELLECTUAL PROPERTY IN PRACTICE

E-mail   The average e-mail message doesn't invoke copyright or trademark coverage. But it is possible to violate these laws using Outlook Express. If you format the body of your message via html and include copyrighted or trademarked images within, you've violated the law. Sending the image is reproduction and display under the Copyright Act and would, technically, be a violation. Likewise for sending copyrighted materials—mp3 files, software, or any other pirated materials—as attachments. It's all copying and distributing.

Will you get caught? Probably not. It's extremely doubtful that the owner will ever find out that you've been moving his work around via the Internet. Still, it's infringement. Wise users will avoid it.

Maintaining a Website   This is where most people get caught with their intellectual property pants down. If you post anyone else's original work on your website without permission, you are infringing on their copyright.

Trademark violations are also very common on the Web. Anytime you display a logo or any other distinctive mark on your website, you run the risk of creating confusion among viewers. This is especially true if your meta-tags or other site construction returns your site when the company name is plugged into a search engine.

If that's the case, you can be sure that the company that owns the mark will find you and shut you down. All of which is well within their legal rights.

Your Lawyer Says:

THE USE EXCEPTIONS ARE FAIRLY LIMITED

The fair use exceptions to copyright law are rather limited. A lot of college students mistakenly think that, since they're at college, all of their uses are educational and thus fair use. This isn't true. Only activities that are directly related to class work are educational uses. Everything else is, umm, unfair use.

You can include materials that reference a brand or company for purposes of criticism (remember that's also a category of fair use), but probably not a corporate logo itself.

DOMAIN NAMES The use of a domain name can be a source of trademark infringement. Cybersquatting—taking someone else's domain name—is certainly an infringement. And courts will definitely award the domain to the owner, no matter who registered it first.

The real questions revolve around domain names that merely *include* a company or organization's name. The most famous of these were the numerous "sucks.com" cases. In those cases, people (usually with some sort of grudge) registered and maintained sites with addresses like Walmartsucks.com or McDonalds sucks.com. One guy even registered Guinnessbeerreallyreallysucks.com (buy a six-pack of Bud and get over it, man).

Generally, courts have sided with the trademark owners in these cases and have shut the sites down. Yes, Mr. Guinnessbeerreallyreallysucks lost his case. But every once in a while one gets through on First Amendment principles. Michaelbloombergsucks.com was allowed to stand because it linked to a site where people could voice their opinions about the company and its owner's politics.

This issue has reared its head in the educational arena a few times. In April 2002 Louisiana State University sued one of its second-year law students for maintaining a site at LSULAW.com. Although the site carried a disclaimer that it was in no way affiliated with the school, it featured the school's colors, a calendar of academic events, and links to the official website. In 2001 the University of North Carolina at Chapel Hill shut down a site titled UNCgirls.com that featured pictures of nude women. In 2000 two students at Claremont McKenna College were forced to shut down their site, claremontmckenna.com, which offered visitors "the dirt on CMC." Even a site named NotHarvard.com was shut down by the Crimson Lawyers.

These are just some examples of school shutting down infringing domain names.

The short of it: If you plan on starting a site titled mycollegesucks.com or hotguysfrommycollege.net or anything else similar, expect a call from the

Cyber Issues

university lawyers and expect, at the very least, a protracted lawsuit. And don't be surprised if the courts take your domain name away; it's probably part of the school's trademark.

Accessing the Internet   Unless you're going to sites that provide illegal serial numbers or other kinds of cracks, accessing the Internet doesn't involve any kind of copyright infringement or intellectual property theft. Technically, by viewing a website you're copying its contents onto your computer, but by posting the information on the site, the owner has granted you an implied license to view the materials. In other words she's given you permission to make those copies and view the materials.

Of course, copying things you find on the net and using them beyond viewing them on your screen could violate all sorts of intellectual property laws.

File Sharing   I don't think I really need to explain that participating in file sharing is illegal. The movies, music files, and software that you download are copyrighted works, and downloading them is theft. You knew that before you ever opened this book.

What you probably are wondering is, "Will I get sued?"

The answer is: "It's hard to say."

Here's what I can tell you for sure. The music and movie industries are really pissed off about what's going on, and they're probably going to keep at it until something works.

The most recent chapters in this saga (at the time of this writing) are the efforts of the Recording Industry Association of America (RIAA). They've been on a tear of late—suing and threatening to sue everyone who's ever even said "Kazaa." And, probably by design, they've been incredibly unpredictable. In November 2002 they announced their intention to start addressing the problem of P2P sharing through litigation. Since then they've filed hundreds of lawsuits (despite a very public statement in August 2003 that they would only pursue those who were gross abusers). Even a few poor college students have gotten caught in the crossfire. Four students from various schools settled their claims for amounts ranging from $12,000 to $17,500.

I'd like to be able to say that if you keep your use to a limit, or only download rather than share files, you'll be safe. But I can't. It's all illegal and there's a chance, albeit a small one, that the RIAA (or whoever takes up the litigation mantle next) will come after you if you do.

Hacking and Electronic Espionage

If you're deep enough into the underside of the Internet for hacking laws to be of any interest, you're probably already well-versed in this type of law. Hackers, hacktivists, and all other electronic criminals make it their business to know about the statutes that might land them in jail. Still, for the rest of you, it's worth it to know at least the basics about the criminal side of cyberspace. Just in case, I dunno, you thought it might be fun to steal U.S. trade secrets online and send them to the Balinese government.

COMPUTER FRAUD AND ABUSE ACT OF 1986

This act criminalizes the unauthorized access to computer systems that are for the exclusive use of either the U.S. government or a financial institution. For the act to kick in, the access has to actually affect—either directly or indirectly—the operation of the computers. So technically, you could probably go sniff around so long as you didn't cause any trouble. But I wouldn't risk it.

Most instances of cybermischief have been litigated under this act. The creator of the original Internet Worm—who was, by the way, a student at Cornell University—was prosecuted under the Fraud and Abuse Act and was sentenced to 3 years' probation, 400 hours of community service, and a fine of more than $10,000.

ECONOMIC ESPIONAGE ACT OF 1996

Hacking your way into private computers is also, under some circumstances, illegal. This act prohibits the concealment, possession, and appropriation of trade secrets through illegal means. If you send those trade secrets to a foreign government knowing that it will benefit them, you're guilty. A single offense carries a fine of $500,000 and fifteen years' imprisonment. Enough said.

Cyber Issues

CHAPTER 12

Campus Safety & Security

Contract guard services (better known as rent-a-cops) are sometimes havens for people who can't get any other job (think: Gary Coleman). If your college employs this kind of security detail, you should ask some serious questions about whether your school is doing everything it can to keep you safe.

Chapter Contents

ollege can feel like it's an entity unto itself, an oasis of safety separated from the rest of the world. In a lot of ways, those feelings are absolutely justified. Campuses are different than most other communities. But, unfortunately, they're not the safe havens we'd like them to be. Real-world problems, including crime—even violent crime—have crept past the ivied walls.

It's an unpleasant truth, but one worth knowing, because a false sense of security is a very dangerous thing. It leads to foolish decisions and compromised safety.

Crime on Your Campus

GET THE LAY OF THE LAND

If you were headed off on a vacation to Europe, or even New York, you'd consider your personal safety both before and during your trip. You'd be more alert, watch your back, do everything you could to make sure you didn't get robbed or worse.

But people arrive at college without giving personal safety much thought at all. Maybe this is because there's so much else to think about when you're leaving for school. Maybe it's the illusion of safety that most campuses portray. Whatever the reason, it's a bad idea.

I can't tell you what the rate of criminal activity is at your specific school. But I can scare the crap out of you by giving you some recent national statistics. In 2001, 859 college students were murdered; 6,446 were raped; 1,617 were sexually assaulted; and 32,595 were involved in aggravated assaults. In addition, 52,727 had their cars stolen; 20,220 were robbed; and 98,862 were burglarized. There were 3,118 campus-related incidents of arson.

And these numbers only represent *reported* crimes. Certainly many more occurred.

More significantly, a high percentage of all of these crimes were committed by one student against another. Don't think that you are safe just because your school is out in the middle of nowhere. Any time you get a few thousand eighteen-to-twenty-two-year-olds together there will be criminals among them.

The Clery Act   You, on the other hand, can quite easily find your school's stats, thanks to a piece of legislation titled the Jeanne Clery Disclosure of Campus Security Policy and Campus Crime Statistics Act.

The law is named for a Lehigh student who in the early morning of April 5, 1986, was tortured, raped, and murdered by a fellow student in her dorm room. At the time, the Lehigh administration had knowledge of a number of violent crimes on their campus, but they did nothing to warn their students or increase security. Clery's assailant walked through three propped-open doors, all of which should have been locked, to get to her room.

Jeanne Clery's murder was the beginning of the end for the culture of campus crime cover-ups. Jeanne's parents championed the cause of effective and open reporting and pushed Congress to enact a mandatory regime. In 1990 the Crime Awareness and Campus Security Act was signed into law. It was renamed for Jeanne Clery in 1998.

CRIME STATISTICS REPORTING   The act requires that all schools publish an annual report that contains three years' worth of crime statistics. The reporting covers crimes on the campus grounds, crimes that occur on nearby "public property that is within the same reasonably contiguous geographic area" as the school, and crimes in off-campus university buildings.

Schools must report the following crimes:

- ✓ murder,
- ✓ sex offenses—both forcible and nonforcible,
- ✓ robbery,
- ✓ aggravated assault,
- ✓ burglary,
- ✓ motor vehicle theft,
- ✓ manslaughter,
- ✓ arson, and
- ✓ arrests or campus disciplinary actions related to liquor laws, drug laws, or weapons possession.

The school must also report whether or not any of the crimes were motivated by race, gender, sexual orientation, religion, ethnicity, or disability—in other words, if they were hate crimes.

These statistics have probably already been made available to you. The law requires that a copy of the report be given to all current students and employees (and prospective students, for that matter). But if you didn't read the report, don't worry. The Department of Education's Office of Postsecondary Education maintains a searchable online database at www.ope.ed.gov/security/. Data on more than 6,000 schools are available there. Go take a look. You'll probably be surprised by the amount of crime that surrounds you.

ONGOING WARNINGS   The act also requires that schools "make timely reports to the campus community on crimes considered to be a threat."

When exactly the duty to warn kicks in is fairly subjective, but any kind of recurring incident where personal harm is a possibility probably rises to the requisite level.

PUBLIC CRIME LOGS   Finally, the law requires that campus security and police forces maintain an extensive public crime log that details all incidents (not just the categories that are required in the report) that are reported on campus. It must include the time, date, location, and nature of the crime as well as the disposition of the case (whether or not an arrest has been made). These logs must be available to the public during regular business hours.

If you're concerned about criminal activity on campus, these logs are the place to look. They're much more detailed and current than the annual report. And they include a much broader range of crimes. It's a bit of a pain to track them down (they're usually kept at the school's security office—call there to find out how to get your hands on them), but I suggest doing it every once in a while just to keep on top of things.

Prevention and Protection

Whether or not crime is prevalent on your campus, it's a good idea to do everything you can to protect yourself from victimization. Crime usually targets the easiest marks.

MANAGE YOUR PERSONAL INFO

One of the best, and most comprehensive, protection strategies is to manage your personal information—don't let too much of it get out. Students, especially freshmen, are inundated with requests for their phone numbers, addresses, and other personal information for use in student directories, facebooks, Greek pledge registrations, and the like. Be very careful about where your personal information is published, especially when it will include a picture. Sometimes facebooks are used for nefarious purposes.

That said, be sure to share *lots* of information with your innermost circle of friends. Let your roommate and your friends know about your class and activity schedule and keep them up-to-date about your plans. Create an ongoing buddy network of people that will worry if you don't show up where you're supposed to. Also be sure that a few of your friends have your emergency contact information so that they can get in touch with your family if they need to.

WATCH YOUR BACK ON CAMPUS

Obviously, you're most vulnerable to crime when out and about on campus. There are two major things you can do that will substantially increase your safety: use common sense and stay alert.

You probably know the basics in these areas: don't walk home alone at night, stick to well-lit walks and paths, avoid ostentatious displays of cash or jewelry, don't talk to strangers. Hell, do all those things you've been told to do since the first grade.

Beyond adhering to those safety fundamentals, I think it's probably worth your time to take a "panic tour" of your school and the surrounding areas. Walk around during the day and take note of things that might help you out if you do face an attacker: Where are the emergency call boxes? Which buildings are usually well populated at night? Are there any security guard posts? Look for any place or thing that might stop an attacker from following you. You're probably not going to be thinking clearly if you're being pursued, so a little preparation while you've got your wits about you could make a big difference.

Finally, trust your gut. If something feels wrong, there's a good chance it is. You're an adult now. You've got twenty or so years of experience at gauging situations and identifying threats. Listen to your instincts and take action if something feels amiss.

IN YOUR DORM

The whole concept of a dormitory—hundreds of students living under one roof—creates some security issues. Thieves, sexual predators, and other criminals know that residence halls are loaded with prime targets. So don't give in to the illusion that once you've crossed the threshold you're home free.

Doors and Windows Entrances—doors *and* windows—are the most important, and most often compromised, security feature of any campus building. They should, of course, all have high-quality locking mechanisms. It should almost go without saying, but don't ever prop doors open or leave windows ajar. In fact, insist that your RA or other security detail patrols regularly and checks to make sure that all entrances are secure.

Individual room doors should also have good locks—deadbolts, really—and should all be equipped with peepholes and chains.

While we're on the subject of locking up, I'd like to say a few words about key technology. By now most campuses have moved from conventional keys to a more modern system, usually a swipe or proximity key card. While there are some privacy issues involved in the use of such a system (the school can track which buildings students go into), there are unbelievable security payoffs (umm, the school can track which buildings students go into). Also, with conventional locks, each time a building key is lost there's a security breach. In order to maintain a secure dorm, the locks would need to be changed and new keys would have to be issued to all of the residents. Most schools simply can't afford to do this. With electronic keys there's no such problem. The lost card can simply be deactivated.

CAMPUS SECURITY EVALUATION

RESIDENCE HALLS

Key System
- ❏ Swipe or proximity card
- ❏ Standard keys
  - Is there copy protection?
  - Yes ❏ No ❏

Doors and Windows
- ❏ Never locked
- ❏ Locked after dark
- ❏ Always locked
- ❏ Propped door alarms
- ❏ Room doors have peepholes
- ❏ Deadbolts
- ❏ Chains
- ❏ Windows equipped with effective locks

Residence Hall Security Detail
- ❏ No Patrol
- ❏ Regular patrols by police or security
  - How often? _____
- ❏ Regular patrols by RAs
  - How often? _____
- ❏ Guard on 24-hour duty

How Are Visitors Dealt With?
- ❏ Phone or intercom available outside
- ❏ Must show ID to guard to enter
- ❏ Must sign in
- ❏ Have unfettered access

Restrooms
- ❏ Private shower and toilet in each room
- ❏ Shared hallway restroom
  - ❏ Doors lock
  - ❏ Stalls lock
  - ❏ No locks

CAMPUS GROUNDS

Security Force
What type of force is used?
- ❏ Proprietary police force
- ❏ Proprietary security detail
- ❏ Contract with local police force
- ❏ Contracted security force

Armed?
- ❏ Yes
- ❏ No

What type of patrols?
- ❏ Foot
- ❏ Horse
- ❏ Bicycle
- ❏ Patrol Car

Is security a constant presence on campus?
- ❏ Yes
- ❏ No

Safewalk or other Escort Service
- ❏ Yes
- ❏ No

Emergency Phones
- ❏ Regularly spaced
- ❏ Clearly marked
- ❏ Connect directly to emergency services

Surveillance Cameras
- ❏ Yes
- ❏ No

INFORMATION SHARING

Up-to-Date Crime Statistics Reporting
- ❏ Yes
- ❏ No

Potential Threats Quickly Communicated?
- ❏ Yes
- ❏ No

If your school is still using conventional keys, I think you should complain. Key cards offer a far higher level of security. Your school should have them. Enough said.

Bathrooms   Shared restrooms, especially women's rooms, are another typical dorm feature that presents safety problems. Those types of semi-public lavatories are often the setting for assaults and peeping crimes. If I was seeing my little sister off to college, I'd do my damnedest to make sure she was in a dorm that had a private bathroom. And I would raise hell if she was assigned to a dorm that had a shared bathroom with no lock on the door.

Parties and Functions   So-called social lubricants do much more than make people lose their inhibitions. They also deaden the senses and affect safety instincts. If you're planning a night of painting the campus red, take a moment before the liquor starts flowing to figure out how you're going to get yourself home safely. Stumbling back to your dorm with limited faculties makes you a prime target for all sorts of crime. So don't do it. Arrange ahead of time to have a sober friend walk or drive you home after the fête.

There are also countless things that can happen to you while you're still at the soiree. Student-on-student sexual assaults occur at an alarming rate. Parties are a prime setting for them. So it's worth your while to keep your faculties about you even while you're at the party. For more information on date rape, Rohypnol, and most of the other potential party horrors, see chapter 15, "Sex & the Law."

AFTERMATH

What you do in the hours directly following a crime is extremely important. Your mental, physical, and legal well-being depends on taking the right steps. Evidence can disappear, statutes of limitations can run out, suspects can leave the area. All of which will make it very difficult for you to bring your assailant to justice.

Of course, your health should always be your first priority, so if there's even the slightest chance that you're hurt, seek medical attention. It seems strange, but you may be more seriously injured than you think. During an altercation the adrenaline is running high in your system and your sensitivity to pain is diminished. You may not even realize you're injured until things calm down a bit. So as soon as it's possible, take a quick inventory of your body—move your legs, arms, pat yourself down. Just see if everything's okay. If something feels weird, go get it checked out.

Sexual Assault and Rape Victims   For victims of rape and other types of sexual assault, the importance of seeking medical attention is even more pronounced. You'll need to collect medical samples (DNA and other things) that can be used to identify the assaulter. There's a very limited window during which physical evidence can be collected—roughly seventy-two hours after the crime.

For a full discussion of sex-crime aftermath, see chapter 15, "Sex & the Law."

Preserve Evidence Stay and keep others out of the crime scene in order to preserve as much evidence as possible. If the crime is a physical assault of some sort, consider your body part of the scene. Don't do anything that will compromise collection like shower or change your clothes.

It's also not a bad idea to take a few quick notes about what happened as soon as possible, before your memory starts to fade. Commit important details, like descriptions of the suspects, the circumstances of the crime, and anything else relevant, to paper.

Take the School's Help Whatever the nature of your crime, you may need medical, psychological, and legal counseling. The school is well-equipped to get you those things. Even though it may not always seem like it, the school really does have your best interest in mind. So, in this case, use their resources. It's almost always the best course of action.

Campus Security Forces

In all likelihood, the first-ever campus security guards were two men named Bill Wiser and Jim Donnelly. They were members of the New Haven Police Department who, after a period of particularly bad town-and-gown relations in the late 1800s, were assigned to patrol the Yale campus full time.

At first Wiser and Donnelly were met with fairly strong opposition. Before their arrival school grounds had been sacrosanct. Police officers never ventured onto campus grounds even if they were pursuing a student. But as time passed the officers gained the trust of the campus and were accepted as members of the school community. A few years after their arrival, they were hired away from the New Haven force and became the first members of the Yale University Police Department.

It's amazing how little has changed in 100 years. The issues faced by Wiser and Donnelly—distrust from students, the perception that their presence damaged the learning environment, strained town-and-gown relations—are still prevalent on most campuses.

THE ROLE OF CAMPUS SECURITY

One of the threshold questions that Wiser and Donnelly faced was: What exactly are we here to do? When they arrived they assumed that their role was to subdue the student population. But over the years their function shifted more to protection of the students from outside interference.

You should ask the same question: What is my school's security force here to do? You can be sure that the administration has considered it—and has drafted policies and granted power accordingly.

Safety & Security

Security functions, and powers, follow a continuum. At one end are watchguard forces that are primarily concerned with protecting college property. At the other are full-fledged forces that perform all of the traditional police duties. As you think about the different facets of how your school's force functions, try to get a gauge on the overall policing theory in

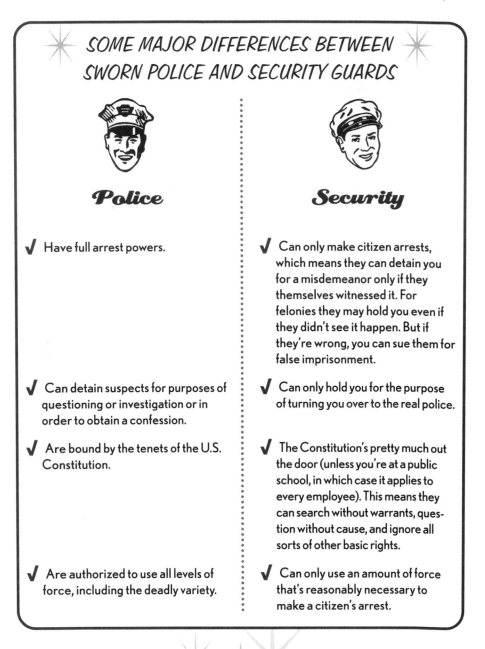

SOME MAJOR DIFFERENCES BETWEEN SWORN POLICE AND SECURITY GUARDS

Police

✓ Have full arrest powers.

✓ Can detain suspects for purposes of questioning or investigation or in order to obtain a confession.

✓ Are bound by the tenets of the U.S. Constitution.

✓ Are authorized to use all levels of force, including the deadly variety.

Security

✓ Can only make citizen arrests, which means they can detain you for a misdemeanor only if they themselves witnessed it. For felonies they may hold you even if they didn't see it happen. But if they're wrong, you can sue them for false imprisonment.

✓ Can only hold you for the purpose of turning you over to the real police.

✓ The Constitution's pretty much out the door (unless you're at a public school, in which case it applies to every employee). This means they can search without warrants, question without cause, and ignore all sorts of other basic rights.

✓ Can only use an amount of force that's reasonably necessary to make a citizen's arrest.

practice. Understanding the mandate of your campus security force, even in broad strokes, will help you decide how to best interact with them.

TYPES OF SECURITY FORCES

Informal Watchguard Details   A watchguard system barely qualifies as a security force. Pre-1890 this type of system was the norm, but today most schools recognize the need for a constabulary that has *some* training. Watchguards are civilians, usually members of the building and maintenance department, who monitor the campus with an eye on protecting university property.

What most distinguishes watchguards from other types of security forces is what they lack—weapons, police training, and any type of police power. Sometimes they appear to be more than they are. They often carry radios, walk regular rounds, or wear uniforms. But they are nothing more than civilians. On small rural campuses, these types of arrangements sometimes work. But if a crisis occurs, these undertrained "officers" usually prove obscenely inadequate.

Contract Guards   Contract guards are employees of a third-party security service that are leased by the school. You may not be familiar with the formal name *contract guards*, but you've certainly heard the colloquial term before: rent-a-cops. The nickname's pretty accurate. Think about the difference in quality between something you rent as compared to something you own, like rented suits. They are usually poorly made, don't fit well (despite the zippered waistlines), and have been somewhat abused by the other people who've rented them. You can't blame the rental place. Their motivation is profit, and they know how the suits they lend out are treated. So why rent out Armani when Men's Wearhouse will do?

Rented security forces have the same kinds of problems:

HIGH POTENTIAL FOR BAD GUARDS   It's a stereotype, but people who work as contract guards are often there because they couldn't get any other job. They're often untrained and lazy. Moonlighters and retirees are also often attracted to these jobs. Both might be sincere and conscientious, but could be physically limited due to fatigue or age, respectively. Worst of all, security companies are havens for urban commandos who have been rejected by or discharged from actual police forces. They're power hungry and often dangerous. I'm not saying that all contracted security guards are bad people. But the likelihood is much higher than on other types of security details.

PROFIT MOTIVATION   The same profit motive that compels Hertz to buy Kias informs hiring decisions at security companies. Their goal is to pay their guards the lowest possible wage while charging the highest possible price to the school. This is not a formula that adds up to a competent security force.

191

LACK OF CONTINUITY Turnover at security companies is relatively high (it's not a particularly good job). And these companies often service hundreds of schools, factories, office complexes, prisons, and other institutions at a time. They'll often shift guards between sites. This lack of continuity inevitably leads to decreased effectiveness. The campus community never builds a rapport with the guards, and, more importantly, the guards aren't able to track trends and changes in campus activities.

REMOVED SUPERVISION Finally, although these guards work at your school, their supervisors are offsite. This means that students and the rest of the campus community have a much more limited ability to voice their concerns about the guards' performance. The guards themselves also have a diminished motivation to react to complaints or criticisms.

Contracts with Local Police Sometimes, instead of leasing a security force from a private company, a school will enter into a kind of service contract with the local police force. While this alleviates most of the training and officer quality problems, other issues arise:

SPOTTY SERVICE Usually, under this type of arrangement, ongoing campus security needs are neglected. The officers' attention is, at best, divided between the school and the surrounding community. In areas where the local town is large enough to have its own crime problems, the campus can be all but ignored. The officers are also often unwilling, or unable due to time restraints, to perform the more routine functions associated with the job—walking rounds, checking for propped doors, and the like. While these tasks seem insignificant, they're the basis for a secure campus.

REMOVED SUPERVISION The same supervisory problems exist under this paradigm. In fact, they're increased. Short of a civil suit against the state, students and professors will find that they have almost no ability to guide the way in which the police function on their campus. Complaints and criticism, if ever voiced, will fall on deaf ears.

Proprietary Security Force By far, the predominant approach on campuses is a university-operated security department—meaning that the university itself hires and supervises a force of nonpolice guards. This allows the university to totally control the quality of the officers and the level of service. The fact that the university directly supervises the force also means that students and professors will have a larger say in the way the patrols operate.

Technically the term "security" refers to guards who are *not* sworn police officers. But often schools that operate fully functional police forces still call them security officers or safety officers. This is entirely for PR purposes and has no bearing on their arrest or other powers. Students and professors generally resist the presence of an actual police force on school grounds. In order to maintain a more low-key profile, the school avoids the title police. The point is: No matter what your school's force is called, you need to find out whether or not they are police officers or simply security guards because they have very different abilities and powers.

Proprietary Police Force A growing trend for schools, especially in urban areas, is to operate a fully commissioned, dedicated police force. Obviously a school, be it public or private, can't just swear in its own police officers. There are a number of ways a school force can obtain police authority for its officers:

LOCAL POLICE Often the school officers are simply sworn in by the local chief of police or sheriff under the auspices of a local ordinance. Usually officers sworn by this means have police authority only on campus property.

STATE ENABLING LAWS Some states have statutes that allow colleges and universities to become a part of the state police force. Under a typical statute, the school must apply to the state police authorizing agency, which conducts an investigation of the force to make sure the training, policies, and officers are adequate.

SCHOOL-SPECIFIC LEGISLATION In states without a broad enabling law, schools sometimes get the state legislature to pass a special law that creates a police force on the campus. Since the legislation is specific to each school, the powers that are granted under this scheme can vary greatly.

Your School's Force If your school cares about safety at all, it will have either a proprietary security or police force. So figure out exactly what kind of security detail your school employs. If your school's got one of the more inadequate kinds of security systems, ask why. You're paying a lot of money for your education. Your school should be able to afford to adequately protect you.

PISTOL PACKING Another critical question for campus security forces is whether or not to arm the officers. Schools with commissioned police forces won't have to confront it. Their police officers will be armed. But for those with a proprietary security force, it's a tough question and one that certainly needs to be addressed on a case-by-case basis. Most are quick to

Your Lawyer Says:

JURISDICTION MATTERS! The territorial jurisdiction of campus police officers is determined by state and local laws and agreements, which vary significantly from school to school. Campus police in New Jersey, for example, have the authority to make arrests anywhere in the state. But authority that is restricted only to campus-owned land and immediately adjacent areas are, by far, the most common. So, if you've been arrested, or even searched, by a campus officer while off campus grounds, it might be worth your (or your lawyer's) time to research the specific laws that apply to your school. Many criminal cases have been won by a defendant simply because he or she was not on university property when the arrest was made.

Safety & Security

condemn the idea altogether. They say that guns have no place on a campus or that introducing weapons into any community will inevitably increase the amount of violence. These arguments aren't particularly persuasive. While I agree that guns really don't have a place at an institution of higher learning, neither do rape, murder, or any other type of crime. And given a choice between the two, I'll gladly choose armed officers over assaults.

The notion that arming officers will increase violence by introducing guns into the equation is bullshit. First, like or not, guns are almost certainly all around your campus, regardless of whether or not your security force has them. Second, there are countless studies by reputable organizations that show that the exact opposite is true: The presence of armed officers quite simply leads to a *decrease* in the amount of crime and violence. Personally I don't think you should need a study to understand that, but if you do, check out the work of Gary Kleck, Ph.D., professor of criminology and criminal justice at Florida State University.

I'm not a particularly big fan of guns, and I certainly don't want them around me. But when considering whether campus police forces should have them I think that "why not?" is a much more important question than "why?"

That said, if your school does arm its officers, there should be strict safeguards in place to make sure that they are safely and responsibly used:

TRAINING

Anyone who is going to carry a weapon should be required to have extensive ongoing training. Many schools administer in-house educational programs for their security staff. I don't think this is wise. There are plenty of outside organizations that can provide the training, and there is a great benefit associated with unbiased, third-party instruction. Officers should also be required to qualify several times on a practical pistol course that emphasizes close-range encounters since most college incidents occur at close range.

STATEMENTS

Armed officers should be required to sign a statement certifying that they will

- ✓ never draw their firearm unless it is necessary to protect the officer's life or the life of another individual,
- ✓ under no circumstances use the weapon to threaten an individual,
- ✓ never use the butt or any other part of the firearm as a club or similar weapon, and
- ✓ never fire a warning shot or a shot that is designed only to disable.

In other words, they should swear that the only time their firearm should leave its holster is if there is a life in danger.

APPROPRIATE EQUIPMENT

There is no need for high-powered guns or ammunition. Guards should carry low-caliber pistols with relatively short ranges and short barrel lengths. They should be carried only in safety-snap or tear-away holsters. Under no circumstances should officers be allowed to carry personally owned weapons. University-issued firearms should be the only weapons in use.

Some forces keep shotguns in the patrol cars. This is probably unwise. Any situation that requires the use of a long-range weapon also requires very specialized expertise—like a SWAT team with sharpshooting training.

Part Three

THE LAW OFF CAMPUS—
GENERAL LEGAL ISSUES
FOR COLLEGE STUDENTS

CHAPTER 13
The Police

Most of what you learned from the movies (and late-night cable) about law enforcement isn't true. Think about it: When was the last time you saw a cop that looked anything at all like Colin Farrell, Will Smith, or any of Charlie's Angels? The difference in the amount of eye candy is just the beginning.

Chapter Contents

ife would be so much easier if we never got into trouble. If that were possible, this book would simply say "Don't ever do anything wrong" and that would be that. But the fact of the matter is this: Everyone reading this page will, at one time or another, pique a policeman's interest and have to deal with what comes next. Being smart when that happens is what really matters because it can mean the difference between being hauled off to the big house or just going home.

Basic Rules for Dealing with the Police

In any interaction with the police, *control* is the operative word. You need to control your words, control your emotions, and control your body.

DOS & DON'TS OF POLICE INTERACTIONS

Be Sure To

✓ Stop when the officer approaches you.

✓ Look the officer directly in the eye.

✓ Stay relatively still.

✓ Keep your hands in sight at all times.

✓ Ask permission before reaching into your pockets or bag or doing anything potentially threatening.

But Don't

✓ Make any sudden or jerky movements.

✓ Ever touch a police officer—he may think you're trying to get his weapon.

✓ Ever run away or resist arrest (these things are crimes).

✓ Get in the way of a police officer chasing someone else (also a crime).

CONTROL WHAT YOU SAY

Be polite and respectful when you speak. Whether or not to issue a citation is often the cop's call. Being an ass pretty much guarantees that you won't get a break—that night or during the officer's subsequent court testimony.

This doesn't mean you have to succumb to the officer's every whim, but if you're going to refuse to do anything, refuse politely. Don't tell the officer to "fuck off." Instead, try something along the lines of, "I'm sorry, officer. What's the purpose of the question? Have I done something wrong?" If you don't want to give up any information, simply say, "I don't think I want to answer that question, ma'am" (unless, of course, your officer is a man—in which case you're in even bigger trouble).

Remember, the police don't know who you are. You could be a dean's list student, a lunatic, or anywhere in between, so the less lunatic behavior, the better.

CONTROL YOUR EMOTIONS

Easier said than done, I know. But we're not talking about getting over the love of your life here. All you have to do is keep it together for a few minutes and put your temper or fear, or whatever else is bugging you, aside so that you can do your best.

Approach an encounter with the police the same way you would a big test. Would you ever start an exam off by writing on the first page of the bluebook, "Screw you, Professor Smith. I just wanted to let you know I'm pissed off and I resent your authority"? Of course not. So don't jeopardize your freedom (and possibly your safety) by letting your emotions guide what you do when you're talking to the police. Act on thoughts, not feelings.

Also, don't be afraid to step back from the conversation if you feel it's gotten away from you. Just slow things down and take another stab at it. If you make one mistake, don't assume that you've totally blown it and make a hundred more.

CONTROL YOUR BODY

This is critical. Making sudden movements near a police officer is risky. Cops have to assume that everyone is armed and dangerous. If you make a jerky movement, they'll react.

And don't ever run away from the police. Resisting arrest is a crime. If that isn't reason enough for you, consider this: If you run, you probably won't get away. As comforting a thought as it may be, Barney Fife and Chief Wiggum aren't really the norm on the force. In fact, sometimes quite the opposite is true. And even if you're faster on your feet than the officers who happen to stop you, the police still have all the advantages—cars, walkie-talkies, other cops with cars and walkie-talkies that can head you off at the pass. And don't forget, they're the ones with the guns.

SAVE YOUR ARGUMENTS FOR THE JUDGE

There's a time and place for everything: If you want to argue the fine points of the law, that time is not while you're still standing on the street in handcuffs. It won't get you released, but it will increase your chances of saying something incriminating.

Likewise, if you think your rights are being violated in some way, don't register your complaint with the officer who's violating them. Wait and lodge a formal grievance with the police department's internal affairs division or complaint board. Of course, don't be shy to say, "Hey, that hurts" if you're being mishandled; otherwise the officer won't know to stop or loosen his grip.

Questioning and Interrogation: Keeping Your Mouth Shut

MIRANDA RIGHTS

You've probably heard them a million times. At the end of every episode of *Law and Order* and at least ten times during each installment of *COPS*, someone delivers them. They're your Miranda rights. And unless you were raised by a pack of wolves, you can probably recite them yourself:

✓ You have the right to remain silent;
✓ If you do or say anything incriminating, it can be used against you in a court of law;
✓ You have a right to an attorney;
✓ If you can't afford an attorney, one will be appointed to you if you want one; and
✓ If you choose to talk to the police, you can stop the interview at any time (this one's usually left out of the script—evidently it's not as sexy as the first four).

Because we hear them so often, everyone who grew up in this country thinks they know all about their Miranda rights. I did long before I ever went to law school. But as a lawyer, I've never fully understood Hollywood's fascination with them. In the grand scheme of things, they rarely make much of a difference. They're dramatic and official-sounding. But when you get down to it, Miranda warnings are pretty insignificant. They affect whether or not evidence can be considered at trial. That's it.

Take a moment and read them again. But this time think about what they mean as you read. I think you'll see that the Miranda warnings aren't particularly complex. If you're being arrested, you have a right to those five things. Still, people attach all sorts of mystical importance to these five little sentences.

COMMON MIRANDA
WARNING MISCONCEPTIONS

The police must always read the Miranda warnings before they ask a civilian a question.

THE TRUTH: The police only have to read them if you're being arrested.

If the police fail to read you your rights, your case will be thrown out and you will get off scot-free.

THE TRUTH: A Miranda omission is not the equivalent of a "get out of jail free" card. If the rule is violated, testimony made after the arrest can't be admitted at trial. That's all. Sometimes that's enough to avoid a conviction, but not usually.

There is a specific Miranda speech, and if the police don't get it exactly right, the warning doesn't count.

THE TRUTH: Come on, this isn't a drinking game. As long as the officer gets the gist of it, the warning is good.

Make your life easier, and just forget about the Miranda game. The substance of the warnings is well worth committing to memory, but the legal effect of their utterance isn't worth your time. It's a technical rule of evidence best left to judges and lawyers. All you need to do is remember if and when they were given, so that you can tell your lawyer later. Leave the rest of it to her.

QUESTIONING BEFORE ARREST

Now let's talk about what really matters in the Miranda warnings: their content. Whether you've been arrested or not—and whether they've been read to you or not—you have the rights spelled out in Miranda. Of course, most important among those is the right to remain silent.

Your Right to Remain Silent Technically, if you're stopped by the police, you don't have to tell them *anything*. Of course, as with any law, there are exceptions:

✓ *Exception One.* If you're stopped in your car, you are obligated to show your driver's license, proof of registration, and proof of insurance.

✓ *Exception Two*. Because some towns have anti-loitering laws, refusing to tell the police who you are and what your immediate business is could get you a citation for standing or sitting around in public. Considered by most scholars to be antiquated and stupid, the police nonetheless use these anti-loitering laws to corral college students. So if you're on the street, it's safest to adopt a universal rule that you'll identify yourself, tell the police your immediate business, then shut your mouth.

QUESTIONING AFTER ARREST

Sometimes, despite being smart, polite, and quiet, you'll end up getting arrested. When that happens, you need to change your strategy.

Your Lawyer Says:

INTERROGATE THEM

What's the best way to tell if you've been arrested? Ask, "Am I under arrest?" Then you'll know for sure.

First, you have to know when you've been arrested. Anytime the police "significantly restrain your freedom of motion" you are technically under arrest—even if the officer doesn't say the magic words. So if the cops cuff you, put you in the cruiser for a substantial amount of time, or even just tell you that you are not allowed to leave, you've been arrested. Of course, if they take you into the station, you've definitely been arrested, but if you couldn't figure that out on your own, just put the book down now. You're hopeless.

As soon as you think that you are being placed under arrest, *ask for a lawyer and say nothing else*. Don't worry about where you're going to get the lawyer, how you'll pay for it, or whether you actually need one. You can work all of that out later on.

Once you ask for an attorney, the police can no longer ask you any questions without him or her there. But just making "the ask" isn't a panacea. If you volunteer information, it can be used against you. So don't ask for a lawyer and then describe exactly how you managed to get all that paint to the top of the water tower. Demand a lawyer and shut up.

One final note: The police have no authority to offer you a deal of any kind in exchange for a confession or other information. Don't take the bait if they try to bargain with you. They may say something like, "Listen, you're not the one we're after, so if you tell us who sold you those drugs, we'll let you go with a misdemeanor." Say, "You can talk to my lawyer about it," nothing more.

Police Stops and Searches: When and Where Can They Look?

RULE ONE: DON'T CONSENT

The law spells out in great detail exactly when the police have a right to search you or your property. But no matter what the law says, if you agree to a search, they can do it. So unless you want the police to invade your privacy, *don't consent to a search*.

It seems so silly, but it's a mistake that's made time and time again. The police are good at lulling people into consenting, so you really do have to stay on your toes. They won't say, "Hello, ma'am. I'd like for you to give me permission to ignore the Constitution and conduct an incredibly invasive search of your home." Instead they'll be friendly and conversational. They'll say something like "Mind if a take a peek?" or "Mind if I come in?"

If an officer asks in any way to conduct any kind of search—of your pockets or the trunk of your car or your house or your backpack—and you don't want them to, make it extremely clear that you do not consent. Say loudly, clearly, and slowly, "I do not consent to any search of any kind." Say it out loud right now. Say it again and again. "I do not consent to any search of any kind." "I do not consent to any search of any kind." Get it tattooed on your arm. Get to the point where you instinctively say it when *COPS* comes on. Make it a knee-jerk reaction because saying that phrase is the single most important thing you can do to protect your privacy. The police still might search you. They may even still have a right to. But it can't hurt, and a lot of the time it works.

STOPS AND SEARCHES OF YOUR PERSON

You're walking down the street, minding your own business, when a policeman approaches you. He asks you to stop. Evidently, there's been an outbreak of shoplifting at a nearby music store. It's generally college-age kids who shop there. He wants to look in your backpack to see if you have any stolen CDs. Can he search you? Can he even stop you? What should you do?

Stopping You   In order to detain you on the street, the police must have what's called a **reasonable suspicion** that you are either doing something criminal or have information about the criminal activity of somebody else.

Legally, you almost always have to stop when the police ask you to. Ignoring the police and walking away creates reasonable suspicion all by itself. Then the officer will have a very solid right to detain you.

Stop and engage the officer. But that's it. Just because the officer can stop you doesn't mean he can search you or question you, right? Well, sort of.

Stop and Frisk on the Street   If you've been temporarily stopped on the street, the police may also pat down your clothing or your bags (sometimes

Vocabulary Lesson

EXPECTATION OF PRIVACY—A person's right to be free of unreasonable searches only applies in places where they have a legitimate and reasonable expectation of privacy. *Bottom Line:* Your intuitive sense of what is "private" will be right in many cases—something in the trunk of your car carries a legitimate expectation; something sitting next to you on the passenger seat doesn't. Unfortunately, there's a significant vague middle ground that not even a judge could instantly evaluate.

REASONABLE SUSPICION—The police need to have a reasonable suspicion to stop you to conduct a precursory investigation or pat you down (a "stop and frisk"). A police officer must be able to support the suspicion with "specific facts that can be articulated." *Bottom Line:* It's less than definitive proof but more than a hunch.

PROBABLE CAUSE—The police need it to make an arrest, to detain someone on the street for any significant amount of time, to ask questions, or to conduct a search. They also have to prove to a judge that it exists if they want a warrant. *Bottom Line:* Way more than a hunch. The officer is supposed to have held a minitrial in her head and found you guilty.

called a "stop and frisk") if they, again, **reasonably suspect** that you have a concealed weapon. Don't resist. Allow them to pat you down and make it clear that you do not consent to any further search.

The reason for the frisk is to look for concealed weapons, but once the search starts the police will be looking for other things. They'll also be attuned to the feel of illegal contraband. They may not turn up a gun or knife, but they could feel a suspicious package, something soft like a baggie of drugs.

If they feel something suspicious through your clothing, they have the right to conduct a more invasive search—they can reach into your pockets and take anything they think is contraband. Why? Because they now have **probable cause** that you're carrying drugs. See how this works? Each search can open the door to the next one.

Frisks can very easily lead to full-blown, lawful searches. Cut this escalation off at the earliest possible point: Avoid carrying suspicious-feeling things in your clothing pockets or the outside pockets of your bags.

Searches of Your Car   If you've been stopped in a car, the "stop and frisk" standards still apply. If an officer reasonably suspects that you have a weapon, he can frisk you. And since you're sitting inside a vehicle, he can also frisk your car, so to speak, by conducting a brief search of the passenger areas. Remember, just because he's looking for a gun or some other weapon doesn't mean he won't find something else, like drugs or open alcohol containers.

Since the vehicular stop and frisk only allows the police to look for a weapon that you could grab at a moment's notice, this search only extends to easily accessible areas of the car—really just the passenger area. If the officer wants to search other places (the trunk, the glove box, closed packages, and so forth), he has to establish **probable cause** for those areas.

And don't forget the cardinal rule of searches: Whether he searches your car or not, make it clear that you do not consent.

SEARCHES OF YOUR HOME

According to the law, your home is the most private of places. People have an ex-

Your Lawyer Says:

USE YOUR PRIVATE PARTS
As a rule of thumb, you're entitled to more legal privacy in places where you expect it. Since the law follows common sense in this area, so should you. Trust your instincts and put things you don't want found in places that seem more private, like the trunk or glove box.

tremely high and legitimate **expectation of privacy** for their own homes. Therefore, the police are not allowed to come inside—whether it's a house, apartment, or dorm room—unless they have a warrant signed by a judge (or unless you consent, but that won't happen, right?). There are only two "emergency" situations where this isn't true—when someone inside is screaming for help or if the police are chasing someone who has run into your house. *Otherwise, the police cannot come into your home without a warrant.*

If they do show up and want to come in, always read the warrant. This may seem silly, but just because they say it's a warrant doesn't mean it is (it's not beyond some police forces to hold up an official looking piece of paper and say it's a warrant). So take the document from the officers, tell them to wait outside, close the door, clear your head, and read the "warrant." Make sure it's for your house, with your name and your address, and signed by a judge or magistrate.

While you're reading the warrant, check its scope. Warrants don't simply name a house and give the officer free reign. It will only authorize the police to search for specific objects at a specified time. One might allow a search of the premises at 212 W. Court Street, between 9 a.m. and 5 p.m., for chemicals, equipment, and other materials used in the production of LSD or other manufactured drugs.

If anything is amiss—if it's unsigned, not for your house, for a different time—point this out to the officers and politely ask them to leave. If they

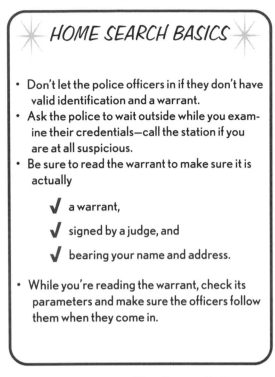

HOME SEARCH BASICS

- Don't let the police officers in if they don't have valid identification and a warrant.
- Ask the police to wait outside while you examine their credentials—call the station if you are at all suspicious.
- Be sure to read the warrant to make sure it is actually

  ✔ a warrant,

  ✔ signed by a judge, and

  ✔ bearing your name and address.

- While you're reading the warrant, check its parameters and make sure the officers follow them when they come in.

refuse, make it abundantly clear that you do not consent. If they leave, find a lawyer immediately because they'll be back soon.

If everything checks out, you have to let them in. Open the door and step aside. While they're searching, stay out of the way, but keep an eye on what's going on. You've read the warrant, so you know if there are any restrictions. If the police go out of bounds, call them on it. Also remember, just because they have a warrant to search your place doesn't mean they can interrogate you. Your rights regarding questioning are fully intact, so stick to the questioning guidelines above.

Roommates, Landlords, and Consent What if the police show up while you're not home? Can your roommate let them in? Your landlord?

The police need permission from the person in charge of an area in order to search it. This means that if you have a roommate, she can only authorize searches of her room and common areas—the living room, the kitchen, maybe the bathroom. Only you can authorize searches of the areas of the house that you alone control.

If you share a house or apartment, don't leave incriminating or suspicious things in common areas. If you live in a dorm room, buy your roommates a copy of this book—that way they'll know not to consent to searches, too.

Your landlord is a different story. He can't let the cops in to search any part of your place. Your monthly rent check guarantees a certain level of privacy—this is true even if you're behind in your rent or in the middle of an eviction lawsuit.

BODILY SAMPLES

There is one final way the police might want to search you: through the use of bodily samples. Believe it or not, if you've been charged with a crime, you can be forced to give samples—hair, urine, blood, or fingernail clippings. It seems counterintuitive, but the Fifth Amendment protection against self-incrimination applies *only* to communications, not to physical evidence. And bodily samples are considered by the courts to be just that. Your urine is treated the same way a fingerprint or a shell casing would: The police just get to take it. There's really not much you can do but pee in the cup. Sorry.

Being Taken into Custody: What to Expect and What to Do

For minor offenses, arrestees are given a citation and sent on their merry way. However, if you're arrested for a more serious crime, the police will take you to the station for booking—your first step into the criminal big leagues. But it doesn't have to be all that bad. By knowing what to expect and keeping your head about you, you can manage fairly well even in these rough waters.

We all have vivid cinematic images in our head about what being taken downtown is like, but it will probably seem more like registering for classes than being on *NYPD Blue*. There's lots of paperwork and a lot of waiting around, and at the end someone takes an unbelievably unattractive picture of you. The similarities aren't a coincidence: Both registration and booking are processes to check you into a system. Of course, at the police station, when it's over you'll be sent to lockup.

Still, if you've gotten to the point where you're being booked into jail, your legal troubles are pretty serious. You may not be on the most-wanted list just yet, but you're going to have to, at the very least, do some legal cleanup over the next few weeks, especially if you think you've been mistreated or improperly accused. Start making your lawyer's job easier by keeping a record of what's going on. Get your hands on some paper and a pencil and write down the important parts of what happened. Include everything you remember that is even remotely related to the incident that landed you in jail. Be sure to include, as near as you can remember, what the police officers said to you and how you replied. Of course, be careful not to record anything that incriminates you. You never know whose hands this paper may fall into.

You should actually start thinking this way as soon as you run into the police. While the scenario is unfolding, take note of the arresting officers' names and badges and patrol car numbers and write them down as soon as you can. Also think about any witnesses to the arrest. Write down things that may help you hook up with someone who saw what happened.

Make records of yourself, too. If you've been injured as a result of the arrest, be sure to take photographs of the injuries as soon as possible, but make sure you get medical attention first if you need it.

THE PROCESS OF GOING TO JAIL

Being booked into jail will be as easy or difficult as you choose to make it. So be smart and choose easy. If you're uncooperative or combative, you'll probably be sent to wait in a solitary location. It may even land you in a higher-security part of the facility when you do get admitted.

Your Lawyer Says:

SPENDING TIME IN JAIL IS NO FUN!

A million things will grate on you while you're there—overcrowding, small spaces, no privacy, irritating levels of noise, poor food, you name it. And you'll almost definitely have trouble sleeping. All of this will make you irritable and will weaken your mental defenses, increasing the danger of doing something stupid. So be on your toes. Remember what you know about questioning. Don't make any confessions or give up any information. And watch your temper; lashing out at someone will get you in trouble, or worse, hurt.

When you arrive, you'll have to go through an extensive booking process before you're sent to a cell. The procedure varies from station to station, but if you're in for something relatively minor, the main points will be fairly consistent.

First, the arresting officer will hand you over to the jail staff or to a "booking officer." You may be asked a few simple questions about your health (to screen for tuberculosis or other communicable diseases). They will also take your possessions—including your wallet, purse, watch, and any bags or packages you were carrying when you were taken in. The police must give you a receipt for everything they take. If you have anything of particular value with you, make sure that you get an accurate slip for it (ask them to write down things like "Rolex" instead of just "gold wristwatch") so there's no confusion later on.

Next, you'll be photographed (mug shot), fingerprinted, and asked your name and address. I know I said to ask for a lawyer then shut your mouth, but do give the police your name and address. They've probably got your wallet anyway, and even if they don't, refusing to give your name out isn't going to help anything at this point.

Sometime during this process you'll be given access to a phone. It may be in the waiting area, or if you've been uncooperative and sent to wait alone, you may be given a specific opportunity. When you get this chance, use it. If you have a lawyer, call her. If you don't, call someone you trust very much that will be able to help you—a parent, a trusted friend, even a professor.

You're going to need some help from the outside, especially if you plan to post bail.

After these preliminaries are over, one of two things will happen. Either you'll be able to immediately post bail and be released or you'll have to wait to be arraigned by a judge.

BAIL

Bail is a security deposit—cash (or the equivalent) that an arrested person gives to a court as a personal guarantee that he or she won't disappear if they're released. If you post bail and show up in court when you're supposed to, your money is returned to you. If you skip town, the court keeps the bail and issues a warrant for your arrest.

You can post bail in three ways: submit the full amount in cash, give over property worth the full amount, or post a bond—a guarantee from a third party that the full amount will be paid if you fail to appear.

Your Lawyer Says:

GET OUT OF JAIL QUICK! Just because you've been arrested and taken to jail doesn't mean you'll have to spend much time there. You can get out as soon as you post bail. So put finding out what your bail is and arranging for it to be posted at the top of your "to do" list.

Most bonds are posted by licensed bondsmen. The defendant pays the bondsman a nonrefundable fee—usually 7 to 10 percent of the bail amount—and gives collateral for the full sum. The defendant then posts the bond instead of cash or property. If you fail to show up in court, the bondsman can cash in on the collateral and has the authority to seek you out and apprehend (arrest) you.

For most minor offenses the amount of bail is already set. All you have to do is post the amount set forth in the bail schedule and you're free to go. But if the crime you're accused of doesn't have a predefined bail amount, it will need to be set by a judge. This is called being arraigned. Unfortunately, this usually won't happen immediately. It could take one to five days.

If you'll be sleeping over, you'll be prepared for your stay. The guards will search you, delouse you (give you a shower with special soap and shampoo), issue you a prisoner's uniform, and place you in a "housing unit."

ARRAIGNMENT

Soon enough, you'll have your arraignment. Hopefully by then you'll have a lawyer to help you, but if you don't, don't worry. You should be able to get through this first court appearance on your own. All that happens is a justice or magistrate officially informs you of the charges against you and asks you to enter a plea. Almost everyone enters a plea of not guilty at this early stage—it's the safest bet. The justice will also set bail (what you've been waiting for) and the date for the next procedural event in your case.

The arraignment is also the point at which a defendant can request the services of a court-appointed attorney, which brings us to the final topic of the chapter:

WHERE TO FIND A CRIMINAL ATTORNEY

If you don't care how good your attorney will be, just flip open the Yellow Pages, pick a name, and dial. If you're lucky, you might get one that's actually licensed to practice law. Otherwise, you're going to have to do a bit of investigation.

Most good lawyers rely on personal recommendations to generate new business. Very few advertise. Because of this, finding a good lawyer is about using your connections. The best place to start is by asking a friend or family member who is an attorney. The vast majority of lawyers do civil (noncriminal) work and won't be able to directly assist you with your problem, but they'll probably be able to point you in the direction of an attorney who can.

If you don't know any lawyers, ask other friends or family members if they've ever used a criminal attorney. It may be an awkward conversation to start ("Uncle Jim, you seem like the type of person who should be locked up; you must know a great criminal attorney . . ."), but if someone you know has used a criminal defense lawyer and was happy with the service he got, that lawyer can likely handle your case well. Remember, you're on a college campus. Connections and information abound—don't be afraid to ask a trusted professor, counselor, or administrator for help.

If that fails, try a local lawyer-referral service. Many state and local bar associations recommend lawyers as a public service. How they operate varies from service to service, but generally a dispatcher takes the call, conducts a brief interview, and makes an initial evaluation of your problem. Based on that assessment, you'll be put in touch with a local attorney who can handle your type of case. Often, referral clients are given a first half-hour consultation at a significantly reduced rate—sometimes for free. A comprehensive list of contact information for lawyer-referral services is included as Appendix B.

What Will a Lawyer Cost? You've asked around and found the best criminal defense lawyer in the state. Now comes the bad part—his fees. How much is the pleasure of this little balding man's company going to cost you?

Well, that depends . . .

Lawyers set their fees based on a number of factors including their level of experience, the complexity of the case, and the geographic region where they practice, so it's nearly impossible to make a definitive prediction.

You can count on one thing: It's not going to be cheap. Expect representation for a misdemeanor to cost between $3,500 and $5,500. For a felony, you'll pay from $17,500 to $30,000. And most criminal attorneys want all or a significant portion of their fees up front.

Court-Appointed Attorneys   I know what you're thinking: "I can't afford that. How do I get a free attorney?"

You'll need to ask the court to appoint one, and in most places, you'll generally have to provide some details about your financial circumstances to show that you really can't afford one on your own.

As I said above, the issue of court-appointed counsel is typically dealt with at the arraignment. The judge will ask you if you have a lawyer. If you don't, you'll be asked if you would like the court to appoint one. If you want them to, say "yes" (am I being specific enough?). Some courts will appoint a lawyer right then and continue with the arraignment. Others will delay the proceedings to a later date and will only appoint an attorney after reviewing your financial circumstances.

Whether or not you'll qualify for free representation depends on where you are. Each municipality has its own rules about who qualifies. In some places it's formulaic; in other places judges need to decide on a case-by-case basis. But don't worry. If you don't fully meet the requirements, most places have partial-payment plans, where you contribute only what you can afford.

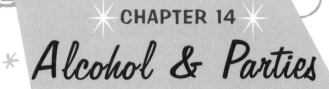

CHAPTER 14

Alcohol & Parties

Lying facedown on your bathroom floor mumbling "I'll never drink again" over and over isn't the worst possible ending to a Saturday night. Lying facedown on a prison floor mumbling the same thing beats it by a mile. Take steps to make sure your partying keeps you on the right side of the law and out of Cell Block 28.

Chapter Contents

As an American you're one of the most privileged and liberated people on the face of the earth . . . except when it comes to liquor. Where alcohol is involved, the "Land of the Free" tightens its grip a bit. The regulatory scheme that surrounds alcoholic beverages in the United States is far more complex, paternalistic, and repressive than those that exist anywhere else. But unless you're willing to drive to Azerbaijan to buy beer, you're going to have to operate under our laws.

I'll be honest with you. I'm not a big fan of the way our laws deal with teenagers and alcohol. I think the current regulatory scheme is unrealistic and ineffective. And by making the consumption of alcohol taboo, it fosters unhealthy drinking (and drinking and driving) habits.

But they're the laws we have, and I can't condone breaking them. Still, just as I've done with every other subject in this book, I'm including information and legal strategies designed to help students, both over and under the age of twenty-one, protect their rights. Please don't think that because I've included this information, I advocate breaking the law. I don't. But I also refuse to leave you without the information you need to protect yourself legally. So please, I beg of you, use this information responsibly.

Underage Drinking Laws

Understanding America's alcohol laws is no simple task. The Twenty-first Amendment, which repealed prohibition, handed regulation of all intoxicating liquors over to the individual states. So rather than one set of national rules, we now have a hodgepodge of local laws. Federal coercion (in the form of threats to withhold highway funding) has had an equalizing effect on most of the major issues. But there are still significant differences in the laws from state to state and, in some areas, even from county to county.

If you're fighting a citation or challenging an arrest, these disparities will be the whole game. But in day-to-day practice most don't make much of a difference. The fact that your state sets the acceptable blood alcohol limit for driving at .10 rather than .08 won't, or at least shouldn't, have any affect on how much you drink when you're out. Likewise, I doubt that anyone has ever said, "What's that? Manufacturing a fake ID is a Class-A Misdemeanor in this state? I thought it was a *Minor* Misdemeanor. Well, then, I guess I should stop what I'm doing right now."

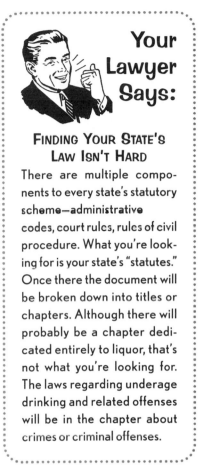

Your Lawyer Says:

FINDING YOUR STATE'S LAW ISN'T HARD

There are multiple components to every state's statutory scheme—administrative codes, court rules, rules of civil procedure. What you're looking for is your state's "statutes." Once there the document will be broken down into titles or chapters. Although there will probably be a chapter dedicated entirely to liquor, that's not what you're looking for. The laws regarding underage drinking and related offenses will be in the chapter about crimes or criminal offenses.

Because of this, the chapter is written fairly broadly. It is by no means a complete survey of state alcohol laws. There simply isn't space to get into that kind of minutia here. Still, it might be worth your time to do a little research on your own. Track down your state's alcohol laws (try FindLaw—www.findlaw.com) and take a careful look at them. But wait until after you've finished reading this chapter—that way you'll be able to understand what they're talking about.

And if you're not that enterprising a drunk, don't worry. The advice included in this chapter is universally applicable, and the most critical state law differences are noted. So you should be just fine.

POSSESSION, PURCHASE, AND CONSUMPTION

As you're well aware, the legal age to drink in every state in the nation is 21. Actually, that's a bit inaccurate. There are three components to "underage drinking"—purchasing alcohol, possessing it, and consuming it. Contrary to popular belief, all three are not illegal in every state. In fact, in fifteen states the actual consumption of alcohol by a minor is not illegal. Only the possession or purchase is prohibited by statute (see the *Overview of State Alcohol Laws* chart for state-specific information).

In many cases the penalties vary depending whether you've possessed, purchased, or consumed. In Alaska, for example, the penalties for possessing and consuming are fairly benign: a fine of $200 to $600, a year of probation, and mandatory alcohol education. But the penalties for purchasing are quite steep: a fine of up to $5,000 and imprisonment of up to one year. And if a false statement was made in the course of the transaction, then the purchasing minor is also guilty of perjury, which is a felony in Alaska.

Wise students will scour their state's law to find out which component of imbibing carries the worst penalties, then take steps to minimize their exposure in those areas.

ATTEMPTED PURCHASE

In some states you don't even have to be successful when you try to buy beer to get in trouble. More than half penalize minors simply for an attempt at it. In most states the penalties are lower, but in some an attemptee faces the same exact penalties as someone who actually got the beer, up to and including suspension of his or her driver's license.

SERVING ALCOHOL TO MINORS

Serving alcohol to, or purchasing it for, a minor is illegal in every state. In most there are exemptions for parents, who can serve alcohol to their children in their home, and for physicians, who are allowed to administer alcohol to minors in the course of treatment (personally, I've never had a doctor advise me that what I really needed was a stiff drink, but I suppose if you've got the right HMO . . .).

The penalties run the gamut from imprisonment of up to one year to small fines and fees. Many kick in regardless of whether the server knew that the person they were serving was a minor. In other words, it's usually your responsibility to know the age of the people you serve.

SOCIAL HOST LIABILITY LAWS

There's a growing trend among the states to hold social hosts civilly liable for the actions of their guests. If a minor who's been drinking or a visibly intoxicated adult leaves your party and causes damage—to themselves, to someone else, or to someone's property—you could be held liable. Usually the host has to have known, or should have known, that the guest was a minor or impaired and that they were planning on driving for the liability to kick in.

Presently more than half of the states in the nation allow for social host liability either through a specific statute or via court-made laws. But even if your state doesn't have a social host liability regime in place right now, there could be one soon. And regardless of the status of the law, there's always the possibility of a lawsuit. An enterprising attorney, aware of the malleability of the laws, might bring a suit even in a state without anything on the books. And even if you eventually win, it will still cost you thousands and thousands of dollars to defend yourself.

Most people are already pretty careful about letting drunks drive away from their parties. But if you're one of the few who still subscribe to the "hey, it's his life" theory, you might want to rethink things a bit.

Fake IDs

Back when I was in high school, we had to make fake IDs the hard way—with an enormous background that looked like a license and a carefully positioned Polaroid camera. Since there was only one giant cardboard template floating around in our little town, we all had the same alias—and to be honest, I don't think any of us made a particularly convincing thirty-two-year-old Benito Verde.

Today ID cards are much more complex. Holograms and encoded magnetic strips are the norm. But the technology available to forgers has improved proportionately. No matter what scheme the authorities come up with, they're quickly outsmarted by America's youth. Present-day forgeries are so sophisticated that police departments actually have to use laboratory equipment to detect them.

ID LAWS

Possession In some states the mere possession of a fake ID is illegal. Chances are you won't get caught if you never try to use your fake. But it could happen. In one instance I know of, an underaged woman's lost wallet was turned in to the local police station. When the cops opened it up to find out whom to contact, they found both her real and her fake driver's licenses. She got her wallet back, but also got charged with possession of a fake ID. The moral of the story: Having a fake ID is a risky enterprise to begin with. Carrying it around with you when you're not planning on using it is just plain stupid.

Lending Many states also explicitly prohibit the unlawful transfer of identification to a minor. It's a fairly common practice: Big brothers and sisters, or just older friends who look somewhat similar, lend their licenses. Under these laws actual owners of the license are guilty of a misdemeanor. Generally the penalties are low—only fines and community service hours. Of course, the minor user will also be subject to charges for use and possession of a fake.

Use In every state except Washington, the penalty for actually using a fake ID to purchase or obtain alcohol involves the loss of driving privileges Washington's

Your Lawyer Says:

USING A FAKE COLLEGE ID IS A BAD IDEA

Some students incorrectly think that if they use a student ID rather than a driver's license, they'll avoid prosecution. This is dead wrong. Most state ID laws are drafted to include any kind of ID at all. Many include wristbands and other much less official items. Some even specifically mention college and university IDs. In fact you're probably worse off using a fake college ID. At most colleges, it's a violation of the university code to steal, falsify, or misuse a student ID card. Getting caught means that you'll open yourself to criminal penalties and get in trouble with the school.

law penalizes misrepresentation of age for the purpose of purchasing alcohol, which includes the use of a fake ID, with only a fine.

Manufacture   The toughest laws concern the manufacture and distribution of fake IDs or the accessories needed to make them. The fines skyrocket—averaging around $5,000. In most states the crime is a gross misdemeanor. In some it's a felony.

A new federal law—the False Identification Prevention Act of 2000—has clamped down on the Internet fake ID trade. It prohibits the distribution of state license templates on United States–based websites. If between one and five IDs are made using the site, violators face up to a year in prison. If more than five are made, the penalty escalates to a maximum sentence of twenty years' imprisonment. Dabbling in the online sale of fakes or the distribution of templates is a foolhardy enterprise.

HOW YOU'LL GET CAUGHT

The guys who work the doors at clubs aren't usually Rhodes scholars. Still, as laws tighten and penalties skyrocket, bouncers and bartenders are getting more extensive and effective training about fake IDs.

Attitude   The number one thing that tips off ID checkers is the demeanor of the cardholder. Bouncers look for all the behavioral cues that indicate dishonesty. Some of the major hints include the following:

- ✓ wandering eyes or lack of eye contact,
- ✓ rapid speech or variable speech patterns and pitch,
- ✓ fidgeting, especially rocking from one foot to the other,
- ✓ exaggerated facial expressions, especially an overly furrowed brow,
- ✓ putting the hand over the mouth when speaking,
- ✓ licking lips or running the tongue over the teeth,
- ✓ inappropriate familiarity with the ID checker,
- ✓ sweating, and
- ✓ shaking.

Most of the things in the above list are pretty hard to control—they're reflexes. Really, the only way to appear relaxed and confident is to actually *be* relaxed and confident. But clever fake holders are able to get their game face on, look the bouncer in the eye, and act calm.

ID Quality   A close examination of the ID itself is the second line of defense for the doorman set. Of course, they'll look carefully at the overall appearance of the ID—to rule out obvious fakes or licenses with crude alterations. And they'll make sure that the picture resembles the bearer. But even on high-quality fakes there are tell tale signs that the license isn't legit. Some of the biggest giveaways are

- ✓ lamination that's too thick,
- ✓ low-quality or incorrect holograms,

✓ a magnetic strip that's covered by lamination (take a look at your real license—see how the magnetic strip is exposed),

✓ signs of alteration, especially in the date of birth area.

Books and Machines Many checkers rely heavily on the use of an ID guide. The one in widest use is published by the California-based Drivers License Guide Company. It gives detailed information about each state's license, allowing bouncers and servers to check the finer points of the card, including the coding of the license number, the angle of the photograph, and the validity of the restriction codes. As with every component of a fake ID, the codes and details can be accurately reproduced. So even a bouncer with a book can be fooled. But a forger without an eye for detail (or a copy of the guide) will probably get nabbed if the bouncer scrutinizes the card.

ID checking machines have also become increasingly common. These devices read either the bar code or the magnetic strip on the license confirm or deny to validity. It's possible to use this technology on the cards issued by most states. The card-reading machines have a reputation for being temperamental, rejecting valid as well as invalid cards. Because of this, many retailers don't entirely rely on them. Often if a card is rejected, it will be examined much more

Your Lawyer Says:

NOT ALL HOLOGRAMS ARE CREATED EQUAL

Most state licenses employ the use of some sort of hologram in their design. Holograms are very difficult to counterfeit and get damaged if they're altered at all. Knowing that fake IDs are usually used out of state, producers—even the high-end ones—usually cut corners by using stock holograms. The problem: Retailers know about this practice and are on the lookout. The most widely used fake holograms in use are the word "secure" or the "lock and key" symbol. No state in the country uses this type of image. If your fake has either one of those holograms on it, using it could be very dangerous. A bouncer with even the slightest bit of ID training will probably be able to spot it as a fake.

carefully, and the owner will be asked to sign a statement that they are of legal age. Then they're let into the bar. This probably won't be the state of things for much longer. As the reliability of the machines increases, so will bars' and stores' reliance on them. And so will their ability to nab fakes.

Quizzes Finally, a suspicious doorman will administer a quick test to see if you're actually the person who's described on the ID. You could be asked to recite your birth date, your address, spell your name, or anything else that appears there. You might also be asked for a second form of ID—a backup. Giving the right answers is only half the battle. The checker will also note how long it takes you to recall the info or find your backup and watch to see if the questioning rattles you.

Keg Laws

Law enforcement officers, legislators, and administrators love to blame things on kegs. There's all sorts of research out there that points to kegs as the reason for every kind of drinking problem—binge drinking, underage parties, and the like. Most also say that it's harder to track how much you've had to drink when there's a keg because guests fill up half-empty cups. Personally I don't buy it. Bored teenagers are the main reason for parties and binge drinking. And no matter what type of receptacle it came out of, after a few beers it's hard to remember how much you've had.

But I don't make public policy (I just criticize it). So the witch-hunt continues, and keg legislation continues to evolve. The most recent trend is toward a keg registration process. At the time of publication, about half of the states required it. Here's how it works: When you buy a keg of beer, you're required to fill out and sign a registration form. Then the keg is tagged with a registration number. That number can be traced back to the retailer and, eventually, to the purchaser. In most states, if the authorities can prove that minors were served alcohol from the keg, they can go after the person who purchased it with criminal charges.

These laws aren't drafted particularly well. The penalties for having unregistered kegs are almost always minimal—usually an administrative fine of a few hundred dollars. They're almost always far lighter than the punishment for serving minors. It makes you wonder how stupid state legislators think their college-aged constituents are. For example, assume that you're a twenty-one-year-old who's throwing a keg party. You think that, despite your best efforts, there might be some underage drinking going on. Which is the smarter move?

1. Leave the registration sticker on the keg and open yourself to all sorts of additional legal problems if the cops do show up; or
2. Carefully remove the sticker or tag (for reattachment after the party) and claim ignorance about who bought the keg when the cops show up.

If you chose option number two, congratulations, you're smarter than the lawmakers thought you would be.

For those of you who answered correctly, here's a bonus question: What's the best way to get around Ohio's law that requires a five-day waiting period for people who want to buy five or more kegs? (Hint: The answer involves two trips to the beer store.)

UNDERAGE DRINKING LAWS

State	Loss of License for Fake ID	Loss of License for Underage Purchase	Attempted Purchase Penalties	Host Liability	Keg Registration	Consumption of Alcohol Is Itself an Offense
AL						
AK	•	•	•	•	•	•
AZ	•	•				•
AR	•	•	•	•		•
CA	•	•				
CO	•	•	•	•	•	•
CT	•	•	•	•		•
DE	•	•	•	•	•	
DC		•				•
FL	•	•	•	•	•	•
GA	•	•	•	•		
HI	•	•		•		
ID	•	•		•	•	
IL	•	•	•	•		•
IN	•	•		•		•
IA	•	•		•	•	
KS	•	•	•	•		
KY	•	•	•			•
LA	•	•				
ME	•	•		•		•
MD		•			•	
MA	•	•	•	•	•	

(continued)

State	Loss of License for Fake ID	Loss of License for Underage Purchase	Attempted Purchase Penalties	Host Liability	Keg Registration	Consumption of Alcohol Is Itself an Offense
MI	●			●		
MN	●	●	●	●	●	●
MS	●	●		●		
MO	●	●	●	●	●	
MT	●	●	●		●	●
NE	●	●	●	●		●
NV	●	●				●
NH	●	●	●	●	●	
NJ	●	●	●	●		
NM	●	●	●	●	●	●
NY	●	●		●	●	●
NC	●	●	●	●	●	
ND	●		●	●		●
OH	●	●		●	†	●
OK			●			●

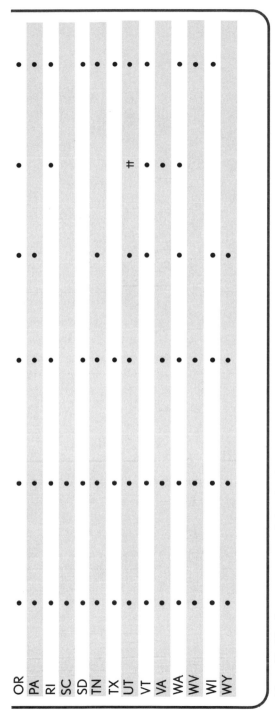

Notes: † In Ohio, keg registration includes a five day waiting period for purchases of five or more kegs.

†† In Utah, no one other than licensed retailers may serve beer from a container larger than two liters.

The Party Throwers' Handbook

Most of the time, when the cops show up and shut down a party, it's because the hosts forget to do the one thing that would have kept them away—think. There's nothing secret or even particularly difficult about avoiding authoritarian party intervention. But party throwers often focus more on picking the right brand of beer than on taking measures to legally protect themselves. The result: unexpected guests wearing jackboots and badges.

The methods outlined here are by no means foolproof. Sometimes no matter what you do the cops will stumble onto your fête and break things up. But if you follow them carefully at each stage of the game—before, during, and after the party—you'll significantly reduce the chances.

BEFORE THE PARTY— PREVENTATIVE STEPS AND SET-UP TIPS

Make Nice with Your Neighbors

The number-one reason parties get discovered is noise. A complaint, usually called in by a neighbor, tips the cop off to some sort of nefarious activity. Smart party throwers will take steps to head off that probability. A few days before the party, walk around to all of the houses that are within earshot of yours and have a friendly chat with the residents. Here's a script for those of you who are conversationally challenged:

> Hi, my name is [insert your name here] and I live over at [insert your address here—if you wish, you may also point in the general direction of your house at this time]. I just wanted to let you know that we're going to be having a party this Saturday night. By all means, feel welcome to come over and have a few beers with us. More importantly, if things get too loud or if there's any other type of problem, please don't hesitate to give us a call instead of the police. I've written down our names and our phone

---

Your Lawyer Says:

GIVE IT UP FOR THE HOUSE OF BOOZE

This part of the chapter is, really, written with off-campus houses in mind. Let's face it, if you try to throw a party with more than 20 guests in a dorm room, you'll get discovered—and shut down—before you can say "RA." Still, dorm residents should read on. Much of the advice is transferable, and if you're willing to keep your soirees small, you can use the information here to avoid hassles.

numbers, as well as the date of the party on this card [hand them the card]. Thanks. [Walk away and go to the next house. Repeat until all houses have been visited.]

Careful readers will note the mention of a card in the above script. Print up a bunch with the time, date, and place of the party, the names of the hosts, and, most importantly, a phone number that disgruntled neighbors can call. A cell phone number is best. If you give out the main phone number to your house, there's always a chance that a drunken partygoer will pick up before you do.

If you want some extra protection, it's never a bad idea to bring a little gift over with you. You'd be surprised how much goodwill a $10 bottle of wine can buy.

> ## ✳ PRE-PARTY CHECKLIST ✳
>
> ### HAVE YOU:
> ❑ Talked to your neighbors and given them your contact information?
> ❑ Performed an outside sound check?
> ❑ Decided on which host or hosts will stay sober during the party?
> ❑ Placed the donation basket as far away as possible from the keg or liquor?
> ❑ Put a stool, a flashlight, and a stamp at the door?
> ❑ Invited people *without* littering campus with posters and flyers?
> ❑ Posted a "21 or Older" sign?
> ❑ Posted a Private Party sign?
> ❑ Read chapter 13, "The Police"?

Alcohol & Parties

Perform a Perimeter Sound Check   A few days before the party, take the time to check how well noise travels around your place. Some afternoon (do it during daylight when you're least likely to disturb anyone) turn your stereo up as loud as you think you'll need it when the party's at critical mass. Then go outside and see what it sounds like. Stand on the street, stand near your neighbors' houses, stand wherever you think non-partygoers might be, and listen. Figure out what level is acceptable and note the settings on your stereo. Then at the party make sure that the volume doesn't go any higher than your predetermined limit.

Also, don't be afraid to change things around to maximize inside noise while minimizing the outside effects. I'm not an expert in architectural acoustics, so my knowledge is a bit limited. But I've walked around on enough campuses late on Saturday nights to know that bass travels much farther than treble does (it has longer wavelengths, I'm told). So be particularly careful not to set the bass levels too high. Also, consider having the music in an interior room or in the basement to minimize seepage.

Invitations   Be careful about who you invite and how you invite them. The chance that you'll have problems is directly proportional to the size of the soiree. The smaller you can keep the party, the better chance you have of coming out legally unscathed. I know, that's not always possible—sometimes there's simply no substitute for a humongous blowout. But, when you can, go small. No matter what the size of the party, *never* put signs up. First, littering campus and the surrounding neighborhood with signs that say "PARTY!" will ensure that the authorities know about your event. More importantly, posting invitations makes your party a public event, open to any and all comers. Legally this could mean that the police are allowed to enter without your permission or a search warrant (not something you want, I assume).

So make all the flyers you want, but stuff them into people's mailboxes, stick them under people's doors, or hand them out personally to your friends.

Fête Financing   It's flat-out illegal to sell alcohol without a liquor license. So charging people to attend your party is out of the question (and a bit gauche, don't you think?). But there are legal ways for you to get funding from your friends to help defray the costs.

First, there's nothing illegal about collecting money before the party and having one person buy the liquor as a representative of the group. Usually just the people who live at the party house or room itself pitch in, but there's nothing wrong with having outsiders contribute.

Second, it's okay for guests to make voluntary donations to the party fund while they're at the shindig. But the donations really do have to be voluntary. You can't post a bouncer at the door that won't let people in unless they make a five-dollar "donation." Set up a contribution table somewhere in your house with a sign that says "Please Donate! Parties Are Expensive" or some such thing. To avoid even the appearance of impropriety, put the table a good distance from the bar—preferably in a different room.

Remember, voluntary doesn't mean unsolicited. So tell people when they come in about the donation basket and point them toward it. And don't forget the power of situational marketing—you'll get more party-aid if people think the revelry is in jeopardy. Here's what my friends and I used to do: Leave half of the booze you bought in your car and, at an appropriate time, announce that you're running out. Pass the hat. Take the cash. Go out to your car and wait ten minutes. Then come back with the replenishments.

Read Up on the Police   If you haven't already done so, be sure to read chapter 13 of this book, "The Police," before the revelry starts. If the cops make an unannounced appearance, you'll need to be ready for them. Party-specific issues are dealt with below, but the general advice included in that chapter will be helpful, too.

DURING THE PARTY—ZEN AND
THE ART OF PARTY MAINTENANCE

Have Designated Hosts   At least one of the people throwing the party needs to stay sober. Really it's best if two of you abstain, but in a pinch you could get by with one. All sorts of things—big and small—could go wrong, and you'll need someone with a clear head to deal with them. For starters, you've given your names and phone number out to the neighbors. If one of them rings up, a lucid person will need to take the call and quiet things down. And if the cops do show up, someone's going to have to talk to them. This is where the second sober host comes in. There should be two cogent people present any time you talk to the authorities—one to do the speaking and one to act as a witness.

It's preferable that one, if not both, of these hosts be over the age of twenty-one. Face it: there's no way that you're going to be able to convince the police that you're having a dry party. They'll know there's beer inside. So it's much better to send out someone who is of legal drinking age and can state with some level of believability that the liquor was purchased and is being distributed legally.

Post Signs There are two types of signs you should post at your party. One that says, "This is a PRIVATE PARTY. No one is permitted to enter unless they have been specifically invited. If you are the police or are working with the police in any fashion, you do not have permission to enter or search this property." And one that says, "You must be twenty-one or over to drink." Put one of each at all of the entrances to your place and one of each anywhere alcohol is being served.

Whether or not your guests follow these posted rules isn't all that important (although, obviously, your life will be much easier if they do). The signs are really mostly for the cops to see. The "Private Party" sign should keep the authorities from walking on in. If they do despite your signs, there's a good possibility that their actions will be deemed an unconstitutional search and that all of the evidence gathered will be excluded in any subsequent hearing.

The "Twenty-one or Older" sign is mostly a prop to use when you're explaining to the authorities that no laws are being broken. Imagine it. You're saying "Officer, there's nothing illegal going on here. Everyone at the party is of age." Then, with a dramatic flair reminiscent

Your Lawyer Says:

AVOID A TRAIL O' TRASH
A trail of empty beer cans and other paraphernalia that leads to your front door might attract the wrong kind of attention. So take steps to ensure that your guests don't leave with anything they'll likely discard a few blocks later. The simplest way to do this: Put a giant trashcan right at the exit of your house or apartment. Most drunks, given the option of heading outside with an empty can or tossing it into a well-placed receptacle, will choose the latter.

of Vanna White, you point to the sign, prominently posted at the main entrance to your house. "See?" you say, "No one who's under twenty-one is allowed to drink, sir." A homemade sign isn't proof positive that you're following the law. But it might sway the officers.

Containment If a squad car drives by and there are fifty kids with plastic cups in their hands on your front porch, the cops are going to take notice. So keep your party inside or in the backyard. Try to avoid having large crowds of people out front (certainly don't ever put the keg out there) and *never* let people drink on your front lawn. Aside from drawing unwanted attention, standing out front with a drink could expose your guests to citations for open container violations. The exact place where your property ends and public property begins is often hard to determine. In most towns state property extends some distance beyond the sidewalk or road. This means that, even if you're standing squarely on lawn, you still may be on public property. Avoid the whole problem by keeping people away from the front of the house altogether.

Also, if the police do show up, you want to have a barrier between them and the party. If there are fifty drunks milling around, nothing will stop them from questioning your guests. And imagine how convincing your statement that you've got everything under control will be if, while you're making it, fifteen of your guests are cheering on some wasted guy doing a beer funnel on your front porch. You get my point. Keep it inside.

Check IDs (or At Least Show That You're Making an Effort at It)
If I were naïve (and hypocritical), here's what this section would say:

> Don't let anyone who's under twenty-one years of age drink alcohol at your party. Have someone who's sober posted either at the entrance or where the alcohol is being served. Make sure your elected ID checker has read the section of this chapter on fake IDs so that he knows what to look for. Give him a stool, a flashlight, and some sort of self-inking rubber stamp (simply writing "OK" on the back of the hands of legal drinkers makes it too easy for minors to stamp themselves). During the party, periodically check to make sure that everyone inside is of age.

But I'm not naïve and not *that* hypocritical. So I know that at least some of you will have parties where minors are drinking. If that's your plan, it's still a good idea to keep up the appearance that you've been requiring a photo ID for admission. Just how much of a façade you want to create is up to you. I suggest going the whole nine yards but having your checker adopt a lax policy. Something along the lines of

> "You twenty-one?"
> "Yes, yes, I am."
> "You got ID?"
> "No, I left it at home."
> "Well, your word's good enough for me." Stamp.

Just like the signs, having a guy at the door who appears to be checking IDs will work wonders during your "there's nothing to see here, officer" speech.

What to Do If the Cops Show Up   Sometimes, despite your best efforts to plan a bust-proof party, the cops will arrive. If this happens, remember everything you learned in chapter 13. Control your body, control your emotions, and control what you say. Be polite and respectful but be firm about your rights.

The first thing you need to do is move the thin blue line away from your doorstep. Step outside, close the door, and take a few steps away from the house. This is where you and your sober witness should engage the officers. I'll talk in detail about this in a moment, but it's extremely important that the police are able to see and hear as little as possible of the party.

They'll ask you if it's your house and will probably ask to see your ID. Legally, you don't have to answer their questions and you don't have to produce ID, but there's really no point in withholding these two bits of information. So answer and show them your license. They may be there because of a noise complaint—if so, apologize and tell them you'll take care of it. If they're there to try to break things up or to try to give out citations, you'll need to rely on your rights to prevent a legal disaster.

AS ALWAYS, DON'T CONSENT TO A SEARCH   There are three things I want you to remember when you're talking with the police:

1. Don't give them permission to come in;
2. Don't give them permission to come in; and
3. Don't give them permission to come in.

As you know from chapter 13, there are only two ways that the police can enter your place without a warrant: one, if there is some sort of emergency and, two, if they are in pursuit of someone who's run into your house. But if you give them permission to come on in, your rights go out the door. So do not, in any way, give them permission to enter your house or to conduct a search of any kind.

If the police ask to come in (and trust me, they will) say clearly, but politely, "I don't want you to go inside. I'm sure that we can work things out here on the front lawn. And by the way, sir, I don't consent to any search of any kind." If they insist on coming in despite your request, state slowly and clearly in front of as many witnesses as possible, "I do not consent to you entering my house, and I do not consent to a search of any kind." They'll probably still walk in, but you'll have made things easier for your lawyer—who can argue that the search was unconstitutional.

DON'T TIP THEM OFF   That's the basic strategy, but in a party setting there are two other evidentiary traps that you might need to sidestep: the **plain view** and **loss of evidence** exceptions.

Under the plain view doctrine, if an officer of the law discovers evidence that's in plain view, then the whole warrant/permission thing is off. For example, if one of your stoner buddies leans out the window of your house smoking a joint while you're talking to the police, it doesn't matter if there's a warrant or not. If they see him, they can charge him.

And if they see something like that, they probably will also have the right to enter your house immediately—without a warrant and without your permission. Why? Because they now know that crimes are being committed and that the evidence of those crimes could easily disappear. Under the loss of evidence doctrine, if delaying a search will create an imminent danger of the loss, removal, destruction, or disappearance of evidence, then the police are allowed to perform an on-the-spot search.

For party throwers this all means one thing. You cannot let the police see or hear anything indicative of illegal activities. If you let that happen, then your right to keep them outside diminishes significantly.

TALK, BUT NOT TOO MUCH   This also means that you can't *say* anything that indicates there might be crimes afoot. The cops will probably try to trick you into admitting something. They'll say things like, "You're serving minors in there, aren't you?" And they'll start questioning you about what's going on. Remember, you don't have to answer their questions. So don't. If they ask anything about what's happening inside, your response should be "There's nothing illegal going on here." That's it. It works for almost any question they could possibly come up with.

"Is everyone in there of age?"
"There's nothing illegal going on here."
"Are there any drugs in there?"
"There's nothing illegal going on here."
"Are you a member of the Mary-Kate and Ashley Olsen Fan Club?"
"There's nothing illegal going on here."

THE END OF THE LINE   At some point the officers will either give up and leave or simply push their way into your house. If they choose the latter, *do not* in any way try to physically stop them: (a) You won't win that fight, and (b) you'll get yourself charged with assaulting an officer. You can continue to verbally object if you want, but at this point, a thousand reiterations of your rights probably won't do a damned thing. In fact it's probably best just to shut your mouth entirely at this point. The only thing talking can do is get you into more trouble.

POST-PARTY DEPRESSION
Legal Cleanup
ASSESS THE DAMAGE   If the cops do make a cameo at your blowout, throwing out half-empty beer cans and wiping unidentifiable muck out of your

bathroom will be the least of your worries. Get all of the hosts together and figure out who got charged with what. As you sort through what's there, you'll probably notice that the citations fall into two broad categories: lesser violations that carry nothing more than a fine and serious charges that mean the loss of your license, probation, or jail time. Obviously you'll need to deal with the two types of charges in very different ways.

LESSER VIOLATIONS If the infractions are limited to the bush leagues of criminal activity, it's probably best to just pay the fines and be done with it. Yes, you could hire an attorney who might be able to get you off the hook. But paying the lawyer will probably cost you more than the fine itself. So why deal with it? Thank your god for limiting the damage. Then send the check in. And be prompt about it. Most fines multiply if you fail to pay them in a timely manner. Left unpaid a $100 fine could very easily turn into $500 in fees and charges and a warrant for your arrest.

Here are a few of the more common lesser violations that party hosts (and guests) often face:

NOISE ORDINANCE VIOLATIONS

This is probably the number-one party charge. Thankfully it's also pretty benign. Almost every town has some type of noise ordinance. (But despite all of the other noisy things that happen all the time, they only seem to be enforced in relationship to parties where there are teenagers in attendance.)

These laws all operate differently. In some municipalities the statute actually defines acceptable decibel levels (65 dB between 7 a.m. and 10 p.m., 50 dB for the rest of the time, for example), and the town has the authority to appoint "noise ordinance officers" who would, I suppose, wander around listening for offenders. Most statutes are a bit less precise. They operate on a disturbing-the-peace model. If an activity interferes with nearby property owners' enjoyment of their place or results in a certain number of complaints, then the activity violates the law.

Often these laws include escalated penalties for repeat offenders. If you've been charged with a noise violation, it's worth your time to check out the local ordinance and see if there are any provisions that treat "habitual" or "repeat" offenders differently. That way you can be extra careful during your noise probation.

OPEN CONTAINER VIOLATIONS, VOLUNTARY OR PUBLIC INTOXICATION

In most towns the above violations are minor misdemeanors. To be honest, they're usually what the police cite you with when they're cutting you a break. So, again: if you're lucky enough to escape with one of these trivial charges, pay your $50 and let it be.

FAILURE TO DISPERSE

In some towns you can get fined for refusing to get lost when the cops tell you to. There's a little more to it than that. Usually there has to be a certain number of people present (usually five), and they have to be likely to cause physical harm, public annoyance, or inconvenience. In other words, the police have to have some sort of reason to tell you to leave. The fines for failure to disperse are generally pretty trivial—usually less than $100.

URINATING IN PUBLIC

A very common party foul is public urination. Long lines, drunken party-goers, and small bladders result in people relieving themselves in the hedgerow. There are two things you should know about these laws. First, even though most are referred to as public urination laws, they include defecation, too. Hopefully this won't ever be an issue for you (and if it is, I think you need to drink a little less when you go out). Still, it's worth knowing. Second, "public" generally means "in view of the public" not "on public property." So even if you're standing solidly on your own lawn, if you're visible from the sidewalk, you could still be charged with urinating in public.

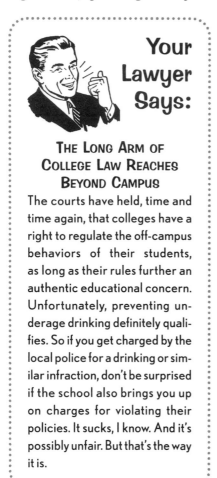

Your Lawyer Says:

THE LONG ARM OF COLLEGE LAW REACHES BEYOND CAMPUS

The courts have held, time and time again, that colleges have a right to regulate the off-campus behaviors of their students, as long as their rules further an authentic educational concern. Unfortunately, preventing underage drinking definitely qualifies. So if you get charged by the local police for a drinking or similar infraction, don't be surprised if the school also brings you up on charges for violating their policies. It sucks, I know. And it's possibly unfair. But that's the way it is.

SERIOUS CHARGES If you've been charged with a violation of the more serious sort—serving alcohol to minors; underage possession, consumption, and purchase; or possession of false identification—you should talk to a local criminal attorney. Detailed information about finding representation is included at the end of chapter 13. Aside from what's said there, if your school has an ACLU chapter or a Legal Services Center, you might want to contact them first. They're usually experts in party infractions.

Barring that, you can use a local lawyer referral service (a state-by-state listing is included as appendix B). Usually, if you find an attorney through these services, your first thirty-minute consultation is extremely cheap or even free. While that doesn't sound like much time, it should be long enough to figure out (a) if you'll really need to hire an attorney and (b) if that specific attorney is skilled enough to handle your case.

Public Relations Aside from dealing with your legal troubles, there are a few other things you should do after the party. First, be sure to clean up areas that are in public view. The police will notice a trashed front yard and will be on the lookout for future events at your place. Obviously, this is much more important if you managed to avoid police intervention. But even if the cops did show up, it's a smart thing to do. You don't want a reputation as a party house.

It's also not a bad idea to touch base with your neighbors again. Even if they didn't call during the party, stop by and casually ask them if they had any problems, if everything was all right. And thank them for their patience. If you're planning on having parties in the future, this bit of consideration will work wonders for you.

Drinking and Driving

If you've read even a few pages of this book, you know I don't often preach. If anything, I err on the other side of things. So the following preachy statement should stand out: Don't drive drunk. It's simply not worth it. People get hurt, become paralyzed, and die every day because they (or someone else) made the stupid and expensive decision to get behind the wheel. It's one of those things that seems like it can't possibly happen to you. But trust me, it could. In fact, there's a 30 percent chance that it will.

According to the National Highway Traffic Safety Administration, three out of every ten Americans will be involved in an alcohol-related traffic accident at some point during their lives. Three of every ten—think about that for a moment. Stunning, isn't it? So are the yearly figures. In 2002 alone 17,419 Americans were killed in alcohol-related accidents. That's roughly one death every thirty minutes.

If the possibility of physical harm isn't enough to scare you off, then think for a bit about the potential legal ramifications. Just under one and a half million people were arrested in 2001 for drinking and driving. That's one DUI for every 137 licensed drivers. The average cost of such an arrest—including court costs, fines, and increased insurance premiums—is roughly $11,000. Getting a competent attorney to defend you in court will cost at least another $5,000. Compared to the ten bucks it costs to call a cab (or the quarter it costs to call your roommate), that's pretty stiff. And of course, if you're convicted, you'll lose your license.

So do yourself a favor and heed the piece of advice that you, as a college student, must hear at least ten times a day: Don't drink and drive.

BLOOD ALCOHOL CONTENT

The beginning, middle, and end of every drunk-driving conviction is the driver's blood alcohol content (BAC). It's measured in number of grams of alcohol per 100 milliliters of blood. So a BAC of .08 means that there are 8/100ths of a gram of alcohol for every 100 milliliters of blood in you. BAC is not technically a measure of how drunk a person is, but it's pretty close. There's fairly good scientific evidence showing that reflexes and motor skills are impaired at a BAC of .05.

There is really only one sure method of measuring a person's blood alcohol levels—taking and analyzing blood. But it can be *estimated* through analysis of the drinker's breath or urine.

BREATH-TESTING DEVICES

The term *breathalyzer* is often used as a generic term for all breath testing devices. Technically a breathalyzer is only one of three types of devices in use. The other two are *intoxilyzers* and *fuel cell detectors*. All three look about the same. They have a mouthpiece and a sample chamber that captures the exhaled air. But the method by which those samples are analyzed differs significantly.

Breathalyzers rely on a chemical reaction to measure the alcohol in the sample. *Fuel cell detectors* estimate alcohol based on the ability of the sample to carry a current. *Intoxilyzers* employ an infrared spectroscope, measuring the reaction of the sample to light.

HOW DOES A BREATHALYZER WORK?

When you drink alcohol it doesn't change chemically. It just moves around in your blood stream as is. When the blood goes through your lungs, specifically the thin membranes of the alveoli (the air sacs), some of that alcohol evaporates into the air. So, if you've had something to drink, the air that you breathe out will contain an amount of evaporated alcohol. Breath testing devices measure those levels. All of the most recent studies show that they are pretty damned accurate. But that doesn't prevent DUI defense attorneys from (successfully) challenging the technology in court. Several factors, they say, can lead to false positives, such as the physical characteristics of the subject, residual mouth alcohol, sample size, shallow breathing, air temperature—even interference from nearby radio signals. And the machines are incredibly delicate (for real). The tests need to be administered with precision and the devices need to be calibrated regularly. Defense attorneys often attack the skills of the administering officer or the maintenance of the machine itself to get their clients off the hook.

If you ever challenge a DUI charge, the type, and probably even the manufacturer, of the breathalyzer will be of paramount importance. Your lawyer will need to attack the accuracy and reliability of the device. In practice, which type a cop pulls out of his cruiser doesn't make much of a difference.

URINE TESTS

Urinalysis is the least accurate way to determine BAC. For starters, it takes roughly one and a half to two hours for alcohol to metabolize and show up in your pee. A urine test, therefore, doesn't show a person's present condition. It reflects their condition one to two hours earlier.

The level of hydration of the subject can also affect the outcome of the test. Someone who is even slightly dehydrated will show much higher alcohol content. So can an individual's metabolism. There's even evidence that the presence of high levels of sugar in the bloodstream could produce false positives. Because of these inaccuracies, this police rarely use urine testing in relation to drinking-and-driving arrests.

LEGAL LIMITS

The chart below outlines the laws in effect in each state. As you'll see, every state now sets the BAC bar at .08. The last two holdouts—Delaware and Colorado—both lowered their limits from .10 in 2004. Of course, there are caveats. The limits are *much* lower for drivers under the age of twenty-one. In most states the "underage" limit is .02, but many set it at .01. Twelve states have a limit of .00, meaning that if you're under twenty-one and there's *any* alcohol at all in your system, you'll be charged with drunk driving.

More than half the states also have *high BAC* laws. These are laws that increase the punishment for drivers with blood alcohol contents higher than .15.

RELATED VIOLATIONS

Child Endangerment   More than half of the states also have *child endangerment laws* that enhance the penalties or create a separate offense for drunk drivers who have minor children in their cars at the time of arrest. The definition of minor child varies from state to state. In some it's as young as fourteen, in others it's anyone under twenty-one.

Open Container Laws   No matter how old you are, no matter how sober you are, in most states simply having an open beer can in a car will get you in trouble. Technically this isn't a drunk driving issue. But it's closely related. The fines for violation are usually pretty low, but it's still a good idea to avoid drinking in the car in those states that prohibit it.

DRINKING AND DRIVING LAWS

State	Allowed BAC Over 21	Allowed BAC Under 21	.15 High BAC	Child Endangerment Laws	Open Container Law	Refusal Penalty Higher than Failing Test
AL	.08	.02			•	
AK	.08	.00	•	•		•
AZ	.08	.00	•	•		•
AR	.08	.02	•		•	•
CA	.08	.01	•	•	•	•
CO	.08	.02	•	•		•
CT	.08	.02	•	•		
DE	.08	.02	•	•	•	•
DC	.08	.00	•	•	•	•
FL	.08	.02	•	•	•	•
GA	.08	.02	•	•	•	•
HI	.08	.02		•	•	•
ID	.08	.02	•	•	•	•
IL	.08	.00	•	•		
IN	.08	.02	•	•	•	•
IA	.08	.02	•	•	•	•
KS	.08	.02	•	•	•	•
KY	.08	.02	•	•	•	
LA	.08	.02	•	•		•
ME	.08	.00	•	•		•
MD	.08	.02		•	•	•
MA	.08	.02			•	•
MI	.08	.02	•	•	•	•

MN	.00	.08
MS	.02	.08
MO	.02	.08
MT	.02	.08
NE	.02	.08
NV	.02	.08
NH	.02	.08
NJ	.01	.08
NM	.02	.08
NY	.02	.08
NC	.00	.08
ND	.02	.08
OH	.02	.08
OK	.00	.08
OR	.00	.08
PA	.02	.08
RI	.02	.08
SC	.02	.08
SD	.02	.08
TN	.02	.08
TX	.00	.08
UT	.00	.08
VT	.02	.08
VA	.02	.08
WA	.02	.08
WV	.02	.08
WI	.00	.08
WY	.02	.08

Where and Why You Could Get Pulled Over

POOR DRIVING

Most of those who are charged with DUI are stopped because of irregularities in their driving patterns. Officers are trained to look for drivers who:

- ✓ turn with an extremely wide radius,
- ✓ straddle the center of lane marker,
- ✓ almost strike objects or other vehicles,
- ✓ weave, swerve, and drift,
- ✓ speed or drive extremely slowly (more than ten miles below legal limit),
- ✓ stop without cause or brake erratically,
- ✓ follow other cars too closely,
- ✓ signal inconsistently with driving actions,
- ✓ have a slow response to traffic signals,
- ✓ turn abruptly or illegally,
- ✓ accelerate or decelerate rapidly, or
- ✓ always drive with their high beams on or with their headlights off at night.

Really, any kind of traffic violation can (and probably will) get you pulled over—from a rolling stop at a stop sign to racing down the highway at 150 miles an hour.

Saturation Patrols and Checkpoints
In areas where there is a high incidence of DUI or at times when there is a spike in drinking in a specific area—such as homecoming or football game weekends—the police will employ these two devices. During a saturation patrol, the department will literally saturate a part of their district with officers and patrol cars for a specific period of time, usually a few hours. The officers will sweep back and forth through the area looking for drunk drivers.

A checkpoint is simply a roadblock. Everyone who passes through is given sobriety tests.

Burgers, Fries, and Cops Knowing that drunks often crave crappy food,

Your Lawyer Says:

CHECK FOR CHECKPOINTS! Strangely enough the times, dates, and locations of saturation patrols and sobriety checkpoints are almost never kept secret. In fact, many state's police departments are required to publicize these events. Usually the department issues a press release detailing their plans. Student who want to avoid hassles should periodically check their local police department's website to see if there are any patrols or checkpoints coming up.

some local police departments have partnered with fast-food restaurants. They actually place officers at the take-out windows to observe the patrons. Slur your speech when you order your Chalupa and you could find yourself being asked to submit to a sobriety test.

Even in towns without a formal program, it's still a really bad idea to drive drunk anywhere near your local McDonald's or Taco Bell. Cops aren't stupid. They know what drunks do. And they monitor the activities near after-hours restaurants closely. So when you're trashed, order in.

Operation Extra Eyes   Cops might not be the only people judging your late-night driving habits. A number of localities have begun to employ volunteer spotters in an attempt to curb drunk driving. They get a few hours training on local liquor laws and how to spot drunks. Then they're set loose on the streets. If they see a person they think is impaired, they call 911 on their cell phones and tail the car until the police intercept.

What to Do If You Get Pulled Over
FIELD SOBRIETY TESTS (FSTs)

If an officer suspects that you are driving under the influence, the first thing she'll do is ask you to exit the car and submit to field sobriety tests—physical trials designed to help her gauge your level of sobriety. The three tests in the widest use are

1. *The Horizontal Gaze Nystagmus Test.* The subjects follow an object, a pen, or a flashlight with their eyes from left to right. If they have consumed too much alcohol, their eyes will twitch involuntarily when moved to the extremes of their field of vision.
2. *The Nine-Step Walk and Turn.* There are really two phases to this test, instruction and performance. The subject is first asked to stand still while given a series of instructions. During this phase the officer will observe the subject's ability to concentrate. Then the subject must take nine steps, heel-to-toe, turn, and walk back in the same way.
3. *One-Leg Stand.* This is also a two-parter with instruction and performance components. In the performance phase the subject must stand for thirty seconds with one foot six inches off the ground, straight out in front of them.

Depending on local practice you may also be asked to recite the alphabet backward, count backward from 100, play patty cake with the officer, repeatedly touch your index fingers to your nose, or do any number of other humiliating things.

You should *always politely refuse to take these tests.* There's no legal penalty for declining. And they all—even the big three—can be inaccurate.

Do a little experiment right now. Try the One-Leg Stand. Can you do it for the full thirty seconds without losing your balance at least a little? Me neither. Even indoors on a solid floor and stone-cold sober, I sway a bit. I'm sure that late at night on a dark roadside, I'd do even worse.

If you agree to submit, all you'll be doing is building the officer's case against you. No matter how well you do, the officer will still be able to say in court that, in her opinion, you performed poorly. But a refusal to take the tests cannot be admitted as evidence against you. So refuse to take them. Clearly and politely explain to the officer that you understand that you have a right to refuse the tests, you know that they're inherently flawed, and you'd prefer not to.

PRELIMINARY BREATHALYZER TESTS (PBTs)

In some states officers carry portable breathalyzers and administer roadside screening tests. The laws vary from state to state, but in most the results of these preliminary tests can't be admitted into evidence as proof. The cops just use them to decide whether or not they're going to arrest you and take you in for a more reliable test. In many states, you have a right to refuse to submit to these field breath tests. But states are continually toughening their DUI legislation. More and more not only require that drivers submit, but also attach stiff penalties (sometimes loss of license) to refusal.

If you're asked to submit to a breath analysis in the field, I suggest you ask the officer about the penalties for refusing. Politely say, "What happens if I refuse?" He can't lie to you. If you're allowed to say no, and you think you're close to the limit, it's probably a good idea to decline. Chances are, the police will arrest you and take you in when you do that, but they were probably going to anyway. As always be polite, but be firm and refuse.

EVIDENTIARY BREATHALYZER AND OTHER CHEMICAL TESTS

At this point the officer will have to make a decision: release you or arrest you and take you in for a "real" blood alcohol test. If it's the former, great. Go home. If it's the latter, then things get a bit more complicated.

You'll be asked, once again, to submit to testing: either a blood, urine, or "evidentiary breathalyzer" test (a more accurate breath-testing device that's kept at the station, the results of which can be used in court). If you refuse at this point, you'll be charged with a violation of your state's **implied consent law**.

Should You Consent? There really isn't an easy answer to that question. It depends on how much you've had to drink and what state you're in. And even then there's some debate about the right course of action.

For first-time offenders it's usually a good idea to submit, especially if you're in a state where the penalties for refusal are stricter than the basic DUI punishment (see the chart above for state-specific informa-

Vocabulary Lesson

IMPLIED CONSENT LAWS— All fifty states have these laws in place that provide that anyone who operates a motor vehicle has implicitly consented to a chemical test of his or her blood, breath, urine, or saliva for the purpose of determining the alcohol content of the blood. So no matter where you are, you do not have a right to refuse when you're asked to submit to the "real" blood alcohol test. The penalties for violating these laws are pretty tough. They are at least as harsh as the corresponding state's DUI penalties and, in many states, much harsher. They're also pretty much impossible to overturn in court. So no matter what happens with your drunk driving arrest, you'll still lose your license under the implied consent statute.

tion). If you refuse you'll definitely lose your license and pay fines under the implied consent laws. But if you submit, you'll still have a fighting chance in court. As you know, the BAC testing methods aren't infallible. If your results fall within a certain range, a good attorney might be able to overturn your conviction.

On the other hand, if you are in a state that has enhanced penalties for high BAC offenders (again, see the chart) and you've had a great deal to drink, it might be wise to refuse rather than risk the increased punishments.

It's impossible to give you a more definitive answer than that, but if you get to the point where the police are asking you these questions, you've got trouble. And no amount of clever legal maneuvering is going to be able get you entirely out of it.

BIKING DRUNK

It's somewhat controversial (among both legal scholars and drunks who don't feel like walking home from the bars), but many states apply drunk driving and other laws to those who operate bicycles on public roads and paths. (Fans of clichéd fraternity rituals will, however, be relieved to hear that getting drunk, putting on a helmet, and racing tricycles on a closed course is still perfectly legal.)

In those states, all of the same tests and procedures for driving drunk apply to pedaling around plastered. More importantly, the penalties are the same. So if you get cited for BUI, you could face steep fines, jail time, and the loss of your driver's license (or be prevented from getting one if you're unlicensed).

And since most statutes extend all traffic laws to bikes, not only could you get busted for drunk driving while navigating your Huffy home, you could potentially get nabbed for reckless operation or, believe it or not, speeding—although you'd have to be one hell of a biker for that to happen.

Alcohol & Parties

Police generally don't enforce the bike laws as aggressively as they do their automotive counterparts. Officers will often look the other way if they encounter a drunk biker—especially on college campuses where they're glad, frankly, that kids aren't driving around drunk. But that should be of little comfort. The fact remains, if you bike drunk, you open yourself to very serious legal troubles.

I know, this whole drunk biking thing seems silly, but these laws exist for a reason. Drunk bicycling *is* actually dangerous. You can't run anyone else over, but you certainly could do a lot of damage to yourself. If you're drunk, call a cab or walk. Either that or invest in a tandem bike and have a sober friend sit in the front seat on the way home.

CHAPTER 15

Sex & the Law

It's easy to let your guard down at college. The scenery's idyllic. There are lots of fun things to do. You're surrounded by kids your age. But just like at Neverland Ranch, a nice setting doesn't necessarily mean you're safe. Sexual assaults on campus are alarmingly commonplace.

Chapter Contents

O n a modern college campus, sexuality has as much to do with avoiding violence as it does with finding a soulmate. As a college student, especially a female college student, you're exposed to so many ambiguous and vulnerable situations. It's horrible to have to think this way, but every party is a potential date rape. Every walk home is a potential sexual assault. And every spurned suitor is a potential stalker.

Because of this, two very different sides of sex are dealt with in this chapter. The first half discusses sex crimes—rape and sexual assault, stalking, and voyeurism. The second half covers the laws surrounding consensual sexual relations—primarily abortion and contraceptive issues.

Sex Crimes

SEXUAL ASSAULT

In the abstract, it's fairly simple to define the two crimes that comprise sexual assault: rape and sexual abuse. Rape is forced sex. Sexual abuse is, basically, an unsuccessful rape—unwanted sexual contact that doesn't involve intercourse. But drafting (and explaining) laws that prohibit these acts is incredibly complex.

Sexual assault crimes are governed by state law. So there are fifty different sets of statutes that deal with these crimes. And the differences are extensive. Even the terminology changes from state to state. Some treat rape and sexual assault as separate crimes. Others fold the entire family of crimes into the sexual assault category. Some use their own special words. Mississippi's law actually refers to rape as the forcible "ravishing" of another person.

The differences in semantics are just the beginning. Each statute takes a slightly different theoretical approach. The crux of the matter in each is how to define—and in turn how a prosecutor must prove—that "unwanted" part. How do you show that the sexual activity was indeed nonconsensual? What types of evidence can be used? What are the critical questions?

These are the types of question that the law always has a hard time answering. The kind that involve getting inside someone's head. Certainly there are clear-cut cases, situations where the assaults take place at gunpoint or after a prolonged physical fight. But in many instances, especially in date-rape cases, it's incredibly hard to determine what either party was thinking beyond a reasonable doubt.

Although no two states have identical sexual assault laws, Richard Posner and Katharine Silbaugh, in their book *A Guide to America's Sex Laws*, identify three broad categories that help to organize them. The first are **statutes that were originally based on the Model Penal Code (MPC)**. The MPC is a theoretical set of laws written by law professors, judges, and lawyers. It has no binding effect, but it's often used as a, well, model for state statutes.

Written in 1962, the MPC is outdated in the way it approaches sexual assault crimes. First, it creates a "grading system" that categorizes each level of the crime. This is, in and of itself, not such a bad idea. But it's applied in an antiquated way. It makes rape of a "social companion" a less serious crime than the rape of a stranger. And it makes the rape of a man a less serious crime than the rape of a woman.

It also focuses pretty heavily on the subjective concept of the consent of the victim. It doesn't outright require that nonconsent be proven. But it does require that it be inferred through evidence that the victim fought back, third-party evidence, or "fresh complaint" evidence (which is evidence that complaint of the rape was made voluntarily and relatively promptly after the abuse). Very rarely are there witnesses to rapes—ones who can testify to the state of mind of the victim anyway. And fresh complaint evidence isn't particularly probative. What this means, in practice, is that if the victim doesn't get beat up or show some other obvious physical signs that he or she resisted, it's hard to convict the rapist.

The second broad category consists of **laws based on the New York statute**. New York's law is a lot like the MPC statute but differs in a few important ways. First, it makes no differentiation based on social-companion status of the victim and assailant. Date rapists can be found guilty of the highest level of the crime. It also depends a little less on the consent of the victim and on proving nonconsent through evidence of physical harm.

Finally, **laws based on the state of Michigan's statute** make up the third category of laws. These take an altogether different approach. They remove consent from the picture entirely. Instead they focus on the conduct of the defendant. The critical component is the amount of force or coercion the assailant used. The Michigan statute doesn't use the word *rape* at all. Instead it uses degrees of assault to define all sex crimes. It is also entirely gender neutral. The crimes are the same, no matter the gender of the assailant or the victim.

Most states loosely follow one of those three models, but also borrow from all three approaches. When you get down to it, they all operate in about the same way—most states have dropped all gender-specific language and none still include social-companion clauses. Still, it's not a bad idea to take a look at your state's statute online via FindLaw (www.findlaw.com).

DATE RAPE

As I said above, states no longer differentiate sexual assault crimes based on whether or not the victim and the assailant knew one another. Therefore date, or acquaintance, rape isn't a separate crime. It's a situation in which rape can occur. The state's standard sexual assault law will be used to prosecute the suspect.

As you can imagine, based on what you read above about these laws, getting a conviction in a date-rape case presents some thorny problems. The difficulty in any rape or sexual assault case is proving that there was no consent. In situations where the two are friends, or even started the evening out on a date, this gets even more complicated. Sure, it might be easy to know what happened if you were there yourself—but three months later in a courtroom, the fact that the victim and the alleged rapist went to dinner and a movie before the crime occurred can have a devastating effect on the other evidence.

Your Lawyer Says:

REPORT SEX CRIMES QUICKLY

The amount of time it takes a victim to report a sexual assault or rape can have an enormous effect on the outcome of a case. Wait too long and the defense could use it as evidence that the incident was consensual. Do it quickly and your lawyer will be able to offer it as evidence that the assault was unwanted.

In fact, less than half of date-rape cases end in conviction. I wish I had something more positive, legally, to say about all of this. But I simply don't. Rape is hard to prove in court. Date and acquaintance rape are much harder.

DATE-RAPE DRUGS

Rapists use date-rape drugs to weaken their victims and make them easier to assault. Their effects run the gamut: from making the target dizzy and woozy, through increasing sexuality and sociability, to simply knocking the victim out cold.

Drugs seem to go in and out of fashion with date rapists (or at least with the media that report on them). Currently three drugs seem to be in common use:

✓ *Rohypnol* is a rapist's dream drug. Sold under the chemical name flunitrazepam and often called roofies or roaches, Rohypnol is a white tablet that's cheap (less than $5 on the street) and dissolves odor- and colorlessly into liquids. Chemically it's a lot like valium or Xanax. It causes both physical and mental impairment, affecting motor skills and judgment. It often lowers sexual and social inhibitions and causes full or partial amnesia.

✓ *GHB* is an acronym for gamma-hydroxybutyrate. On the street it's often referred to as Liquid Ecstasy, Vita-G, or G-Juice. It's a clear, odorless, and colorless liquid that acts as an overall depressant to the central nervous system. In low doses it creates an effect somewhat like inebriation. In higher doses it can cause loss of consciousness, respiratory failure, and coma.

✓ *Ketamine* is an animal tranquilizer. It can be found in liquid, pill, and powder form. It causes dissociation, amnesia, hallucinations, and unconsciousness. It's often referred to as Special K or Vitamin K.

Those are the three drugs that are commonly called "date-rape drugs," but any substance that has a sedative or amnesiac effect can be used to accomplish date rape. Lots of other drugs, really all drugs, can and are used in date-rape scenarios. The most obvious example is alcohol—which is used far more often to illegally take advantage of women than all date-rape drugs combined.

TIPS FOR PROTECTING YOURSELF FROM DATE-RAPE DRUGS

✓ Never leave your drink unattended.

✓ If you do lose sight of your beverage, don't drink it. Throw it out and get a new one.

✓ Don't accept drinks from people you don't know. If someone wants to buy you a drink, take it directly from a bartender or server.

✓ Avoid drinking out of open or communal containers, like punch bowls. If possible, stick to drinks that are sealed or come out of taps.

✓ If your drink looks, smells, or tastes funny (especially if it tastes salty), don't risk it. Just throw the damn thing out.

✓ Consider using a test kit. A company called Drink Safe Technology (www.drinksafetech.com) makes coasters and credit card–sized cardboard testers that can detect the common date-rape drugs. They're cheap, easy to use, and available at many convenience stores and Drink Safe's website.

DATE-RAPE DRUG LAWS

All rape statutes include a clause about mental incapacity. Maryland's law, for example, makes it a felony to "engage in sexual penetration by force or threat of force against the will and without the consent of the victim, or where the victim is mentally defective, *mentally incapacitated, or physically helpless.*" Clearly drugging someone to the point where they weren't able to think, then taking advantage of them would fall under this, general, definition of rape.

Other states have gone a bit further and have added specific language about date-rape drugs to their rape statutes. Maine's is a good example. Its definition of rape includes sexual contact when

> the actor has substantially impaired the victim's power to appraise or control his or her sexual acts by administering or employing drugs, intoxicants, or other similar means where the victim did not voluntarily consume the substance with knowledge of its nature or did so pursuant to medical treatment.

It also states, in a separate section that

> It is a felony to engage in sexual contact with a person who has not expressly or impliedly acquiesced in the sexual contact; where the victim is unconscious or otherwise physically incapable of resisting and has not consented to the sexual contact.

In practice all of the rape statutes—from the ones that simply mention incapacitation to those with drawn-out drug language—operate in the same way. They allow the defendant to be convicted on the basis of the victim's incapacity. This significantly simplifies the consent questions. If a woman was drunk or drugged beyond reason, then the prosecution's need to show evidence of resistance or subjective nonconsent almost disappears. It can make obtaining a conviction much easier.

Federal laws have also targeted the more common drugs themselves. GHB is classified as a Schedule I drug, making possession outright illegal. Ketamine and Rohypnol are Schedule III and IV drugs, respectively. It's possible to legally possess them, but you have to have a prescription.

In 1996 Congress passed the Drug Induced Rape Prevention and Punishment Act in response to the use of date-rape drugs. It makes the distribution of any controlled substance with the intent of committing a rape, or other violent crime, punishable by a sentence of twenty years' imprisonment.

WHAT TO DO IF YOU'RE A VICTIM

If you've been assaulted or raped, your health should be your number one concern. No matter what, get yourself to a doctor, hospital, or other medical facility, even if you don't think you're injured. It's not uncommon for assault victims to be unaware of their injuries. You might be in shock or you might have internal damage that you can't feel.

After that, and I mean right after that, your priority should be to preserve as much evidence as possible.

The most important evidence will be any DNA left behind by the assailant—skin from under the fingernails, blood stains, semen, hair samples. Signs of physical trauma are also important and should be documented. These types of evidence are often called a "rape kit" (the rape kit is the evidence itself, not some device or package used to obtain it). You should tell the doctor or nurse you've been sexually assaulted and ask for a *medical-legal exam*. It's important to use this legal term rather than simply requesting a rape kit test. It will ensure that the exam is kept confidential.

From an evidentiary standpoint, it's usually best to go to a hospital

Your Lawyer Says:

TAKE STEPS TO PRESERVE

The sooner the medical-legal exam is performed the better. To be useful at all, it needs to happen within forty-eight hours of the attack. Don't do anything before the exam that could destroy the evidence. Specifically:

- Don't shower, bathe, douche, brush your teeth, wash your hands, or smoke a cigarette.
- If possible, try not to urinate.
- Don't change your clothes. Keep what you were wearing at the time of the attack on. If you absolutely must change, bring the clothes with you to the hospital in a paper (not a plastic) bag.

emergency room rather than a private doctor's office. They're equipped to administer post-assault examinations. On-campus health centers are also usually experienced in medical-legal examinations.

You have one chance to gather this evidence before the critical window closes. So even if you think you that you don't want to press charges, get the exam. That way you'll have the option later on.

There's a specific law that helps college students navigate the sexual assault aftermath. The Campus Sexual Assault Victim's Bill of Rights (also called the Ramstad Act) requires colleges and universities to provide victims with certain basic rights and to inform them of their options. Under the law victims must be

✓ given information about how to report the crime to local authorities, including on-campus and local police,

✓ given assistance by a college employee in contacting the authorities if they ask for it,

✓ given information about on- and off-campus counseling, mental health, or other services for sex-offense victims, and

✓ given information about options to change their living or academic arrangements in light of the attack.

In other words, the school is required by law to help you out. So ask for assistance. The school will be able to help you make a report, press charges, get counseling, and even change rooms or lighten your academic load.

CRIMINAL TRANSMISSION OF A DISEASE

If you've been the victim of a sexual assault, you'll probably have to have an STD test. This brings us to a loosely related crime: the criminal transmission of a sexually transmitted disease. Although it's not often discussed, many states make the act of passing, or even exposing another to, an STD a crime.

California's law, for example, provides a "three-year sentence enhancement for the commission of certain specified crimes, such as rape and sodomy, when the offender commits such offenses with the knowledge that he or she has AIDS or the HIV virus at the time of commission." California also has a separate law (drafted way back in 1957) that simply makes it a misdemeanor to expose another person to any venereal disease, regardless of the circumstances.

Other states have more complex legislation. Florida's statute also has a sentence enhancement for sex crime offenders. It requires that anyone convicted of a sexual assault be tested for HIV. If they are found to be infected, they are also guilty of the felony transmission of the AIDS virus—regardless of knowledge or intent.

Just more than half the states have specific transmission statues. But even in the half that don't, a person could still be held criminally liable for these kinds of acts under more general criminal laws, such as reckless endangerment, attempted murder, or, in the case of actual infection with HIV, manslaughter or murder.

STALKING

Roughly 15 percent of all college women will be stalked in one way or another during their time at school. Stalking is a crime that often leads to even more serious, and violent, crimes: 76 percent of intimate-partner homicides involved an incident of stalking within a year of the crime.

Behaviors that can legally constitute stalking are practically limitless. You can be stalked via e-mail, over the phone, through the mail, or via the old-fashioned, creepy, following-you-around-in-a-raincoat way. Because of this,

Sex & the Law

stalking is defined in the statutes more by its effect on the victim than the actions of the stalker.

Like most other sex crimes, stalking is defined by state law and the statutes vary significantly: Some only kick in if the victim fears physical harm. Others are much broader and include most "harassing" behaviors. But all of the statutes contain, in some form or another, the following three components in their definition:

1. intentional acts on the part of the stalker,
2. that communicate a threat to the victim, and
3. create fear in them.

Intentional Acts   Someone who keeps bumping into you by accident is not a stalker. His acts need to be intentional. In most states the prosecution must also prove that the stalker was committing the acts in order to threaten and cause fear.

Threat   The threats can be explicit or implied; there's no requirement that the threats be imminent at all. They can be for the indefinite future. Of course, in most cases the threats are implied (few stalkers call up and outright say, "I'm going to hurt you"). In those implied cases the threat can be inferred by what the stalker says or how he acts. And any special knowledge that the victim has about her stalker—most often a prior history of violence—can be taken into account.

The standard is that of a reasonable person. This means that if a reasonable person would feel threatened by the acts, then it's stalking.

Fear   In explicit cases the threat and the fear are two distinct things. But in the implicit-threat cases, which are the majority, proving that there was a credible threat and that the victim was afraid will be about the same thing.

Not all states follow this three-part definition, but it's still a useful tool in addressing a situation in any state. If the stalker's actions meet this test, it's probably legally actionable. Still, it's not a bad idea to take a look at your state's specific law. The National Center for Victims of Crime has an online stalking resource center (www.ncvc.org/src). It lists the regulations for all fifty states.

Technology and Stalking   Stalking doesn't need to involve any in-person contact. We have a million ways to communicate with one another these days, and the use of any of them to threaten or harass could be stalking. Some states have language that targets specific types of stalking. Colorado's statute, for example, singles out crank calling, stating that anyone who "[m]akes repeated communications at inconvenient hours that invade the privacy of another and interfere in the use and enjoyment of another's home or private residence" is a stalker.

Cyberstalking is another area that's gotten a lot of attention lately. Justifiably. Electronic communications factor into more than 30 percent of all stalking cases. State stalking statutes have been modified accordingly. Forty-five statutes specifically mention e-mail and other forms of electronic contact. And the laws in the others are inclusive enough to include e-mail, even though they don't explicitly discuss it.

Telephone calls and e-mails are just two examples. Any unwanted harassing contact can be stalking. You could even be stalked via the FTD florist. If someone sent you flowers every day with a weird note, it would probably meet the legal standard.

What to Do If You Think You're Being Stalked Even on the smallest campus there will be resources to help you. Most schools have a women's crisis center or a similar facility staffed by someone who's well versed in stalking and other sex-related crimes. They'll be able to help you assess the situation, make a decision about what to do, and give you good advice about how to protect yourself and your privacy. They'll also know the specifics of how to file a complaint or apply for a protective order in your jurisdiction.

This book is great (if I do say so myself), but an on-site professional who can talk with you about your specific problem is irreplaceable in stalking cases. So seek out the help that, I'm sure, abounds at your school.

Legally, the most common, and effective, tool you can use to combat a stalker is a protective order. In most states, if a victim can show a violation of the anti-stalking

> ## ☆ *RESTRAINING ORDER TIPS* ☆
>
> - The time directly surrounding the filing of the order is, statistically, the most dangerous. Often the stalker will retaliate. Be extra careful right after you file.
> - Remember, a restraining order is absolutely useless against someone who doesn't care about it.
> - Report even the tiniest infraction of the order after it's been granted. If you let your stalker slide, even a bit, he might start to try to push your limits. Don't invite this.
> - If you report something, don't worry about witnesses or proving that you saw your stalker. Once the order is issued, the police have to take your word on its face.

laws, a judge can issue what's called a "stalking protective order." This makes it outright illegal for the perpetrator to continue his harassing behavior and allows the police to arrest him immediately if he crosses the line.

So what exactly should you do? Is it really necessary to get one of these protective orders? Stalking very often leads to other, much more serious crimes like assault or even murder. I know. Crank calls and murder are on opposite ends of the criminal spectrum. But no matter how benign your stalker's actions may seem, they're not normal. The situation needs to be regarded with concern.

VOYEURISM

Voyeurism laws are much older than those of most other sex crimes. Evidently people have been peeping into each other's windows since the early days of our nation. Less than half of the states have specific voyeurism statutes—only twenty-three—but in states that don't, peeping toms can usually be prosecuted under trespass or invasion of privacy laws.

In those states that do have specific voyeurism statutes, the laws are pretty simple. My favorite of all of them is Michigan's, which just says, "It's unlawful to be a window peeper. A person is guilty of being a disorderly person by being a window peeper."

Generally, window peepers (I really like writing that) don't need to actually see anything to be guilty of a crime. Simply trespassing with the *intent* to invade someone's privacy is enough. The crime is a misdemeanor and carries fairly low penalties in most jurisdictions.

PUBLIC NUDITY

I have this friend—we'll call him Todd—that used to always take his clothes off when he got drunk at a party. Sometimes he'd do naked tricks for us. But usually he'd just scream and run around. Every once in a while he'd even manage to get outside and run up and down the street scaring the neighbors. We all thought it was a bit strange at the time. But we really didn't give it much thought. If Todd wanted to be the naked guy, that was his choice and we weren't going to stand in his way.

Technically, though, Todd was probably breaking the law. Every state in the nation has laws that prohibit public nudity in some way. They're all different in what they outlaw and how they define unlawful exposure, but there are a few overriding themes.

Most of the statutes only outlaw exposure of the genitals and the anus—making most of your butt and your breasts A-OK for public display—although a few do specifically include those lesser private parts. Arizona, for example, prohibits exposure of the "areola or nipple of the breast" as well as the other stuff. A number of other states simply list the exposure of "privates" as off-limits, which could include buttocks and breasts.

But the lists of specific body parts aren't half as entertaining as the intent requirements that are included in most state public indecency statutes. Almost all of the laws have some sort of language that requires either that the exposure be "reckless" or intended to cause "alarm."

The Texas law is a good example. Title 9, Chapter 21 of the Texas Penal Code defines indecent exposure in the following colorful way: "A person commits an offense if he exposes his anus or any part of his genitals with intent to arouse or gratify the sexual desire of any person, and he is reckless about whether another is present who will be offended or alarmed by his act."

Similarly, Title 9, Chapter 42 of the code states that a person who "exposes his anus or genitals in a public place and is reckless about whether another may be present who will be offended or alarmed by his act" can be charged with disorderly conduct.

Now, where the line between safe and measured exhibitions and reckless ones falls is hard to tell. Ultimately it would be up to a judge or jury to decide.

But just because baring your assets is, to a certain extent, legal under state law doesn't mean that you can flash to your heart's content. Many campuses have their own rules and regulations. Middlebury College, for example, prohibits nudity if it's used as a part of fraternity or sorority hazing rituals (at all other times, I assume, nakedness is sanctioned).

Most schools simply vaguely list nudity or seminudity as "inappropriate behavior" that is subject to discipline. Check the student handbook to see if there's any such rule in existence. Depending on what it says, you could, theoretically, get in trouble for something as benign as tanning topless — but I doubt it. Those rules are aimed at people who streak at football games, not quiet bronzers.

Finally, if you really want to be super safe you should check the city and county ordinances to see what they say about public nudity. Look online, or call the local police station and (anonymously) ask if they can tell you a bit about the laws.

Girls Gone Wild   While we're discussing public nudity it makes sense to talk about the *Girls Gone Wild* (and now, I suppose, *Guys Gone Wild*) phenomenon. In my opinion, the biggest risk you take when you get naked in public isn't the chance that you'll get cited with a misdemeanor or punished under some school code. It's the possibility that someone could photograph you and distribute your naked likeness over the Internet, via video, or use it in a commercial that airs during the *Howard Stern Show* on E!.

You have zero expectation of privacy when you're, say, riding on a float in the middle of Mardi Gras or hanging off a balcony in Ft. Lauderdale. So if someone snaps a picture of you, or films you, they own it. Technically they're supposed to get you to sign a model release before they use it for anything. But most don't bother. They just use whatever they can shoot.

Even if you don't really mind the fact that there are naked pictures floating around of you, you should get pissed off about the financial injustice. The producers of these videos and websites make millions and millions of dollars. And you won't get one red cent of it. Hell, even your school's art department will pay you $25 an hour to model nude. So if the *Girls Gone Wild* people approach you with some sort of profit sharing and royalty scheme, consider it. Otherwise, screw 'em. Let them get rich off of someone else's body.

Listen, I'm all for drunken nudity. It's a part of the college experience that we should all get to enjoy. But please, use some caution. Restrict your naked beer slides to small gatherings of close (camera-free) friends. Don't do them in front of thousands on spring break.

Consensual Sex Problems

Strangely enough, the law can affect sexual relations between two consenting participants. In fact, if you're lucky enough to be sexually active while you're in school, there's a good chance that you've broken some strange law. Fornication, sexual intercourse between two unmarried people, is illegal in seventeen states. So those of you in D.C., Florida, Georgia, Idaho, Illinois, Massachusetts, Michigan, Minnesota, Mississippi, New Mexico, North Carolina, North Dakota, Oklahoma, South Carolina, Utah, Virginia, and West Virginia should think twice before taking your date up to your dorm room for a little whoopee.

And for those of you who are sleeping with your married professors, watch out for prosecution under your state's adultery laws. Yes, in twenty-six states it's illegal (sometimes even a felony) to engage in sexual relations with a married person who is not your spouse.

I wouldn't worry too much about any of these laws. They're almost never prosecuted. They're really only used in combination with charges for sexual assault, either to add to the charges or in cases where a conviction on the primary charge is too difficult to secure. Still, I think it's always good to know when you're breaking the law. And in this case I think it's even okay to brag about it. "I broke the law four separate times last night!"

STATUTORY RAPE AND AGE OF CONSENT

I can remember people discussing statutory rape when I was in college. At least once a year someone would say to me, "Having sex with anyone under eighteen is illegal in this state, you know. It's statutory rape. So if you sleep with a freshman, you could go to jail." I would generally nod and try to look interested, but I never cared much. I had never heard of anyone being convicted of statutory rape. With date rape and all of the other violent crimes that abounded on campus, it didn't seem like anything that was worth my time.

It turns out, I was right. Just like the fornication and adultery statutes, statutory rape laws are rarely enforced. And even when they are, it's usually in extreme cases or in conjunction with some other, more serious crime. Certainly the police have never busted into a college dorm room and arrested two consenting college students just for having sex.

Still, since it's bound to come up in conversation, I feel I should set the record straight: There are both state statutes and a federal law that governs the age of consent, so the statutory rape laws vary depending on where you live. But very few of these laws, four by my count, set the age at eighteen. And one of those four is Mississippi's law, which sets the bar at eighteen only if the person was "previously of chaste character." For the unchaste the limit is fourteen.

And almost all of the statutes set limits based on the relative ages of the two people, requiring that the offender be a certain amount of years or months older than the victim. The federal law is a good example of this. Under that statute it's a felony to have sex with "another person under sixteen, and at least four years younger than the offender." So, sixteen-, seventeen-, eighteen-, and most nineteen-year-olds would be well within the legal limits even if they were sleeping with a fifteen-year-old.

You'd have to be a pretty old student and be sleeping with someone who's really young—like fourteen or fifteen years old—to break most of these laws. So most of you have nothing to worry about. And if you've read this and still *are* a little worried, well, first, *gross*. And second, take a look online to see where the actual limit lies in your state.

CONTRACEPTION LAWS

I doubt this will be a big problem on any college campus. Generally, free condoms and other forms of contraception are readily available at, or near, schools via health centers and clinics. But it bears mentioning that *there are currently no laws that limit a minor's access to contraceptives in any state in the country*. This means that if you attempt to purchase, or ask your doctor to prescribe, a form of contraception, they can't withhold it. Your doctor, for medical reasons, could suggest a different method. But they can't outright refuse to prescribe it.

And there are no laws that require parental notification either. You have a right to buy condoms, get a 'scrip for the pill, or anything else without qualification. Again, I doubt you'll run into trouble in this area, but you should know your rights just in case.

ABORTION

When I was in high school you couldn't turn around without someone shoving some pamphlet about teen pregnancy in your hands. So I'll spare you the long lecture about what a hard decision abortion is and where to turn for help. I'm sure you already know about that. But I do want to talk a bit about a specific legal issue: notification—both to the parents and to the father of the child.

It's well-established law that the father of a fetus has no right to be notified of an intended abortion. On that front, the decision is the woman's alone to make.

But parents are a different story. A majority of states have laws that require parental involvement in the decision-making process. These statutes vary a great deal: Some require the consent of both parents, others only the notification of one. A few simply require a counseling session that includes a discussion about telling your parents. Of course, the laws only apply to minors. So if you're over the age of eighteen, you can do whatever you want to and have no legal obligation to talk to anyone about it.

But there is another option. Most states that require parental notification also allow for something called a **judicial bypass**. This means that, with court approval, the notification requirement can be waived and a minor can get an abortion without telling her parents. Presently the only states without a judicial bypass option are Alaska, Florida, Maryland, and Utah. All of the others either don't require notification or have a judicial bypass process in place.

Appearing in court may seem far more intimidating than telling your parents. But if that's the route you want to take, there are often local organizations that represent young women in judicial bypass proceedings for a nominal fee or even free of charge. Your local Planned Parenthood Clinic or ACLU can tell you where to get help. And the Center for Reproductive Rights (www.reproductiverights.org) has a great deal of information available on its website.

CHAPTER 16

Off-Campus Housing

If one of your roommates
storms out mid-lease, your
first thoughts are probably
going to be about revenge.
Retribution is a worthy goal.
You should definitely try to
stick it to your new ex–best
friend—but not just yet.
Your immediate concern
should be preserving
your relationship with
your landlord.

Chapter Contents

W ater that cuts out mid-shower, toilets that barely flush, spotty heating, leaky roofs, and pretty much every other housing trouble you can think of are continuing problems in student rentals. And knowing that the majority of their tenants won't have the required knowledge or ability to stand up for their rights, college-town landlords often capitalize on that ignorance through flagrant neglect. Not knowing any better, most college students accept their sorry state as a part of the college experience. But I'm betting that you're not like most college students. To start with, you have this book—which not only denotes that you have impeccable taste, but also means that you probably don't like being taken advantage of.

Don't get your hopes up too high. Knowing about landlord-tenant law won't work miracles. A shithole is a shithole, and no amount of legal posturing is going to change that. But there are certain rights that are guaranteed to everyone—from the guy who rents the $5,000 a month penthouse to the slob in the $300 basement hovel.

Leases and Rental Agreements

At the very center of the landlord-tenant relationship is the lease or the rental agreement. That document you signed at the beginning of your stay is the contract that binds the two (or more, if you have roommates) of you. It dictates, to a great extent, all the ways that you and your landlord must interact.

Go get your contract right now and take a look. I think you'll be surprised to see how comprehensive it is. If you ever have a problem with your apartment or house, your first line of inquiry should be a look at that contract itself. Chances are, there will be language within that explains both your and your landlord's responsibilities and obligations.

Of course, it's not quite as simple as that. If it were this whole chapter would just say "read your lease" and that would be that. The lease sets out the basics of your relationship. But there is a complex set of rules and regulations that govern how you operate within that contractual bond. There are even a few discreet areas where you have rights regardless of what you've agreed to.

THE BASICS OF YOUR CONTRACT

Who Should Sign the Lease?   If you're renting the apartment alone, you and your landlord will be the only parties to the agreement. But what if you're renting a house with six other people? Should every last one of you sign on to the contract? It depends.

Vocabulary Lesson

LEASE VS. RENTAL AGREEMENT— Leases and rental agreements are essentially the same thing—contracts that dictate the terms of the rental. But technically they're two distinct types of documents. Most apartments are rented through a **lease** that binds the tenant and the landlord for a set period of time—usually a year. **Rental Agreements** bind the two for a much shorter period of time, but are continuous. Often they're referred to as month-to-month rentals. The agreement automatically renews at the end of each term. There are advantages to both. Under a lease you're locked into your agreement for a long period of time. So your landlord can't unexpectedly raise the rent or kick you out. But if you want to leave early, you'll probably run into troubles. On the other hand, walking out on a rental agreement is usually pretty easy. But so is upping the rent or evicting a tenant. The vast majority of college-town landlords use leases. They don't want the constant turnover that month-to-month renters would bring.

First, you may not have a choice in the matter. Your landlord might require that everyone who's going to live at the place sign the contract. This is the best option for her because it binds everyone, equally, to the terms. In law this is called **joint and several liability**. It means that you're all in the boat together—you're all equally responsible for paying all of the rent and you'll all get in equal trouble if one of you breaks the rules. So, if there's rent due, your landlord can sue every last one of you. It doesn't matter who bounced a check, you're all responsible.

In most cases this is the best course of action for the tenants, too. It creates a direct legal relationship between each roommate and the landlord, *and* it creates a legal relationship between roommates. If something goes awry, you'll be on much stronger legal footing.

The only potential downside is: It's a bit harder to kick out a crappy roommate if they've signed the lease themselves. We'll go into this in detail later, but signing the lease gives each roommate direct rights of occupancy with the landlord. If you're the only one on the lease,

then you have more control. Still, for most college students, it's best to simply have everyone who's going to live with you sign on.

The Term of Rental The contract will also denote the length of the tenancy. Despite the fact that most college students won't use their apartments for two or three months over the summer, most landlords will insist on a lease that runs for the full calendar year. You can try to negotiate your way out of it, but don't expect to get anywhere. In a college town, with so many prospective tenants, landlords can usually afford a take-it-or-leave-it stance on that issue.

Rent   Obviously the contract will spell out exactly how much you're going to have to pay to live there. In the case of a lease, the rent will usually be described as one amount paid in monthly installments (e.g., tenant shall pay landlord the sum of $9,000; payment shall be made in 12 payments of $750).

Usually the contract will also specify how the rent must be paid. Contrary to popular belief, a landlord can demand that the rent be paid in a certain fashion. Most won't accept cash, for example. The lease may also set out where the money is to be taken or, more often, mailed. If you go the postal route, usually the due date is the day on which the check must *arrive* in the mail, not the day it needs to be postmarked by.

Grace Periods   I'm not sure why, but most renters seem to think that there's a built-in grace period for paying the rent. "It says it's due on the first, but I don't really have to give it over until the fifth," I've been told by numerous students with great conviction (and limited information).

This simply isn't true. The date on the lease is the date the money is due. Sure, your landlord might not do anything if you're one or two days late, but that doesn't mean you aren't technically breaking a term of the contract. The only exception to this is when your due date falls on a weekend or a federal holiday. Generally, rent paid by the next business day is considered to be timely.

Late Fees   Most landlords will impose a fee if you ever pay your rent late. Generally these fees are minor and are only meant as an annoyance to push you to pay on time. But in some instances they cross the line of legality.

First, if there is no late-fee clause in your lease, your landlord cannot impose one. However, most leases do include a clause that calls for late fees—so the majority of renters have to live with the reality of paying a fine when they send their rent check off a week late.

Still, every state in the country requires that late fees, and the circumstances in which they come due, be reasonable. What does "reasonable" mean? It varies from state to state, but if your landlord attempts to charge a fee more than 5 percent of your monthly rent, it's probably unreasonable.

So what should you do if your landlord is attempting to impose an unreasonable late fee? Unless the fee is really out of line, it may not be worth the fight. Use your head—creating ill will over a few dollars probably isn't a wise move.

The best way to make sure you don't get boned by an inordinate late payment penalty is not to agree to one (or always pay your rent on time). Before signing, check to see how much you'll have to pay if you're not on time. If it's more than 4 or 5 percent of the monthly rental fee, ask for it to be changed. Politely tell the landlord that, while you don't plan on ever paying late, the fee is excessive. Point out that fees over 5 percent are routinely struck down in court and ask that it be adjusted. Chances are she'll knock it down a bit.

You can also try this approach after you've signed the lease, or even after you've been hit with the fee itself. But you'll have a much lower chance of success.

SECURITY DEPOSITS

Roughly half the states in the country have laws that limit security deposits. Most cite either one or two months' rent as the acceptable amount. In the states that don't have these laws, the landlord is free to charge whatever he wants, but market factors usually keep things in check—anyone who demands a security deposit equivalent to six months' rent would probably have some trouble finding a tenant.

Chances are your landlord knows what the limit is (or what he can get away with if he's in a nonregulated state) better than you do. So unless he's asking for more than two months' rent, there's probably not much you can do about it. Still, if you think you're being had, it's not a bad idea to check your state's laws. Look in your phone book's government section for a housing authority or building authority in your county. They'll be able to help you with your state and local landlord–tenant laws.

Even if your landlord has a right to ask for a deposit, it doesn't mean you can't haggle a bit. If it's more than you can afford—or simply more than you want to hand over—ask him to reduce it. Try to give him a reason to cut you a break. Show him great references from past landlords or your high GPA. If that fails, ask if you can pay it off in installments over the course of the rental.

Some states, roughly one-third, also require that the landlord put the security deposit in an interest-bearing account and give the interest over to the tenant. Regardless of your state's law, it's never a bad idea to ask your landlord for documentation that shows where your money's gone.

Getting Your Security Deposit Back Of course, most of us never give the security deposit a second thought—until it's time to try to get it back. Then we're mad as hell when it arrives minus a $300 "excessive cleaning charge." This is an area where college students perennially get screwed over. And it's totally unnecessary. By taking a few proactive steps, you can significantly increase your chances of getting the full amount returned.

WHAT CAN YOUR LANDLORD LAWFULLY DEDUCT? Your landlord can use your deposit to return the rental to the condition it was in on the day you moved in. This can mean cleaning, repairing, or replacing things. The deposit can also be used to cover unpaid back rent or, if you move out early, future rent (see "Breaking Your Lease" below). Most deductions fall into the cleaning and repairing categories.

But the security deposit can't be used for damages that are normal wear and tear—degradation of the condition of the apartment from its standard and intended uses. Example: The wear of your carpet from a party where you had a few friends over to watch a movie is "normal wear and tear." The damage to the carpet (and walls, ceilings, and everything else in your apartment) from a keg party with a band, a foam pit, and 250 guests in your one-bedroom apartment probably isn't.

Document the Move-In Condition   Clearly, the best way to ensure that you don't pay for someone else's holes in the wall is to show that they're, well, someone else's holes in the wall. So be sure to document the exact condition of the apartment when you move in. If your landlord provides an inventory sheet, fill it out carefully and completely. And don't be afraid to write in the margins if there's damage that doesn't fit into one of the designated categories.

If you aren't asked to perform an inventory, do one on your own. Go through every room in the place with a fine-tooth comb and note every last piece of the damage. If there's anything particularly distressing, it's not a bad idea to take a picture or two. Send a copy to your landlord. That way he'll be on notice.

BE SMART ABOUT MOVE-OUT

The vast majority of deposit deductions are made because of cleaning issues, not wear and tear. The best thing you can do to get your money back is clean the place really thoroughly. Rent a steam cleaner ($20 at the supermarket), mop the floors, and, most importantly, remove every last bit of your stuff. Chances are if the place is sparkling, the remnants of your mishaps won't get noticed.

Second, don't let a landlord charge you for the full replacement cost of something that was old and grungy when you moved in. Say you accidentally burned a big hole in the carpeting. You definitely ruined it. But it was in bad shape when you moved in; it probably only had one or two years left in it anyway. Your landlord might try to hit you with the total cost of recarpeting the room. Legally you're only responsible for the cost of those one or two years of carpet life you took off the end. How do you calculate that? Simple math. If a carpet costs $600 to replace and usually lasts five years, then a year's use costs about $120. The same reasoning goes for holes in the walls and scratches on the floor. Before you pay for anything to be totally redone, find out the last time the place was painted or the floors were refinished. If replacement was due, refuse to pay any more than your fair share.

Finally, be a bit proactive about the whole process. A month before you move out, send a letter to your landlord detailing what you plan to do on

Your Lawyer Says:

BE CAREFUL ABOUT YOUR LAST MONTH'S RENT

It might seem like a good idea to shortcut this whole process by not paying your last month's or last month and half's rent. But it's a gamble that comes with some risks. First, college landlords are ready, at the drop of a hat, to move for eviction. Withhold your rent without notice and you can expect a lawsuit. And in some states that kind of action is specifically illegal. Try a security deposit change-up and you'll get fined. The bottom line: It's almost always best to play by the rules.

move-out day. Tell her that you'll steam-clean the carpets, scour the floors and the kitchen, remove all of your belongings, and so forth, and that you'll expect your full deposit back. If she doesn't respond, you'll be on strong legal footing to sue in small-claims court for any unwarranted deductions. In any case, it will put her on notice that you know your rights and ought not to be messed with.

Repairs and Maintenance

Over the course of a year in even the nicest apartments, something's going to go wrong. And even the most conscientious landlord drops the ball on fixing things from time to time.

YOUR LANDLORD HAS A DUTY TO PERFORM ALL MAJOR REPAIRS

In every state in the nation, renters are entitled to a safe and habitable home regardless of how much the apartment costs or whether or not the repairs needed to be done when you signed the lease. This right, however, only extends to the basic requirements of a livable home—things like hot and cold running water, heat, sturdy walls, a roof that doesn't leak, and the absence of dangerous substances like lead paint or asbestos. It doesn't cover anything cosmetic or not altogether necessary to make the apartment livable. This concept is called the **implied warrant of habitability** and it basically means that by renting the apartment or home to you, the landlord has guaranteed that the place is, indeed, habitable.

So what does habitable mean? The answer is a little tricky. Certainly landlords are required to keep the building or apartment free of violations of all applicable sanitation and housing codes. In practical terms, these codes are relatively similar in every state and cover similar situations regardless of where you live. But regardless of code coverage, some problems denote inhabitable conditions: A toilet that won't flush in a one-bathroom

Off-Campus Housing

Your Lawyer Says:

WHEN SAFETY'S AT STAKE, ACT FAST

Your landlord is responsible for maintaining the safety of your rental unit. But if you think you're at risk, don't hesitate to take matters into your own hands. Certainly call your landlord and see if she can solve the problem quickly, but if she hesitates or is unavailable, consider arranging things on your own and asking to deduct the cost from your rent. Being safe is always more important than being legally right.

apartment and no hot water are problems that a landlord would have to fix in every jurisdiction. Many states also prohibit such behaviors as storing refuse in public areas or having insufficient ventilation.

The duty of your landlord to provide a *safe* home is also relatively universal. That means that your landlord needs to take action to stop dangerous activities (such as drug dealing, which almost always brings dangerous side effects) in your building. He's also required to fix problems that physically compromise your safety (such as a broken lock or dead bolt on the front door).

THE ABOVE RIGHT ONLY APPLIES TO DAMAGES CAUSED BY "NORMAL WEAR AND TEAR"

Now hang on a minute before you decide to host your college's first-ever indoor bonfire party. This warrant of habitability doesn't mean that you can do whatever you want to wreck the place, then call your landlord and have him clean up the mess. In fact, the landlord is only responsible for repairs that result from—you guessed it—"normal wear and tear."

Furthermore you, as a tenant, have certain repair and maintenance responsibilities that you must meet yourself. If a major repair needs to be done because you didn't keep up with your end of the bargain, your landlord isn't responsible. So what are your duties? They are basically what you would imagine. You need to keep the apartment, and its plumbing fixtures, as safe and clean as their condition allows; fix things that you break; dispose of all waste (garbage, rubbish, and other refuse) in a safe and sanitary manner; use all fixtures (such as appliances, heating and ventilation systems, and electrical outlets) in the proper manner; and, in most places, notify your landlord in a reasonable amount of time when something major breaks.

YOUR LANDLORD MAY ALSO HAVE TO MAKE MINOR REPAIRS

Most of the repairs that tenants need performed don't fall into the "major" category. More often we want our landlords to repair annoying

dripping faucets, repaint dirty (or very, very ugly) walls, or something similarly trifling. Clearly these types of repairs do not affect the habitability of your apartment. Still, there may be ways for you to put the burden on your landlord. First, check your lease or rental agreement. Often rental contracts will include promises made by the landlord to repair specific or general parts of the rental. Further, if the lease mentions that certain items, such as a washing machine, cable TV, or use of a community pool, are included in the rental fee, the landlord has made an implied promise to keep those items in working order and should repair them.

Second, sometimes local building codes will, in addition to covering the major items like hot water and structural integrity, set standards for the more minor aspects of your rental such as the number of electrical outlets each room should have and other lesser details. Check your local code. Again, your county's or city's housing authority should be able to help you find your way.

Finally, look at the ad you responded to when you rented the apartment (if you still have it). If it listed specific features, you have a right to them. Such an advertisement acts essentially as a contract. By advertising the feature the landlord has promised to keep that feature in working order. For example, if the ad for your apartment said "Cable TV Included!" your landlord is responsible for keeping your cable working.

HOW TO GET YOUR LANDLORD TO MAKE REPAIRS

Just because your landlord is legally responsible for a repair doesn't mean it's going to be easy to get him to make it. It's probably going to take a bit of prodding on your part.

Asking is the first step. Start with a call. Then if you don't get anywhere, send a letter. Be sure to follow up on any promises made in writing, too. Hopefully a few phone calls and letters explaining the situation are all it will take. But if that doesn't get the job done, you might have to take the next step.

Withholding Rent   Rent withholding is a dangerous game, and I don't suggest doing it without help. The basic theory is pretty simple. You refuse to pay the rent until your landlord makes the needed repairs. Of course, in practice it's much more complicated.

First, this measure can only be used for major repairs—ones that interfere with the livability of the rental. Second, it's only legally allowed in specific states and under certain circumstances. In the states that do allow it, there are strict rules about how it's to be done. Usually you don't get to "withhold" the rent. You have to give it to the court, or put it in an escrow account.

In the states where it's not explicitly allowed via statute, withholding is even more of a gamble. You have to operate a bit outside of the law to make it work by withholding the rent and then, when your landlord tries to evict you, using the unmade repairs as a defense.

Off-Campus Housing

No matter what kind of state you live in, this is not something for the legally inexperienced. There are plenty of places to find help. Big universities usually have off-campus housing offices that can assist you. Or there may be a legal clinic in a nearby town that could give you some guidance. You could even hire a local attorney. It should only take an hour or two of her time to help you out.

Repair and Deduct   Repairing and deducting is the little brother of withholding. Its theory is just as simple. You pay for needed repairs out of your own pocket, then deduct the cost from the next month's rent. Legally, it's not quite as complicated as withholding and the potential consequences aren't as dire. Still, I wouldn't do it without representation of some sort.

Like withholding, it's only allowed in some states—roughly half. And again, it's really only allowed for remedying habitability problems. Most states also put a limit on the amount you can spend—an amount equivalent to one month's rent no more than two times a year, for example.

Your Lawyer Says:

A CAREFUL THREAT CAN WORK WONDERS

You may not be prepared to jump through the legal hoops that withholding or repairing and deducting require. But your landlord doesn't know that. If you seemed to have reached a dead end in your negotiations, it's never a bad idea to send a certified letter that outlines your "intentions" to withhold. The simple fact that you know about those options may be enough to stimulate some action on your landlord's part.

Privacy in Your Apartment

Your home is your palace, and your landlord needs to treat it that way. Or at least he has to be careful about dropping in too often. The law sets forth pretty specific guidelines about when and why landlords can invade their tenants' privacy and enter their apartments.

WHEN CAN YOUR LANDLORD ENTER?

Landlords can always enter your apartment if you give them permission to do so. Many leases include provisions for a walk-through a few times a year to inspect for damages or needed repairs. If you're lucky enough to have a landlord who asks to come in and look for things to fix: Invite him in for a cup of coffee and show him your leaky faucet. Of course, if the visits are excessive to the point of being harassing (e.g., every other day instead of twice a year), you might want to take some action.

A landlord can also enter your place if there's an emergency. He has a right to come in and protect his property, so if the pipes burst or the electrical work is starting fires, he can come in without giving you notice to patch things up.

In the case of less dire repairs, he (or a contractor he hired) can come in, but he needs to give you notice. Most states require at least twenty-four hours, but it varies. Some call for two full days while others simply require that the notice be "reasonable"—which probably translates to somewhere between twenty and thirty hours.

Use your head before you take the hard line on these laws. If you've been asking for the landlord to replace the crappy showerhead in your bathroom for months and he sends a plumber over with only a few hours' notice, you might want to waive your rights in order to get the job done. I would.

Finally, if you're moving out or if your landlord's selling the building, you've got to accommodate his efforts to re-rent or sell the place. He's entitled to enter for a reasonable number of showings to prospective tenants, buyers, bankers, or mortgage offices. This doesn't mean that you have to make the apartment available to hundreds of tours or host an open house every weekend. But you can't impede his ability to move his unit. Use your common sense and only allow reasonable entry.

STEP OFF, BIYATCH: GETTING YOUR LANDLORD TO RESPECT YOUR PRIVACY

If you think that your landlord's overstepping her privacy bounds, there are really only two things you can do: complain or sue.

Usually a forceful complaint will do the trick. This is especially true if it's someone other than the owner that's bugging you—like the superintendent. Often owners don't know everything that's going on in their buildings. So a phone call to tip them off to the indiscretions will probably solve things.

But if it's the owner that's the problem, you're probably going to have a more difficult time of it. You should probably try a frank discussion with her first. But I think it's wise to start putting things in writing and sending letters as soon as the problem starts. If things do escalate to a lawsuit, you'll want to have as much proof about your requests as possible.

So send a letter outlining your complaints and ask that the invasions stop. Let her know that you understand your rights and that you'll take legal action if necessary. It might also be worth your time to research the specific laws that govern privacy in your state and quote them.

You should do everything you can to work things out at this level because after this you really have no choice but to lawyer up and sue. And, frankly, that's not much of an option. There are a number of potential causes of action—invasion of privacy, breach of contract, trespass. But they're all pretty hard to prove in court except in the most extreme cases. And a win in court won't necessarily make your life easier. You'll have to live with a really pissed-off landlord for the rest of your lease. And you can be sure that you won't be able to renew and live there for another year when the term ends.

Breaking Your Lease

Sometimes you need to leave your place before the agreed move-out date. Maybe you're transferring. Maybe there's been a change in your budget and you can no longer afford to live on your own. Maybe you simply can't stand another month with your annoying roommates. Whatever the reason, you'll need to step carefully to avoid major problems.

If you've rented your house or apartment under a rental agreement, you shouldn't have much of a problem. The agreement itself should spell out in detail the steps you'll need to take to terminate the contract. Generally thirty days' notice to the landlord, in writing, will be required. So give the notice, wait it out, then hit the road.

But if you're locked into a long-term lease, the process is going to be a bit more of a hassle. What you'll be doing is called breaking the lease. In essence, you'll be breaching the contract you have with the landlord—the contract where you agreed to pay the full rent for the term of the lease. So, technically, you're liable for all twelve months of rent. But it won't necessarily turn out that badly. You'll probably end up paying an extra month or two's rent. But if you're smart—and a little bit lucky—that should be it.

The first thing you should do is so simple, many tenants don't think to try it. Ask your landlord if he'll let you out of the agreement. You never know. He may hate you and be dying to get rid of you. Or maybe he's been planning on selling the place and was hoping to vacate it anyway. Maybe he's just a really great guy and doesn't feel like sticking it to a poor college student. He'll probably say no, but it's worth a try.

If he does say no, you'll have no choice but to pull the trigger. So tell him that you're really sorry, but you've got to go. It's important to do this as soon as possible because you want to give your landlord as much time as possible to **mitigate his damages**. "Mitigate?" you may be asking yourself. "Whaaa?"

Here's the deal: When a tenant breaks a lease, the landlord doesn't just get to sit back and collect the rent on the empty apartment until the end of the lease. He has to take reasonable steps to re-rent the place. That means advertising and showing the unit. He can, and I'm sure will, pass the costs for doing these things on to you. But he has to do them.

But the law only requires reasonable steps, not superhuman effort. In college rental markets that may not be enough to move the unit quickly—especially if you break the lease out of sync with the academic schedule. So you need to do everything in your power to facilitate the process. Give your landlord as much notice as you possibly can. Make the place look nice when prospective renters come around. Try to find your own replacement. Because the sooner your apartment gets rented, the more money you save.

CONSTRUCTIVE EVICTION

The above rules apply if you move out for your own reasons. If you break your lease because your landlord has breached the warrant of habitability, then you're not liable for any future rent. This is called constructive eviction. Of course, you have to give your landlord a chance to remedy the problems. You can't just move out because the toilet broke that morning. But if your apartment needs major repairs and your landlord refuses to make them despite your requests, then she's, effectively, evicted you.

Expect a lawsuit if you try to move out under this theory. You'll want to be able to stand up in court and prove that it, indeed, was a constructive eviction. So keep careful records that document both the problems with your apartment and your unanswered requests that they be repaired.

Subletting

There are two ways to sign your apartment over to someone else. The first is called **assigning your lease**. Legally speaking, this is the cleaner of the two methods. The original tenant ends their relationship with the landlord, and a new tenant takes it over. Technically, it's not a sublet. It's a transfer of the contractual obligation. But since it involves one person taking another's apartment, it's often generically called a sublet.

If you don't plan on returning to your apartment after the sublet is over, this is absolutely the best way to pass off your responsibility. It takes you, the original tenant, entirely out of the picture. So if anything goes wrong in the future, it's between the new tenant and the landlord. You won't be involved at all.

Most leases include a clause that prohibits assignments without the express permission of the landlord. So you'll have to ask permission. Many landlords will refuse, especially those in college towns. They're under no obligation to grant your request, and they don't want to be bothered with the hassle of checking out the new tenant.

This is why most apartments that change hands mid-lease do so as an actual **sublet** or sublease. Standard leases usually require the landlord's okay for sublets, too. But because their original tenant remains bound, they're much more lenient about granting them.

In a true sublet, the original tenant enters into a separate agreement with the new occupants—called subtenants. The legal relationship then works like a ladder. The tenant is bound to the landlord. The subtenants are bound to the tenant. Legal matters have to follow the same hierarchy. If the subtenants don't pay the rent, the landlord can only sue the person he has the contractual relationship with—the tenant. The tenant can then sue the subs.

Sublets are most common in situations where the original tenant is absent. Students go home for the summer and let their apartments to dorm dwellers for the summer term. But this isn't always the case. Roommates can also enter a tenant-subtenant relationship. One roommate signs the lease with the landlord, then the other roommates sign subleases with him.

At some point in your renting life, you're probably going to have or be a subtenant. You shouldn't go into either side of this lightly. Treat the relationship as carefully as you would one with a "real" landlord. And certainly don't ever enter one without a written contract. Use one of the sample subleases that abound online.

Roommate Issues

By and large, the vast majority of college housing problems come from within the apartment itself. I am, of course, talking about roommates. After living together for only a few months, people you used to call your best friends turn into "that ass I live with" or "the slob that never does his dishes." This is a book about the law, so you're on your own with the dishes and most other niggling roommate annoyances. There are, however, a few drastic roommate situations that do require legal knowledge.

WHAT TO DO WHEN SOMEONE WALKS OUT

Your first instinct, when a roommate skips out, will be to think of revenge, to focus your energy at going after the deadbeat and making her pay what she owes. These are good thoughts. But your first priority, as a remaining roommate, should be to preserve your relationship with your landlord.

As with most things, communication—early communication—will be the key. I suggest contacting your landlord as soon as possible and letting him know what's going on. Tell him straight up that one of your roommates has walked out on their responsibility and ask him for some patience.

He'll probably ask you what your plans are regarding the apartment. Are you going to stay on? Or are you going to have to leave, too? So be prepared to give, at least, a preliminary answer. This conversation might also be a good time to gauge the likely consequences of your choices. Ask a few questions of your own. Will your landlord be a hard-ass if you break your lease? Is he willing to be a bit lenient about the rent or even reduce it until you can find a replacement?

After you've covered your bases with your landlord, it's time to go after your former roommate (and, I assume, former friend). The situation operates essentially the same way as a broken lease. Whether she signed the lease as a cotenant or subtenant, your roommate made a legally enforceable promise to you. (You *did* record your agreement with your roommate in writing, didn't you?) By walking out, she's breached that contract and you can go after her.

I would start with by sending a letter, via certified mail, that states your claim and threatens a lawsuit if things aren't made right. Send a copy both to your former housemate and to her parents (they're much more likely to pay up).

If that doesn't work, file a claim in your local small-claims court. I know that sounds intimidating, but small-claims courts are designed specifically with nonlawyers in mind. It's really easy to fill out the forms and start an action. And you won't have to spend much time at all preparing your case. All you'll need to do is show the judge your lease, say "Your honor, she walked out," and you'll win.

One final note: Just like a landlord you'll need to take reasonable steps to mitigate your damages. So do your best to find a replacement or minimize any other ill effects of your roommate's departure. Otherwise you'll have a hard time holding her responsible in court.

GETTING RID OF A CRAPPY ROOMMATE

Eviction laws are set up in favor of the tenant. They have to be. Otherwise it would be far too easy for landlords to extort their tenants with ongoing threats of being kicked out. So evicting someone under the most extreme of circumstances isn't easy to do. When the evictee is one of your roommates, it's even harder.

In order to legally evict someone, you first have to go to court to prove that she's done something that justifies the termination of the lease. Nonpayment of the rent is the most common reason, but any material breach of the agreement will suffice. In a landlord-tenant relationship, this is pretty clear-cut. But with cotenants it can be a bit sticky. As you know, if you've all signed the lease, then you're all jointly and severally liable for meeting your contractual obligations. If your roommate fails to pay her half of the rent, but you cover for her by paying double, there really hasn't been a breach. Sure, she may have screwed you over, but technically the terms of the contract have been met.

The logistics get a bit simpler in a tenant-subtenant situation. If you're the tenant and your deadbeat roommate is your sub, her nonpayment is a breach of the agreement between the two of you. It will be much easier to move for eviction in front of a judge. This is the one major advantage to being the sole tenant on the lease and having your roommates sign sub-lease agreements: expediency in showing someone the door.

But a legal eviction isn't the best way to go. For starters, you'll probably need a lawyer to help you make it happen—which could cost you more than simply paying double rent for a year. I would try a straight-up conversation first. Just sit down and talk through why the arrangement isn't working out and ask her to leave. Give her a specific move-out date and cite the reasons that you could, if you wanted, move for eviction.

If that doesn't work, you may have to be a little more creative. Bribery is often a good way to move someone along. Offer a little cash or a rebate in the last month's rent if she's out by a certain time. Or, if things get really bad, you may want to get your landlord involved. Generally landlords don't want to get in the middle of roommate problems, but you never know. If she's not listening to you, a threatening call or letter from the owner of the building might do the trick.

CHAPTER 17
Money Issues

There's absolutely no reason to pay your bank lots of money for checks with frolicking kittens or cartoon characters on them. Choose the simplest, cheapest ones they offer—and ask if you can have them for free. If you must have SpongeBob SquarePants on your checks, buy them online. They'll be about half price there.

Chapter Contents

Banking, and all financial dealings for that matter, are sort of like plumbing—when everything's working fine you hardly think about it, but when there's a problem, your whole world turns upside down. Finding out you're out of cash at the wrong time can be just as shocking to the system as a sudden lack of hot water in the shower.

The good news (and the bad news, I suppose) is that there's no real trick to avoiding cash catastrophes—you just have to stay on top of things. Keeping your eye on the money ball is the simple secret to keeping it all together.

Banking

Banks may all seem exactly the same (certainly they seem to all have the same decorator—one with a strange penchant for polished brass and pens on chains). But how they work for you can vary significantly. There are two major areas you should consider when choosing a bank: convenience and account rules.

BANK CONVENIENCE

As a college student, your number one point of interaction with your bank is probably going to be at the ATM. So before you open your college account, go for a long walk and take note of all the ATMs. If there's one bank that has significantly more, it's probably worth serious consideration. You'll save loads of money (in $1.50 increments) over the course of your education.

Also, consider the actual branches. If possible, it might be wise to consider a bank that has branches both near your school *and* near your parents' house. That way, when money's getting thin, all you have to do is ask mom or dad to go downtown and make a deposit. Not everyone will be able to find a bank that operates both at home and at school (or have parents that are willing to funnel beer money into their account on a regular basis), but it's worth looking into.

ACCOUNT RULES

Despite the fact that almost every bank in the country has at one time or another advertised "Totally Free Checking," maintaining a checking account can be expensive. The average person racks up roughly $200 a year in charges.

Your Lawyer Says:

WATCH THE FEES!

If you let them, the bank will gouge you every chance they get, so be clear up front about when and what they're going to charge you. Some common reasons are

- monthly "maintenance" fees
- writing more checks than your account allows in any given month
- using nonsystem ATMs
- overdrafts
- other person's bounced checks (sometimes called a deposit item return fee)
- doing bank business with the teller at the branch rather than via the ATM
- using online banking services

All banks charge fees, but the specific policies can vary significantly.

So evaluate each bank's policies carefully. Take a moment to figure out how you're going to use the bank and make sure the fee structure jibes with your needs.

STUDENT ACCOUNTS

A lot of banks (especially those near campuses) offer special "student" or "no frills" checking accounts. They cost a lot less, but they often come with severe restrictions, like limits on the number of transactions you can make a month. They're worth checking out, but just because they bear the label "student" doesn't mean they're right for you.

OPENING AN ACCOUNT

Once you've decided which bank is going to keep all your swag for you, it's time to, literally, sign on the dotted line. If at all possible, open the account up a few months before you start school. Some banks put restrictions on new accounts that, among other things, extend the time it takes for a check to clear. You don't want to be waiting around to have access to cash your first few months of school.

And don't waste your hard-earned money on fancy checks with gold leaf and marbled accents. Check printing is one of the areas where banks really take advantage. So ask to see the simplest and cheapest checks the bank offers. In fact, ask for your checks for free; often they'll waive the printing fee just for the asking.

And if their prices are outright ridiculous, remember, you can go elsewhere to get your checks printed. There are countless places online that print checks up at much cheaper rates than the banks themselves. All you need is your account and your bank's routing number. This is an especially good option for those of you who absolutely have to have the checks with

Money Issues

kitty cats or butterflies on them. Those kinds of checks are always a humongous rip-off at the bank.

BREAKING THE BANK: MAKING SURE THEY DON'T TAKE ADVANTAGE OF YOU

Here are my two simple rules for interacting with your bank. Number one: Keep a close eye on what's going on. Number two: If you don't like something, complain.

Show Me the Money

There's absolutely no way to know whether or not you're getting screwed unless you know what's happening in your account. This means: When you get your statement in the mail, open it and scrutinize it. Reconcile the withdrawals and deposits with your records. And keep a close watch on instances where the bank itself has charged you a fee.

Do not look at the balance, think, "Hmm, is that how much money I have in my account?" and move on.

If you're technologically inclined, an even better way to keep track is via online banking. Do what I do: Make a commitment to go online and check your accounts twice a

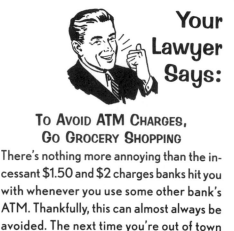

Your Lawyer Says:

To Avoid ATM Charges, Go Grocery Shopping

There's nothing more annoying than the incessant $1.50 and $2 charges banks hit you with whenever you use some other bank's ATM. Thankfully, this can almost always be avoided. The next time you're out of town and need cash, instead of looking for an ATM, look for a grocery store. Most take ATM cards at the register and will give you extra cash free of charge. So go buy a pack of gum and get $40 cash back. 35¢ is a lot less than $2. And you get gum!

month—the first and the fifteenth. Then, on those days, jump online and check out what's been going on.

Give Me Back the Money   If you see a charge on your statement, complain until someone reverses it. Call them on the phone and ask questions like, "Can you explain this $25 service charge to me?" Then outright say, "I'd like it reversed, please." More often than not, if you manage to pull off the right combination of charming and stern, they'll give you your cash back. I can't tell you how many charges I've gotten reversed simply by being nice to the woman who answers the phone at my bank's 1-800 number. Some may say flirting for money is immoral. I think charging a $30 service fee is worse.

Avoiding Overdraft Charges   For a minimal yearly fee, you can get $500 to $10,000 worth of overdraft protection from your bank. The system works almost exactly like a credit card—if you write checks for more than you have in your account, the bank pays the amount on credit. It's a good idea to get at least a few hundred dollars' worth of protection. It will save you money in the long run.

One word of caution: Do not use overdraft protection like a credit card. The interest rates on these accounts are often outrageously high. So if you need to buy something on credit, get a Visa card. Leave the full amount of your overdraft credit there to do what it's supposed to.

UNCOLLECTED FUNDS Depending on where a check you deposit is from (out of state, from your bank or another, etc.), your bank may not make that money available to you for a number of days—which could mean trouble if you try to draw on those funds too early.

If you need the money sooner, ask the branch manager to release the funds. He'll probably give you a hard time. He'll tell you that the federal government regulates how long the checks are held. He may even show you a little chart with check routing numbers and corresponding holding limits. This is an outright lie—the federal government regulates how long banks are *allowed* to hold checks, not how long they *have* to. The bank can release the cash any time they want. So call the manager on this lie and politely ask for your money.

The whole check-holding process should improve in the near future. In October 2004, a law entitled the Check Clearing for the 21st Century Act (Check 21 for short) went into effect. Check 21 makes it easier for banks to transfer money electronically, eliminating the need for original paper checks and making processing times much faster. Check 21 didn't change the maximum hold limits (because banks aren't required to switch to electronic processing, they're just allowed to). But, depending on how Check 21 works out, a change in that law may soon be coming.

Credit Cards: The Siren Song of "Free Money"

Some of the smartest people I know have at one time or another gotten into credit card trouble. When I was in law school, I ran up a $6,000 debt buying important things like beer and fancy meals for me and my friends. A lawyer I knew in Manhattan got herself $30,000 in the hole on cashmere sweaters and leather jackets. Another, quite inexplicably, found himself owing Visa more than $12,000. He hadn't been paying attention to his spending for a few months, and it all just crept up on him. In fact, almost everyone I know has at some point overspent on a credit card.

The system is set up to encourage this kind of stupidity. The credit card companies make money when you carry a debt. So they grant obscenely high limits to people who have no business walking around with $10,000 of

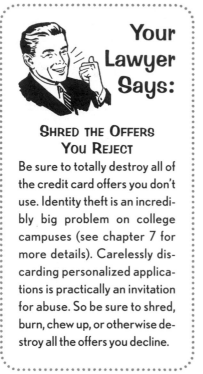

spending power. Properly used, credit cards can be a great tool for managing cash flow problems. But I'd be negligent if I didn't start this section out with a few gruesome Visa tales because misused credit can truly be the stuff of horror stories.

CHOOSING A CREDIT CARD

If you don't have a credit card, college is a good time to get your first. You'll have plenty of offers to choose from, and using it well will help build your credit history. To find the best deal, just hang on to every offer you get for a few weeks—pick them up around campus, keep the ones from the mail, and so forth. In almost no time, you'll have accumulated a pretty big pile. Somewhere in that mountain of letters and pamphlets is the right card for you.

Don't Get Too Excited about Being Pre-Approved Many of these offers will tell you that you're one of the lucky pre-approved customers. Don't buy into this crap and feel special. Just because you've been pre-approved doesn't mean you'll be issued a credit card. All it means is that you met some initial criteria for receiving the offer. For you, just being a college student was probably enough to get on the mailing list. These offers aren't necessarily bad, but watch out. The credit card companies often use pre-approval as part of a bait-and-switch scheme. They pre-approve you for a card with very attractive terms, then issue you one with a much higher interest rate or fees.

Evaluating the Terms

INTEREST RATES The card with the lowest initial rate may not be the best deal. Some cards have introductory rates that increase automatically after four to six months. Others have rates that skyrocket if you miss one or more payments or go over your spending limit. The bottom line: Pick a rate that will be the lowest in the long term, not just for the first couple of months.

All interest rates are not created equally. There are three different methods for calculating interest. The most attractive for you is called adjusted balance, where payments that are received during the billing period are subtracted from the balance at the beginning of the billing cycle and new purchases are not included in the calculation. Try to pick a card that uses that method. By all means, avoid cards that use what's called a two-cycle balance calculation. These include the previous month's balance in calculating charges, which means higher payments.

GRACE PERIODS   The grace period is the amount of time between the close of your billing period and the day the payment is due. It's usually thirty days, but can be more or less. If you're the type of person who pays off their bill every month (and by the way, everyone should be the type of person that pays off their bill every month), then this will be an extremely important feature of your card. A ten-day difference in the amount of time your credit card is willing to float you can make a big difference.

FEES   Next, read the fine print and make sure there aren't any hidden charges or fees. Actually, first make sure there aren't any fees out in the open. Don't ever get a card that charges you an annual membership fee. Credit cards make money every time you use their card. They get a fee of anywhere from 1 to 2.5 percent of the purchase amount from the merchant. This is plenty, and they know it. If you already have a card that charges such a fee, call them up and ask them to waive it—they will, without much of a fight at all. If you're applying for a card, only consider ones without the annual shaft.

Then take a look at the other fees that are associated with the card. Are cash advances subject to an exorbitant finance charge? Will there be late fees if you're a few days late? Will they charge you fifty bucks if your zip code ends in an eight? Credit card companies are very creative at figuring out new and interesting ways to charge you penalties. The latest shaft: Many card agreements now include a clause that allows the company to change your rate based on your behaviors with other creditors. In effect this means that you could see a spike in your interest rate based on the fact that you were late with your payment on *another* credit card.

THE SCHUMER BOX   Finally, don't be fooled by the Schumer Box—a disclosure chart that credit card offers must include by law. It contains most of the important information about the card, but not all of it. It's a good way to get the general idea of the offer, but to really know what the terms of the card are, you have to actually read the fine print.

Of course, if you have any trouble understanding the terms, call the company's 1-800 number and ask. They'll be a bit biased, but they'll be able to help you figure out what the actual deal is.

How Much Credit Do I Need?   I have friends who walk around with four or five credit cards in their wallets. Whenever they make a purchase, they do some weird mental calculations, trying to remember which card has how much left on it. Then, they tentatively slide one across the counter, hoping they've chosen the right account. If you're playing this kind of credit roulette game with your cards, you're using them incorrectly.

Everyone's finances are different, so look at how much you're likely to spend a month, then add a few thousand dollars for emergencies—needing a last-minute plane ticket, medical care that your insurance will eventually pay for, etc. I'm sure many of you live much more extravagantly than I do, but I would think a limit of $5,000 to $7,000 would be *plenty* for almost any college student.

And do yourself a favor and get as little extra credit as possible. Having more credit than you could ever pay off will bring you nothing but trouble.

USING YOUR CREDIT CARD

Approach your relationship with your credit card company the same way you deal with your bank: Keep your eye on what's going on and complain, complain, complain when you don't like something. Aside from that, here are a few more specific suggestions on how to tame the plastic beast:

Forget the Whole Idea of Minimum Payments "Minimum payments" are designed to stretch your indebtedness out as long as possible and, in turn, make you pay the credit card company a shitload of interest.

Here's an eye-opening example: Stick to an average card's minimum payment schedule, and it would take you more than 20 years to pay off a $2,000 debt. And you'd pay more than $2,500 in interest on the loan. That's in addition to paying back the $2,000 you borrowed in the first place.

Use your own definition of minimum payment—as much as you can afford until you've paid the damn card off. Using theirs will keep you in credit-card-debt hell for eternity.

Keep a Close Watch on Your Account As soon as you start using your credit card, the company will probably try to change things up on you. So watch them like a hawk. One of the most common ploys is to simply, without warning, raise your interest rate. Believe it or not, credit card companies do not have to inform you in advance if they're going to change your rate. They'll definitely raise your rate if you miss a payment. But you don't have to do anything quite that obvious to raise their ire (and your rate). Making a big purchase on another card could be enough to skew your credit rating and justify the hike.

Charges, including the infamous annual fee, may also unexpectedly appear on your bill—even if the initial terms of the card said that there would be no such fee. Sometimes a company will even inexplicably lower your credit limit then slam you with both penalty charges and an interest rate hike as a penalty for going over that new limit.

Don't Take the "Skip a Payment" Bait Credit card companies often do this around the holidays, when cardholders are feeling pinched for cash. They'll say it's okay for you to skip a payment—they'll even put "$0.00" in the little minimum payment box.

It's tempting, but it's a really bad idea. If you take the bait and send nothing but your best wishes for the New Year, you'll open yourself up to all sorts of extra fees and payments.

For starters, the credit card company will just tack the interest you would have paid this month on to your existing balance. This means they get to charge you even more interest on your next bill, which means a longer repayment period and, in the long run, hundreds of extra dollars out of your pocket and into their coffers.

Second, if you pushed the credit envelope, skipping a payment may put you over your spending limit. This means a penalty fee and, most likely, a significant increase in your annual percentage rate. Again, the ultimate result is more money out of your accounts and into theirs.

The bottom line: If there's any way you can manage it, make the payment. Even if you can't swing what you usually send in, try to pay off some amount—2.5 percent of your balance is usually just enough to cover the interest and make a small dent in the principal. That should keep you safe.

Bitch, Bitch, Bitch   Just as with the bank, if your creditor does anything to you that you don't like, call them on it. Dial the 1-800 number and bitch and moan until you get some satisfaction.

Credit Ratings: What Kind of Credit Grades Have You Earned?

Before a company extends you credit, they'll take a look at your financial history to see what kind of risk you are. If you've totally screwed up in the past, they may only offer you a loan or a credit card at the highest interest rates. Or they may refuse you a credit line altogether. If you've been squeaky clean and done everything right, they'll give you the sweetest deal possible.

There are two tools major tools they'll use to evaluate you: credit reports and a Fico score.

CREDIT REPORTS

A credit report is a detailed history that shows your borrowing habits for the past seven years. It's the financial equivalent of a report card. It shows all of your financial accounts, past and present—credit cards, bank accounts, mortgages, department store accounts, etc.—and all of the activity associated with them. Most significantly, it's a record of your payment histories. If you've ever paid a bill late, it will be noted in your credit report.

Credit reports also show any collections and court actions relating to your finances, like tax judgments and bankruptcies. And it includes a

Money Issues

listing of the businesses that have requested your report—in other words all the places where you've applied for credit.

Most information stays on your report for seven years. Bankruptcies stay for ten.

There are three companies that collect and distribute this information: Experian (www.experian.com), Equifax (www.equifax.com), and TransUnion (www.transunion.com). These three companies are commonly referred to as the big three. Because each company operates independently, each probably has different information on you. In fact, your credit could be very good with one and unacceptable with another.

FICO SCORES

If credit reports are report cards, then your Fico Score is your GPA. Named for the Fair Isaac Corporation, your Fico score is your entire credit history reduced to a single number. Fair Isaac takes a credit report from one of the big three and, using mathematical models, turns all of that information into a number between 300 and 850. The higher the score, the more likely a borrower is to pay their bills on time.

HOW TO CHECK THEM?

It should be abundantly clear by now that your credit history and the Fico Scores that are derived from it are very important. Your ability to get any kind of loan depends on the information in them. Not such a huge deal now, but since the information stays on there for so long, what happens now could affect you down the line, when you're trying to get a car loan or a mortgage for your first house.

Your Lawyer Says:

DON'T OVER-APPLY YOURSELF! Every time you apply for credit it shows up on your credit history as an inquiry. Since applying for too much new credit can have an adverse affect on your Fico Score, be careful about your attempts to get it. It's best to make credit applications in a concentrated period of time—Fico scores differentiate between multiple applications for a single loan and applying for numerous credit lines. Of course, checking your own credit doesn't count as an inquiry, so feel free to check it as often as you like.

This means you need to do two things. First: Don't be stupid. Be careful with your credit. Second: Regularly check the information in your reports and challenge all of the negative marks.

It used to be a pain in the ass to check your credit ratings. You had to fill out forms and send formal written requests to the big three. Until 2001 Fico scores weren't released to individuals—they were only for the lenders to see. Today it's not so bad. You can find out everything you need to know in about twenty minutes online. And now, you can do it once a year for free. An amendment to the Fair Credit Reporting Act requires each of the national credit reporting companies to provide you with a free copy of your report, at your request, once every twelve months. The law is being phased in regionally, but by September 2005, it will be in full effect everywhere in the country. If you've already gotten your free credit reports for the year, you can still buy them. They're not expensive—$10 to $15.

Fixing Problems on Your Report   You'll notice that two paragraphs ago I said that you should challenge *all* the negative marks, not just the incorrect ones. I meant what I said. You should challenge anything on your credit report that adversely affects your rating, regardless of whether or not it's true. When you challenge an entry, it places the burden of proof on the entity that reported the activity. They then have thirty days to affirm the mark, or it's erased. So if there's an entry that shows that you paid your Citibank Visa bill ninety days late in 2002 and you challenge it, Citibank has thirty days to offer some proof that this is true. Usually they can affirm the negative information. But a lot of the time they simply don't respond, or at least don't respond in time. This is especially true of smaller companies that may have limited resources or spotty records.

Challenging negative information is extremely easy online. The process varies at each of the three agencies, but it's basically the same. You simply select the entry you want to challenge and complete an online form about why the information is wrong. Don't worry; it's a multiple-choice form— there are pull-down menus with choices like "I never paid this account late" or "This is not my account." And it doesn't really matter what you say, just so long as you challenge it, the burden shifts. So pick whatever strikes your fancy.

You can only challenge entries at the site of the agency that has the information. You'll be offered countless times during this process "3-in-1 plus Fico Scores"—credit reports from all three agencies plus a Fico Score for $5 less than what it would cost you to visit each site. Don't do this. Because lenders may look at any one, or all three, of these reports, you need to clean each up. The 3-in-1 won't allow you to do that. And by all means, don't sign up for one of those credit-monitoring services that try to entice you with a free credit report. They're nearly impossible to terminate, meaning they'll charge you $70 a year for the rest of time.

Watch Out for Credit Repair Scams   There are a number of credit repair companies out there that are making unbelievable claims, stating that they can "repair your bad credit 100 percent guaranteed" or "create a new credit identity legally." Basically it's a load of crap.

Most of these places are absolute scams. They'll ask you to pay hundreds or even thousands of dollars up front, then do nothing at all to improve your credit rating or, even worse, will just disappear with your money.

There are some nonprofit organizations that, for a small fee, can assist you with credit rating problems, but they can't do anything you can't do yourself—check your reports and challenge the negative information. They can also help you develop a repayment plan that fits your means. But even these services aren't entirely on the up-and-up. These agencies are usually funded by the credit card companies themselves and are, therefore, more interested in ensuring that the credit card company gets their money than they are in actually helping you with your problems. Mention the word "bankruptcy" to them and they go crazy.

Tuition and Financial Aid

The subjects of tuition and financial aid are immense. Volumes could be written about federal aid programs alone. Of course, these books would be spectacularly boring—detailing the minutia of the policies, extrapolating figures from the mathematical need models, differentiating between Perkins Restaurants and Perkins Loans, and so on. That level of detail isn't really appropriate here. Most of you have already started school or are, at most, only a few months away from entering. Either way, you have already navigated the rough waters of the FAFSA and have a financial aid package in hand.

Because of this, my discussion of financial aid will be confined to a few distinct areas where legal rights and funding most prominently intersect. For those of you who are in the very early stages of figuring out your aid, I'd like to point you in the direction of another resource—*The Smart Student Guide to Financial Aid*. Available online at www.finaid.org, it covers all of the nuts and bolts of the financial aid process: everything from calculating potential costs to line-by-line instructions for filling out most of the common forms. And it manages to do so without spectacular (or any other sort of) boredom.

RESIDENCY REQUIREMENTS

The Holy Grail of the student at a public university or college is status as an in-state resident. Students at private colleges have nothing much to gain from being declared residents. But at a public school, native standing means a humongous tuition discount. Unfortunately, colleges can, and often do, require fairly ridiculous requirements to prove that you are, truly, an in-stater. Where I went to law school, conventional wisdom was, "Don't even try to declare yourself an in-state student unless you were born here; it's just a waste of time." While that advice was probably a bit dramatic, it wasn't all that far off.

The burden of proof falls on the student in this area, and in most cases there's a lot to prove.

✓ Most states require that the student be domiciled in the state continuously for at least one year before the start of classes, although in some states, such as New York and Tennessee, it's possible to declare residency immediately upon arrival. Utah has one of the toughest waiting period rules. A student must live in Utah for one year prior to the start of classes and must not leave the state for more than 30 days during that year(!).

✓ Minors (under eighteen) and dependents (declared as such on tax returns) will usually be considered residents of the state in which their parents live. In order to buck this assumption, the minor will have to be legally emancipated.

✓ Often the requirements tighten for students who have already started school. Texas, for example, requires that "students who seek reclassification as residents must withdraw from school and be gainfully employed in Texas for 12 months before reentry into an educational institution."

✓ Often an intention to make the state a permanent residence after school—which can be shown by acceptance of an offer of full-time employment or the purchase of a home—will factor in.

To find out what the rules stipulate in your state, visit the College Board's website (www.collegeboard.com). They maintain a state-by-state directory that details the requirements for each public school system.

These issues have been litigated with some regularity. Students have challenged both the rules themselves and their application to specific situations. Unlike other areas of higher-education law, the students win fairly often—about half of the time. So if you really feel like you're getting the shaft, litigation might be an actual option for you. Of course, seeing this type of case through to the bitter end will cost thousands of dollars (probably more than you stand to save through the in-state discount), and it will likely take longer than your entire college education.

Also, by now, most state rules have already been examined by the courts. Meaning that there are few questions left as to what's an acceptable requirement and what would be over-the-top and unconstitutional. Certainly one-year waiting periods and travel prohibitions are perfectly legal.

In practice, this is one of those situations where the best way to win is to play by the rules. If you want the cheaper rate, go online and get a copy of your state's policy. Study it. Learn it. Live it. Find out exactly what they want you to do to prove you are a full-on resident. Then put a plan into action. And by all means be meticulous. Details are of paramount importance in these situations. Remember, the school *wants* to prove that you're not a resident, so they won't cut you any slack.

SCHOLARSHIP RULES

Scholarships sometimes come with rather draconian constraints and restrictions. Usually the requirements are academic in nature—minimum GPAs and the like. But often the requirements seep into the personal arena. The most restrictive ones are usually associated with scholarships funded by religious organizations. It's not uncommon, for example, for the

Money Issues

recipient of a church scholarship to be prohibited from drinking, smoking, or anything else that would result in damnation.

Why can a scholarship donor impose these types of boundaries on your personal life? The simple answer is: Because you agreed to their terms when you took the money. You entered a contract just like any other at that point. For example, no one can come to my house and force me to spend ten hours a day laboring in a coal mine. But if I agree to do so for money, then I either have to go down the shaft or not get paid. You get the drift.

If you find yourself under the thumb of such a group, protect yourself by being informed. Get a copy of the scholarship agreement and see exactly what's forbidden. Take note of any vague terms or conditions that allow the directors or some other people decide about specific behaviors on a case-by-case basis or make rules as they see fit. If the agreement contains that kind of language, you're pretty much beholden to the decision maker. Chances are they won't arbitrarily pull the scholarship out from underneath you, but it's a good thing to know that they can. That way you can be sure to behave yourself when you're in their presence and say nice things to them at cocktail parties.

But no matter what the agreement says, if you want to keep your scholarship, you've got to play by the rules of those who administer it. A wrong step could result in your scholarship not getting renewed or, worse yet, taken away midterm.

SCHOLARSHIP SCAMS

Each year, students and parents are fleeced for more than $100 million through scholarship scams. The swindles come in many guises, but they all have one component in common—they ask for money up front. In fact, any financial aid opportunity that involves an investment of anything more than postage is probably a scam.

Some common ploys are

- ✓ *Loans with fees.* Students are offered an educational loan at an extremely low interest rate. But in order to get the money, they need to send in a processing or application fee. The company takes your fee, but the loan never shows up.
- ✓ *The unexpected scholarship.* Students receive a letter telling them they've won a scholarship or prize they've never applied for. Of course, to claim it they'll need to send the company a redemption fee. The fee goes, and the scholarship never shows.
- ✓ *Guaranteed scholarship searches.* Some companies advertise that, for a fee, they'll cross-reference your information with available scholarships and awards, and they *guarantee* that you'll receive some sort of award. Most just take your money and disappear. In fact, almost any fee-based scholarship service is a waste of money. All of the same information is available for free on the World Wide Web.

✓ *For-profit prizes.* This is the simplest scholarship scam. It's an award that requires the applicant to pay some small fee—$50 or so—to submit an application. These places do give out a few small awards, just to maintain some semblance of legitimacy. But mostly they just keep the money.

Please adopt a rule that you will never send any money to any person or organization that promises you a scholarship. They are almost all scams.

And while we're talking about money for scholarships, it's also a good idea to avoid the whole genre of financial aid consultants. Or at the very least be very careful about engaging one. Some do provide valuable services and can offer some good strategies about maximizing your or your parents' eligibility for aid. But mostly, they can't do anything that you can't do for yourself. Many will try to charge you exorbitant fees to fill out simple forms or for other simple tasks.

DEALING WITH YOUR LOANS

Unfortunately, being awarded a financial aid package—be it loans, scholarships, work study, or a combination thereof—is just the beginning of the process. There will be things to do at every step along the way. And none of it will be fun. You'll also probably be confronted with at least one financial aid surprise during your time at school. And it won't be the good kind. It will be a last-minute notification that some sort of funding has disappeared or is being withheld. When this type of thing happens, I want you do two things:

1. First, calm down. These events are par for the course. They're shocking and scary as hell, but they're not uncommon. It will get worked out. But it will require prompt and careful attention on your part.
2. Go immediately to your school's financial aid office and commence the aforementioned process of working it out.

The Financial Aid Officer, Your First Line of Defense The financial aid office at your school is an unbelievable resource. So use it. They have a professional staff that does nothing but deal with financial aid matters. And, even though sometimes it might not seem like it, they're on your side. They *want* you to be able to pay for school.

But the staff members at these offices are often extremely overworked and underappreciated. And many of them have to spend most of their time dealing with very frustrating companies and people. Spend a few hours trying to get a straight answer out of someone at the Direct Loan Office's 1-800 Center, and you'll have a whole new appreciation for anyone who deals with this stuff for a living.

So the last thing you want to do is become yet another annoyance for whomever you're dealing with. In other words, make them *want* to help you.

Clearing up an aid problem is usually more a matter of tenacity and persistence then anything else. So you need your school's staff to keep your file at the top of the pile and to be willing to put the time in to make things right. The best way to ensure that they won't is to go in and whine or make demands.

Also, be willing to do your share of the work. The people at the aid office will know how to work the system, but they can't be expected to be your personal secretaries. You need to keep on top of all of the documentation. Keep neat files and have copies available to hand over to them. Make it as easy as possible for them to help you.

Going to the Source   Sometimes you'll need to take matters into your own hands and deal directly with the lending agency. Unfortunately, there's no magic formula that will always yield favorable results. But here are some guidelines that will help you wind your way through the mire:

- *Be obstinate.* As I've said above, persistence and tenacity are the keys to getting satisfaction. So be prepared to spend lots of time on hold, have your call dropped, deal with incompetents, and all sorts of other things. Don't let these things stop you. Just keep at it. It's the only way to win.
- *Always work your way up.* Never take a "no" from a person who isn't authorized to tell you "yes." The first person who answers the phone at a call center usually doesn't have the ability or authority to do much more than pull up your file and tell you what's in there. So don't deal with people on this level. Be polite and give them a rough outline of the problem, then say something like, "Can I talk to your supervisor? I think she may be able to help me out." First-line reps are trained to try to avoid bumping calls up, but if you're persistent they will.
- *Take names (and no prisoners).* Always get the name and identification number of whomever you talk to. If possible, also try to get the direct dial number of the upper-level representatives you speak with. Being able to call someone whom you've dealt with before is a huge advantage.
- *Document everything.* Keep a log of all of your communications that includes dates, summaries of each topic that was discussed, and contact information for each person you talked to. It will help you immensely if you're able to say "I talked to James, ID #4572, on May 2, and he assured me that this form would be returned to me within the week. Then I spoke to Nancy, ID #4590, on May 7 and . . ."

Let Your Representative Represent   As a last resort, try calling your congressional representative. If you're dealing with a federal program, the congressional staffers will have access to people you could never get to. Once when I was having a particularly hard time with the people at the Direct Loan Servicing Center, I gave my representative (the Honorable James Greenwood) a call. A member of his staff managed, in one day, to clear up a problem that I had been wrangling with for three months.

CHAPTER 18

Student Activism

Statements made to the media can be admitted as evidence of guilt in a trial. So if you're talking to the press, keep the details of your ecoterrorism to yourself. Also, resist the urge to give a "shout out" to anyone including your "peeps." It sounds really unprofessional.

Chapter Contents

I t's tempting to revert to clichés when you think about student activism. Visions of picketing hippies, shantytowns, and people with flowers painted on their faces generally spring to mind. It's also easy to think of student activists as a thing of the past, a phenomenon of the sixties that gasped its last breath sometime during the 1980s. The media certainly paints both of those pictures—inundating us with grainy footage of Woodstock and describing today's youth as slackers who are disengaged and uninvolved in the world around them.

But neither conception is particularly true. You, today's college students, are by most accounts more involved in social causes than any other generation—including the Flower Children of the sixties. It's just that you go about it in a new, different way. Traditional protests do still occur with some level of regularity on our nation's campuses. So there's still a place for some good old-fashioned hassling of The Man, if that's what you're into. But most modern student activists have set their signs and armbands aside for more advanced and effective methods.

You're also, as activists, much less unified in your choice of causes. Sixties students rallied around two national issues, civil rights and the Vietnam War, which created an easy-to-see (and measure) level of involvement. Today, students are concerned with an incredibly diverse range of social problems on local, national, and global levels.

My point is: Don't listen—in fact don't take it—when someone calls your generation politically detached or socially disconnected. Correct them. Tell them that just because you don't all burn your bras or march on Washington every other weekend doesn't mean you don't care. And it doesn't mean you aren't involved. So tell off whoever tries to say that kind of thing to you, because, as a generation at least, you *are* involved. The collective activism of you and fifteen million other college students is formidable.

But enough about aggregate activism. It's impressive, yes. But I want to talk about the prospect of you as an individual activist. Perhaps you're already knee deep in rallies and petitions. If so, good for you. But if you're one of the uninitiated, I'd like you to consider getting involved. Activism is one of the most important ways to apply what you know about the law. Yes, making sure that the cops don't bust your party up is a fine use of legal knowledge, too. But there are so many other incredible things you can accomplish with that same effort.

I'm not a hippie (technically I don't think lawyers are allowed to be hippies). And I'm not advocating that you become one. All I ask is: The next time you see something you don't like, consider the possibility that you might be able to change it. Margaret Mead said it best: "Never doubt that a small group of thoughtful, committed citizens can change the world. Indeed, it is the only thing that ever has."

Organizations and Organization

There's a reason the word *solidarity* is so closely associated with activists. It's a hell of a lot easier to move a social agenda forward with a group than as an individual. If you're concerned about some social cause, you *could* just set up a table in the student union and start yelling at whoever walks by. But things will probably end up pretty badly. Imagine how much more bargaining power a group of twenty-five like-minded protesters would have. They'd be a force to be reckoned with—a voice of the students rather than the opinion of one cranky undergrad.

RECOGNITION

Finding a bunch of people who believe in your cause is only the first step. To be truly effective you're going to have to get official recognition from the university. Schools usually only let official groups use their space—indoors or out—and equipment, reserve halls, recruit members at functions, or be included in printed listings and other resources. You'll generally need official status to do something as simple as set up a table in a public space.

And being official entitles you to money. Or at least it will enable you to apply for it. Colleges have loads of dough set aside specifically for distribution to student groups. Remember that student activities fee you pay every year? That cash gets handed out to university groups who ask for it. Why pay for posters out of your pocket when the school will?

The process for gaining recognition varies from campus to campus. Mostly

Your Lawyer Says:

CONSIDER JOINING FORCES
You don't necessarily have to start your own group to get access to university resources. It's just as effective to join forces with an existing group. Before you go through all the effort of applying for recognition with your student government, check around to see if there's an established club that might take on your cause. It means giving up a bit of your autonomy, but you'll save a lot of time and hassle.

it will involve filling out a bunch of forms. You'll probably also have to submit some sort of proof that there's interest in your proposed club—the signatures of a number of people who will join is the most common. You'll probably also have to appoint officers and coerce a professor into being your faculty adviser. Your school's student governance association will be able to tell you everything you need to know.

EDUCATE YOURSELF

Once you've figured out your group dynamics, take some time to really educate yourself about your issue. Too many young activists skip this step and try to propel themselves with uninformed fervor. Please don't be one of those people. Do some research. Read the important books, see what's on the Web, contact any national and international groups that are involved and ask them for information and guidance.

And be sure to verify your facts *before* you make any kinds of accusations. If you're interested in child labor issues and are worried that your school may purchase insignia wear from sweatshops, find out about the actual companies that your school deals with before making potentially baseless charges. Do they belong to any watchdog groups? Do they have their own standards? Have they adopted an institutional policy? It's easy to assume that your school is a cruel, heartless institution. But think about it. People don't become college professors (or even college bookstore managers) to further their evil agendas. Most educators are a pretty caring lot, and they may have thought about your issues already.

While you're getting educated, it's also probably also a good idea to read chapters 8 and 13 of this book—"Free Speech" and "The Police," respectively. Chances are those two areas will play a role in your future activities.

SET GOALS

Finally, set concrete goals for your group. A lot of activist organizations get bogged down in the mire of actually being a group—holding meetings, having elections, paying dues, etc.—and lose sight of their cause. So set a goal directly related to your issue. It doesn't have to be anything monumental. It could be as simple as raising awareness on campus about your cause. But it could also be as far-reaching as sending a group of aid workers overseas. Then focus your group on meeting those goals.

Here's an example of what not to do. I once worked with a gay rights group that was circulating a petition to "end homophobia." Ending homophobia is a laudable goal, to be sure. But it's not the type of thing that you can take affirmative steps toward as a group. And it's certainly not the type of thing you can accomplish with a petition. What do you do with it when you've got enough signatures? Show it to the homophobes on campus and say, "See? No!"?

As a theoretical mantra, ending homophobia was just fine for this group. But they needed to focus on things that were more tangible, more real. Working to strengthen the school's anti-discrimination policies or trying to get individual departments to offer gay and lesbian literature or history courses, to name two examples, would have been much better targets.

Events

At some point after you've gained recognition, educated yourself, and set group goals you're going to actually want to *do* something. Congratulations. You're ready for your first event.

THINK OUTSIDE THE RALLY

Just because your overarching goals involve social good doesn't mean your only event options are sit-ins and flag burnings. The ways you can move your issue forward are almost limitless. Panel discussions or guest lectures are really good ways to generate interest and educate the community about a certain problem or topic. So are film screenings.

But your event doesn't have to directly relate to your issue. In fact, some of the most successful campus events have nothing at all to do with the cause of their sponsoring group. Consider things like bringing in a band, or any entertainment, and having someone get up before the show starts and give a short talk about your organization and its agenda. This kind of thing is especially effective for newer groups. You get a captive audience, one that probably wouldn't have shown up at a "Save the Whales" or some similar type of rally. You'll raise the profile of your group in a different demographic.

Of course, you shouldn't be totally sworn off of civil disobedience. It still has its place in the world and will probably, at some point, have its place in your group's history. But it really only makes sense in certain situations, and it's only appropriate after you've exhausted the other avenues available to you. So many young activists miss this point. They jump right to storming the administration building. They ignore all of the other ways they could resolve the situation. Like, I don't know, making an appointment with the president of the school and just *asking* that things change. You never know, he might agree with you wholeheartedly and work with you to address your complaints. He might also shoot you down—and if he does, then it's time to get out the megaphones and picket signs. It's *always* best to try to work things out amicably. There will be plenty of time for rallies, protests, and chaining yourself to stuff later on. So give the businesslike approach a try first.

EVENT PLANNING

There are no real shortcuts or tricks that make planning an event simple. And there's no way to guarantee that it will be successful. Really it's careful

planning and hard work that will give it the best chance of doing well. I suggest that you approach a potential event the same way you attacked the formation of your group itself.

Set Goals   There's no point in doing something if you're not going to get anything out of it. So sit down and figure out what you want to accomplish before you plan your event. Don't make the rookie mistake of thinking of a cool thing to do first, then forcing it into your agenda after the fact.

Make a Plan   Red tape abounds on college campuses, so make a distinct plan. Then investigate all of the things you'll need to do to make it happen. Do you need a permit to set up? Is there a limit to the number of people you can have in your chosen space? Is there equipment you need to use? How do you reserve it?

Chances are you won't be able to think of every last thing on your own. So get help. If your school has a student activities committee or some similar organization, go to them for advice. They'll be able to help you navigate all the procedural hoops. If there isn't such a group at your school, go to the office of student life. Plop yourself down in the dean's chair and say, "My group wants to bring Star Jones in to speak. How do we do that?"

Make a Budget   Financial matters should be a critical part of the planning process. It's easy to gloss over this area and forget about incidental, but critical, expenditures that have to be made. Don't just think, "We have to pay Star Jones $7,500 to come and speak—so the budget's $7,500." There are probably lots of other things that will need to be arranged. How is she getting from the airport to the campus? Where is she staying? Who's responsible for reinforcing the stage so that it can support her? Do you have to feed Star while she's on campus? How many cheeseburgers will she require a day?

Again, look to your student activities committee or Office of Student Life for guidance. They'll probably be able to show you some sample budgets or at least tell you about the common expenses associated with events like yours.

Divide and Conquer   After you've got everything planned out, just go down the list of what needs to be done and divvy it up among your membership. You're a group for a reason, and this is it. Of course, this makes the event easier on everyone. But spreading the responsibility out also prevents a core group of members from taking over and marginalizing the ideas or views of the group as a whole.

Post-Event Documentation   After everything's over, it's not a bad idea to put all of the paperwork that was produced in a file folder. And if you have the time, it's a good idea to jot down a few notes about how things went—what the problems were, things that worked particularly well, unexpected problems that came up. Keeping records like that will be extremely helpful to future members of your club. Four years later, when you're long gone, your successors will be able to learn from your experiences.

Student Activism

The Media

You can't overestimate the importance of the media in the current activism landscape. Coverage can make an otherwise failed event spectacularly successful. Think about it. A protest with only a few people in attendance doesn't do much of anything for anyone. But a protest with a few attendees that gets media coverage is, in most ways, a huge victory. So be media savvy as you approach each event. Take affirmative steps to ensure and exploit news coverage.

LEARN TO FIND THE HOOK

Important and newsworthy are two entirely different concepts. Why do you think that national nonprofits get celebrities involved? Because celebrities are newsworthy. Protecting animal rights might be really important. But, in and of itself, it probably won't merit the front page. Get Pamela Anderson involved, however, and all of the sudden it's a top story. Have her wear little or no clothing, and it becomes national news.

You probably won't be able to get major celebrities involved in your efforts. But there may be local figures or minor celebs that are willing to help you out. Don't hesitate to call the mayor's office or a local sportscaster and ask them to come to your event. You'd be surprised what a regional personality can do for your coverage quotient.

Celebrities aren't the only way to gather media momentum. Do whatever you can to make your event as sexy and interesting as possible. If you're sponsoring a guest lecturer, find out what her more provocative views are. Emphasize those points in your advance publicity. Or if her message is relevant to an already hot topic, point that out.

If you don't believe me, just go to a newsstand and pick up the first newspaper you see. Take a look at what gets coverage. I think you'll see a distinct pattern in the stories that are printed. In fact, reading the papers and watching the news carefully is the best way to teach yourself about the concept of newsworthiness. Read and watch enough of it, and you'll start to develop an internal sense of what's important to the people who run the media.

PUT IT IN WRITING

A good press release makes so many aspects of covering an event simple for the reporters. It frames the story, provides a few interesting quotes, gives the necessary background information, and presents pretty much all the pertinent information a writer or correspondent needs to cover an event. In short, it does a lot of the work for them.

You should always prepare a press release and send it out a week or two in advance of an event. And don't forget to make it newsworthy. Give it a catchy title. Write a lead paragraph that entices the reader to continue. Also make sure that your contact information is included and easy to find.

Writing a press release is pretty simple. Still, it's a skill that not many college students have honed. But there are lots of places on a college campus that will be able to help you. If your school has a journalism department, go there and ask a professor for help. Even if you don't have a J-School at your college, there's definitely a public affairs office. Their whole job is to get media coverage for the school. They will be absolute experts at writing effective releases. And, even though they're not teaching faculty, they'd probably be happy to help you out with your media relations (unless, of course, you're planning on protesting the school itself—then they'll probably be a little less enthused about your project).

Finally, make sure that you send your releases to the right people, not just the right places. Figure out which reporters will be most interested in your event and address your press packet to them. Don't be afraid to send multiple copies of the release to different people at the same organization. If there are three reporters at a paper that cover environmental issues, send a release to all three. It doesn't cost much more, and it will increase your chances of getting coverage threefold. Again, your school's public affairs office or journalism department will be able to offer you guidance in this area. They'll probably even have a media directory that will make identifying media targets incredibly easy for you.

HAVE A MOUTHPIECE

At the event itself, appoint a designated media contact—someone who's job it is to talk to reporters. It's generally best if your designee is someone who holds an office, or has a title, in your organization. Reporters would rather quote Kim Johnson, President of Students Against Child Labor, than Kim Johnson, student. If your most media-friendly member doesn't have a title, just give them one (how do you think I got to be the executive director of CO-STAR?). Tell everyone else who will be at the event not to talk to the media, to instead point any reporters in the direction of your spokesperson.

Your talking head should take a few steps to prepare for the event. Of course, she should be well-educated and well-

Your Lawyer Says:

WATCH YOUR MOUTH WITH THE MEDIA
Never say anything legally incriminating to a member of the press. Statements that appear in newspapers or on television can be admitted into evidence and used against you in a court of law. So steer clear of any topics that could come back to bite you in the ass.

versed in your organization—its goals, the surrounding issues, the history of your group, and things like that. But you should also take some time, as a group, to prepare in a more specific sense. Think about what questions the media is likely to ask and rough out answers. For example, you can be sure that every reporter will ask, "What does your group hope to accomplish with this event?" So have an answer ready.

You should also think about what your want your group's key message to be. Public affairs firms call these talking points. Think of one or two important things you want to communicate to the media and prepare some short, canned statements. This ensures that you'll get your most significant information across, and it gives your media contact something to fall back on if she blanks.

Finally, train your media rep to keep it simple. As my PR agent always says to me: "If you only say thirty words to a reporter, those are the thirty words he'll have to use in his story." Being concise gives you a great deal of control over your message.

STICK TO THE TRUTH

When you talk to a reporter, there's going to be a huge temptation to lie or exaggerate about what's going on. Don't. Sooner or later you'll be found out, which will hurt your credibility in both the short and the long term. And you can be sure that whatever media outlet you lied to will *never* cover one of your events again.

MAKE MEDIA FRIENDS

Finally, do what you can to develop long-term professional relationships with your media contacts. Be friendly and polite to anyone who's covering your event. Put any contempt you have for the media aside and kiss their asses because like it or not, you need them.

Be sure to get the contact information and follow up after the event. Send them a quick e-mail thanking them for their interest in your organization. Offer yourself for a follow-up interview.

And keep your media friends in the loop in an ongoing sense. Put them on your newsletter mailing list. Send them clippings from other news sources. A current and friendly relationship with a few key reporters is one of the most valuable things an activist can have.

Debunking Popular College Myths

'm always surprised by the things people are willing to believe. With no more substantiation than "I read somewhere that . . ." or "No, really, it's totally true," people will swallow the most outlandish fabrications. "Mikey died from eating Pop-Rocks, then drinking soda; *really, it's true.*" "*I read that* Green M&Ms are an aphrodisiac." "*Seriously*, Bill Gates is giving away his entire fortune; all you have to do is forward an e-mail to ten people, and you'll get fifty bucks." God, I feel silly even typing those words. But every day people pass these lies, and hundreds of others like them, off on the gullible people of the world.

Maybe it's that we all sort of want these things to be true. I suppose it *is* more interesting to think that Mikey's stomach exploded than to imagine him working as a security guard or an accountant or whatever else he might actually be doing with his adult life. That's one of the reasons folklorists generally point to anyway—a need to truly believe that the world is strange and remarkable, rather than the boring, static place that we actually occupy.

Whatever the reason we believe, urban legends have practically become a national pastime. And students are not immune. In fact, college campuses are hotbeds for this kind of misinformation. Every urban myth makes its way through the campus circuit at some point or another. I'd love to take the time to set the record straight on all of these lies, but there simply isn't space here. Still, there are a few myths that are so directly related to academia and the law I'd be remiss if I didn't address them:

SORORITY BROTHELS

The sorority house brothel story is one of the most widely circulated campus urban legends. I remember hearing—and believing—it when I was

an undergraduate. Students across the country cite an outdated law as the reason that women aren't allowed to live in the sorority houses on their campus. The law, according to the stories, outlaws any arrangement where more than ten (or some other number of) unmarried women live under the same roof, because such buildings are automatically considered to be brothels.

There are a bunch of versions and variations, ranging from stories about sororities that actually *are* high-class brothels to tales of entire Greek systems being shut down due to similar, Prohibition-era laws.

But all of these stories are just, well, stories. They're interesting, but not true. There is no record of any such law in any town or at any college.

Just think about it logically. The brothel law explanation doesn't make any sense. Most schools probably have women's dormitories that are older than the sorority houses. So why were they allowed to be built and occupied under this law? In fact, if these laws existed, how did women *ever* attend these schools? Did the college build a separate house for each coed? Or were the women just forced to stay outside all the time?

If you attend a college with nonresidential sorority houses, they're probably that way due to good old-fashioned gender discrimination. When the Greek housing was being built, back in the fifties or earlier, women weren't afforded the same privileges as men. So while the guys built giant houses where they could live and drink and do whatever it is that fraternity men did back then, the women were forced to live in the dormitories.

Personally, I've never understood why sorority members allow this kind of gender discrimination. Where I went to school, not only were the sororities nonresidential, but they weren't allowed to have alcohol or even male guests in the building. Meanwhile the frats were a bacchanalian paradise. Maybe I'm wrong, but that seems unfair—in fact, unconstitutional— to me.

SUICIDE STRAIGHT As

This is another one of the most popular college legends. If your roommate commits suicide, or in some versions, just dies, you'll get straight As for the semester. Everyone who went to college has heard one version or another. And a surprisingly large number of college students buy it. According to some surveys, as many as 85 percent believe it to be fact. Its reach is so pervasive that it spawned not one, but two major (albeit abysmal) motion pictures in the last few years. So you're in good company—or at least you have lots of company—if you believed this one. But in reality the grades-for-grief rule is pure bunk.

There's not a single college or university that ever had such a rule. This includes suicides, accidental deaths, murders, or whatever other interpretation of the dead-roommate-equals-straight-As story you might have heard. To put it as simply as possible: No one has ever gotten As because their roommate died, and in all probability, no one ever will.

Colleges aren't entirely unfeeling toward the bereaved. If your bunkmate buys the farm, they will, generally, make some special arrangements for you. Most allow the victim's roommates to withdraw without academic penalty or, at the very least, delay completion of the term. And, of course, all schools offer extensive counseling services.

I know, sessions with the school shrink and a few extra weeks to write your final papers won't get you into grad school, but those are the breaks. And when you really think about it, wouldn't you rather have more quality time with your roomie than some silly Ph.D. from Yale?

ALUMNI-REQUIRED SWIMMING TESTS

Rich alums are blamed for a disproportionately large number of campus ills. Ugly buildings, strange rules, and bad classes are often blamed on a wealthy graduate who demanded that things be that way. Often their eccentric demands are linked to some personal tragedy they've suffered or irrational fear they have.

One of the more popular versions of this type of story explains a requirement that all graduates of a specific college pass a swimming test before graduation. According to the myth, at some point in the school's history an undergrad drowned while at school. Her wealthy parents made a large donation to the school in memory of their late daughter. But in order to avoid such tragedies in the future, they conditioned the gift on a requirement that all students learn to swim.

The variations on the crazy alumnus theme are almost limitless. According to the legends, eccentric graduates have done everything from demanding that ice cream remain on the cafeteria menu (because someone's daughter once died of anorexia) to specifying how the colored lights should be arranged at the holidays.

These stories, at least the ones in wide circulation, are untrue. Certainly strange things have transpired in the course of every school's history in regard to alumni donations. But if your school requires you to learn to swim, it's because the faculty thought it was an important thing for you to know how to do. And if there's always ice cream available at your cafeteria, it's because ice cream is delicious and students like to eat it, not because some old woman threatened to withhold a bequest.

CAKES AND ALE

According to the most popular version of this legend, a student, most often at Cambridge or Oxford, demands cakes and ale from his professor during an examination. When the confused professor refuses, the student produces an ancient copy of the school's rules. In some versions it's written in Latin. Among the many rules on the old piece of paper is one that entitles students taking examinations to be served cakes and ale by the professor on request. The professor, not one to ignore strange rules, runs off and gets some modern equivalent—donuts and milk, burgers and soda. The details vary.

Of course, the professor exacts his revenge on the wise-ass student the next week by fining him under another ancient (and apparently enforceable) school rule that requires all students to wear a sword to class.

This story is usually set in Europe, but there are American versions. The U.S. rendition is usually set in Texas or one of the other frontier states. The drink is usually whiskey or rye, and the sword is replaced with a rifle or musket. But other than that, the story's the same.

As you've probably guessed, these stories are patently false. No schools, even the centuries-old ones in Paris and London, have or had rules like these.

OVERPAYING SPEEDING TICKETS

This theory about overpaying your ticket is one of the most prevalent (and in my opinion—silliest) urban legal legends going around. It's not technically an academic myth, but it gets repeated on college campuses so often, it bears debunking. Here's how the story goes:

If you get a speeding ticket, when you're paying the fine make out the check for five dollars more than what you owe. The state's department of motor vehicles will then cash your check and send you a refund check for the extra money you sent. If you don't cash the refund check, the case will somehow remain "open" at the DMV, which will prevent them from ever reporting your ticket to your insurance companies or adding points to your license.

This theory is not only false, acting on it will get you increased fines and trouble.

Most courts won't even accept a payment for the wrong amount. They'll just send it right back to you with a terse letter. Meanwhile, you'll probably get an increased fine for failure to pay in a timely fashion. And since you haven't officially responded to the citation, if your appointed court date passes, you could get charged with failure to appear, which means another fine and, maybe, a warrant for your arrest.

So if you get a speeding ticket, just make the check out for the right amount or challenge the citation the right way. Messing around will cause you nothing but trouble. And for future reference, legal loopholes that seem too good to be true generally are.

APPENDIX B

Local Lawyer Referral Services

Specific information about how to find an attorney is at the end of chapter 13. The absolute best way to find a competent lawyer is to use your personal connections. Talk to your friends, family members, and colleagues about your situation and ask them for a recommendation. If that fails, try one of the services listed below. But be wary. The amount of screening done varies from service to service. Many of them don't do any at all. So the level of competency can be spotty. Certainly, you should never simply assume that because you found your lawyer through one of these services, she's good enough to get the job done. That simply isn't true. Treat the situation just like you would if you were hiring anyone to do anything. Keep your eyes and ears open and look for signs that she knows what she's doing. If it doesn't feel right, call back and get another referral.

State	Sponsoring Organization	Geographic Area Covered	Fee	Online Referral Service	Contact Information
Alabama	Alabama State Bar	Statewide	$25 for an initial 30-minute consultation	Yes	Phone: (800) 392-5660 E-mail: lrs@alabar.org http://www.alabar.org
Alaska	Alaska Bar	Statewide	$50 for an initial 30-minute consultation	No	Phone: (800) 770-9999 E-mail: info@alaskabar.org http://www.alaskabar.org/
Arizona	No referral service available. State bar organization provides free lists of certified specialists in the areas of bankruptcy, criminal, estate & trust, family law, injury and wrongful death, real estate, tax or workers' compensation by calling (602) 340-7300.				
Arkansas	No referral service available. Online list of attorneys, searchable by county and area of practice, available at http://arkansasfind alawyer.com. Attorneys pay to be included in the database, and the entries are not screened by the Arkansas Bar Association.				
California	San Bernardino Bar Association	San Bernardino and Riverside Counties	$30 for an initial 30-minute consultation	No	Phone: (909) 888-6791 http://www.sbcba.org/
	Alameda County Bar Association	Alameda County	$25 for an initial 30-minute consultation	No	Phone: (510) 893-8683 http://www.acbanet.org/LRS.htm
	Humboldt County Bar Association	Butte, Colusa, Del Norte, Glenn, Lake, Lassen, Mendocino, Modoc, Nevada, Placer, Plumas, Shasta, Sierra, Siskiyou, Sutter, Tehama, Trinity, and Yuba Counties	$20 for an initial 30-minute consultation	No	Phone: (707) 445-2652

Organization	County/Counties	Fee	Online	Contact
Contra Costa County Bar Association	Contra Costa County	$30 for an initial 30-minute consultation	Yes	Phone: (925) 825-5700 http://www.cccba.org/cclawyer/lrs.htm
Fresno County Bar Association	Fresno County	$30 for an initial 30-minute consultation	Yes	Phone: (559) 264-0137 E-mail: FCBA@worldnet.att.net http://www.fresnocountybar.org/
Tulare County Bar Association Lawyers Referral Service	Kings and Tulare Counties	$20 for an initial 30-minute consultation	No	Phone: (559) 732-2513
Los Angeles County Bar Association	Los Angeles County	$25 for an initial 30-minute consultation	Yes, including real-time chat with an attorney	Phone: (213) 243-1525 E-mail: lris@lacba.org http://www.smartlaw.org/
The San Fernando Valley Bar Association	Los Angeles and Ventura Counties	First half-hour consultation is $25 if registered online, $30 if registered via phone.	Yes, with $5 discount	Phone: (818) 227-0490 E-mail: info@sfvba.org http://www.sfvba.org/
Marin County Bar Association	Marin County	$35 for an initial 30-minute consultation	Yes	Phone: (415) 453-5505 E-mail: info@marinbar.org http://www.marinbar.org/
Merced County Bar Association	Merced County	$30 for an initial 30-minute consultation	No	Phone: (209) 383-3886
Monterey County Bar Association	Monterey County	$30 for an initial 30-minute consultation	No	Phone: (831) 375-9889 E-mail: sgood@redshift.com

(continued)

State	Sponsoring Organization	Geographic Area Covered	Fee	Online Referral Service	Contact Information
California (continued)	Orange County Bar Association	Orange County	$25 for an initial 30-minute consultation	Yes	Phone: (949) 440-6747 http://www.ocbar.org/
	Riverside County Bar Association	Riverside County	$35 for an initial 30-minute consultation	No	Phone: (909) 682-7520 or (909)568-5555
	Sacramento County Bar Association	Sacramento County	$30 for an initial 30-minute consultation	Yes	Phone: (916) 444-2333 http://www.sacbar.org/
	San Bernardino County Bar Association	San Bernardino County	$30 for an initial 30-minute consultation	Yes	Phone: (909) 888-6791 http://www.sbcba.org/
	San Diego County Bar Association	San Diego County	No charge for an initial 30-minute consultation	Yes	Phone: (619) 231-8585 http://www.sdlawyerreferral.com/
	Bar Association of San Francisco County	San Francisco County	$25 for an initial 30-minute consultation	Yes	Phone: (415) 989-1616 http://www.sfbar.org/lrs/
	San Joaquin County Bar Association	San Joaquin County	$30 for an initial 30-minute consultation	Yes	Phone: (209) 948-4620 http://www.sjcbar.org/
	San Luis Obispo County Bar Association	San Luis Obispo County	$30 for an initial 30-minute consultation	No	Phone: (805) 788-2099 http://www.geocities.com/slocountybar/
	San Mateo County Bar Association	San Mateo County and Santa Clara Counties	"Nominal fee" charged for an initial 30-minute consultation	No	Phone: (650) 369-4149 http://www.smcba.org/

	Organization	Location	Fee		Contact
	Santa Barbara County	Santa Barbara County	$35 for an initial 30-minute consultation	No	Phone: (805) 569-9400 http://www.sblaw.org/
	Santa Cruz County	Santa Cruz County	$35 for an initial 30-minute consultation	No	Phone: (831) 425-4755 E-mail: sccba@aol.com http://webserver.firstecc.com/santa_cruz/html2/
	Solano County Bar Association	Solano County	$35 for an initial 30-minute consultation	No	Phone: (707) 422-0127
	Sonoma County Bar Association	Sonoma County	$30 for an initial 30-minute consultation	Yes	Phone: (707) 546-5297 http://www.sonomacountybar.org/
	Stanislaus County Bar Association	Stanislaus County	$30 for an initial 30-minute consultation	No	Phone: (209) 571-5727
	Ventura County Bar Association	Ventura County	$35 for an initial 30-minute consultation	Yes	Phone: (805) 650-7599 E-mail: lrs@vcba.org http://www.vcba.org
Colorado	Numerous Local Bar Associations	Denver, Boulder, Ft. Collins, and other selected communities	$35 for an initial 30-minute consultation	Yes	Metro Denver/Boulder: (303) 831-8000 Fort Collins: (970) 226-2455 http://www.mlrsonline.org/
	El Paso County Bar Association	El Paso County and surrounding areas	No set fees	Yes	Phone: (719) 636-1532 http://www.elpasocountybar.org/
Connecticut	Connecticut State Bar Association	Statewide	No set fees	No	Hartford, Litchfield, Middlesex, Tolland, and Windham: (860) 525-6052

(continued)

State	Sponsoring Organization	Geographic Area Covered	Fee	Online Referral Service	Contact Information
					Fairfield: (203) 335-4116 New Haven: (203) 562-5750 New London: (860) 889-9384 http://www.ctbar.org/
Delaware	Delaware State Bar Association	Statewide	$35 for an initial 30-minute consultation	No	New Castle County: (302) 478-8850 Kent and Sussex Counties: (800) 773-0606
District of Columbia	Bar Association of the District of Columbia	Districtwide	$40 for an initial 30-minute consultation	No	Phone: (202) 296-7845 http://www.dcbar.org/
Florida	Florida State Bar Association	Statewide	$25 for an initial 30-minute consultation	No	Phone: (800) 342-8011 or (800) 342-8060 extension 5844 http://www.flabar.org/
Georgia	Atlanta Bar Association	Atlanta and surrounding areas	$35 for an initial 30-minute consultation	No	Phone: (404) 521-0777 https://www.atlantabar.org/
	DeKalb Bar Association	DeKalb, Fulton, Gwinnett, and Cobb Counties	$40 for an initial 30-minute consultation	No	Phone: (404) 373-2580 or (404) 370-0843
	Cobb County LRS	Cherokee, Cobb, Fulton, Douglas, and Paulding Counties	$35 for an initial 30-minute consultation	No	Phone: (770) 424-7149 E-mail: contact@cobbbar.org http://www.cobbbar.org/
	Savannah Bar Association	Chatham County	No set fees	No	Phone: (912) 236-9344

State	Organization	Coverage	Fees	Online	Contact
Hawaii	Hawaii State Bar Association	Statewide	No set fees	No, but list of screened attorneys by area of practice is available online.	Phone: (808) 537-9140 E-mail: LRIS@hsba.org http://www.hsba.org/
Idaho	Idaho State Bar Association	Statewide	$35 for an initial 30-minute consultation	Yes	Phone: (208) 334-4500 http://www2.state.id.us/isb/
Illinois	Illinois State Bar Association	Statewide	$15 for an initial 30-minute consultation	No, but a searchable list of attorneys is available.	Phone: (217) 525-5297 http://www.illinoislawyerfinder.com/
	Chicago Bar Association	Cook and surrounding counties	$20 for an initial 30-minute consultation	Yes, services are only available online.	Phone: (312) 554-2000 E-mail: info@chicagobar.org http://www.chicagobar.org/
Indiana	Indianapolis Bar Association	Statewide	No set fees	Yes	Phone: (317) 269-2000 Fax: (317) 269-1915 http://www.indybar.org/referral.cfm
Iowa	Iowa State Bar	Statewide	$25 for an initial 30-minute consultation	No, but a searchable database of lawyers is available.	Phone: (800) 532-1108 or (515) 280-7429 http://www.iowabar.org/
Kansas	Kansas Bar Association	Statewide	$15 for an initial 30-minute consultation	No	Phone: (800) 928-3111

(continued)

State	Sponsoring Organization	Geographic Area Covered	Fee	Online Referral Service	Contact Information
Kentucky	Boyd, Greenup, and Lewis County Bar Associations	Boyd, Greenup, and Lewis Counties	No set fees	No	Phone: (606) 326-1313
	Fayette County Bar Association	Bourbon, Clark, Fayette, Franklin, Jessanine, Madison, Scott, and Woodford Counties	$25 for an initial 30-minute consultation	Yes	Phone: (859) 225-8644 http://centralkylawyers.com/
	Louisville Bar Association	Jefferson, Bullitt, Hardin, Henry, Meade, Oldham, Shelby and Spencer, and Indiana Counties	No charge for an initial 30-minute consultation	No	Phone: (502) 583-1801 E-mail: cgiesin@lba.win.net http://www.loubar.org/
	Northern Kentucky Bar Association	Campbell, Kenton, Boone, Owen, Gallatin, Carroll, Grant, and Pendleton Counties	$15 for an initial 30-minute consultation	No	Phone: (859) 781-1300 E-mail: nkybar@one.net http://www.nkybar.org/
Louisiana	Louisiana State Bar Association	Statewide	$25 for an initial 30-minute consultation	No	Phone: (888) 503-5747 http://www.lsba.org
Maine	Maine State Bar Association	Statewide	$20 for an initial 30-minute consultation	No, but faxable questionnaire available	Phone: (800) 860-1460 http://www.mainebar.org/
Maryland	Anne Arundel Bar Association	Anne Arundel County	$30 for an initial 30-minute consultation	No	Phone: (410) 280-6961 E-Mail: AABA@circuitcourt.org http://www.aabar.org/

State	Bar Association	Area	Fee		Contact
	Bar Association of Baltimore City	Baltimore and surrounding areas	$30 for an initial 30-minute consultation	No	Phone: (410) 539-3112 E-mail lris@clark.net http://www.baltimorebar.org/
	Baltimore County Bar Association	Baltimore County	$25 for an initial 30-minute consultation	No	Phone: (410) 337-9100 http://www.bcba.org/
	Montgomery County Bar Association	Montgomery County	$40 for an initial 30-minute consultation	No	Phone: 301-279-9100 http://www.montbar.org/law_ref.htm
	Prince George's County Bar Association	Prince George's County	No set fees	No	Phone: (866) 757-7785 or (301) 952-1440 http://www.pgcba.com/law-ref.htm
Massachusetts	Massachusetts Bar Association	Statewide	$25 for an initial 30-minute consultation	Yes	Phone: (866) 227-7577 In Boston: (617) 654-0400 E-mail: lrs@massbar.org http://www.masslawhelp.org/
	Boston Bar Association	Boston and surrounding areas	$25 for an initial 30-minute consultation	No	Phone: (617) 742-0625 E-mail: lrs@bostonbar.org http://www.bostonbar.org/lrs/index.htm
Michigan	Michigan State Bar Association	Statewide	$20 for an initial 30-minute consultation	No	Phone: (800) 968-0738 http://www.michbar.org/
Minnesota	Minnesota State Bar Association	Statewide	$25 for an initial 30-minute consultation	No	Phone: (800) 292-4152 http://www.mnbar.org/
Mississippi	No attorney referral services are available in the state of Mississippi.				
Missouri	Missouri State Bar Association	Statewide except St. Louis, Kansas City, and Springfield	$25 for an initial 30-minute consultation	No	Phone: (573) 636-3635 http://www.mobar.org/

(continued)

State	Sponsoring Organization	Geographic Area Covered	Fee	Online Referral Service	Contact Information
Missouri (continued)	Bar Association of Metropolitan St. Louis	St. Louis and surrounding areas	$25 for an initial 30-minute consultation	No	Phone: (314) 621-6681 http://www.mobar.org/
	Kansas City Metropolitan Bar Association	Kansas City and surrounding areas	$25 for an initial 30-minute consultation	No	Phone: (816) 221-9472 http://www.mobar.org/
	Springfield Metropolitan Bar Association	Springfield and surrounding areas	$25 for an initial 30-minute consultation	No	Phone: (417) 831-2783 http://www.mobar.org/
Montana	Montana State Bar Association	Statewide	$30 for an initial 30-minute consultation	No	Phone: (406) 449-6577 http://www.montanabar.org/
Nebraska	Nebraska State Bar Association	Statewide	Not a formal referral service, but the legal aid department will aid in finding an appropriate attorney.	No	Phone: (800) 742-3005 http://www.nebar.com/
	Omaha Bar Association	Douglas and Sarpy Counties	$35 for an initial 30-minute consultation	No	Phone: (402) 280-3603 E-mail: lrs@omahabarassociation .com http://www.omahabarassociation .com/
Nevada	Nevada State Bar Association	Statewide	$45 for an initial 30-minute consultation	Yes	Phone: (800) 789-5747 E-mail: ileanav@nvbar.org http://www.nvbar.org/

New Hampshire	New Hampshire State Bar Association	Statewide	No set fees	No	Phone: (603) 229-0002 E-mail: lrsreferral@nhbar.org http://www.nhbar.org/
New Jersey	Atlantic County Bar Association	Atlantic County	No set fees	No	Phone: (609) 345-3444
	Bergen County Bar Association	Bergen County	$30 for an initial 30-minute consultation	No	Phone: (201) 488-0044 15 Bergen Street Hackensack, NJ 07601
	Burlington County Bar Association	Burlington County	$35 for an initial 30-minute consultation	No	Phone: (609) 261-4862 http://www.burlcobar.org
	Camden County Bar Association	Camden County	$30 for an initial 30-minute consultation	No	Phone: (856) 964-4520 http:// www.camdencountybar.org
	Cape May County Bar Association	Cape May County	$35 for an initial 30-minute consultation	No	Phone: (609) 463-0313
	Cumberland County Bar Association	Cumberland County	$20 for an initial 30-minute consultation	No	Phone: (856) 692-6207
	Essex County Bar Association	Essex County	No set fees	No	Phone: (973) 622-7753 E-mail: info@essexbar.com http://www.essexbar.com
	Gloucester County Bar Association	Gloucester County	$35 for an initial 30-minute consultation	No	Phone: (856) 848-4589
	Hudson County Bar Association	Hudson County	$25 for an initial 30-minute consultation	No	Phone: (201) 798-2727 583 Newark Avenue (at the corner of Newark and Baldwin) Jersey City, NJ 07306

(continued)

State	Sponsoring Organization	Geographic Area Covered	Fee	Online Referral Service	Contact Information
New Jersey (continued)	Hunterdon County Mercer County Bar Association	Hunterdon County Mercer County	No set fees $25 for an initial 30-minute consultation	No No	Phone: (908) 735-2611 Phone: (609) 585-6200 E-mail: mcba@gte.net
	Middlesex County Bar Association	Middlesex County	$35 for an initial 30-minute consultation	No	Phone: (732) 828-0053 http://www.mcbalaw.com/lrs.htm
	Monmouth Bar Association	Monmouth County	No set fees	No	Phone: (732) 431-5544
	Morris and Sussex County Bar Association	Morris and Sussex Counties	$25 for an initial 30-minute consultation	No	Phone: (973) 267-5882 http://www.morriscountybar.com/
	Ocean County Bar Association	Ocean County	$30 for an initial 30-minute consultation, $50 for one hour	No	Phone: (732) 240-3666
	Passaic County Bar Association	Passaic County	$35 for an initial 30-minute consultation	No	Phone: (973) 278-9223
	Salem County Bar Association	Salem County	No set fees	No	Phone: (856) 935-5629
	Union County Bar Association	Union County	$35 for an initial 30-minute consultation	No	Phone: (908) 354-5984 E-mail: info@uclaw.com http://www.uclaw.com/
	Warren County Bar Association	Warren County	$25 for an initial 30-minute consultation	No	Phone: (908) 637-8055 E-mail: lgarno@gos.com

State	Association	Coverage	Fee	Referral	Contact
New Mexico	Albuquerque Bar Association	Statewide	$30 for an initial 30-minute consultation	No	Phone: (505) 243-2615 E-mail: ABQBar@aol.com http://www.abqbar.com/
New York	New York State Bar Association	Statewide	$25 for an initial 30-minute consultation	No	Phone: (800) 342-3661 Albany: (518) 487-5709 http://www.nysba.org/
	Association of the Bar of the City of New York	New York City, all boroughs	$25 for an initial 30-minute consultation	Yes	Phone: (212) 626-7373 E-mail: LRS@abcny.org http://www.abcny.org/
North Carolina	North Carolina Bar Association	Statewide	$30 for an initial 30-minute consultation	No	Phone: (800) 662-7660 Raleigh: (919) 677-8574 http://www.barlinc.org/
North Dakota	State Bar Association of North Dakota	Statewide	$15 for an initial 30-minute LawReferral/ consultation	No	Phone: (800) 932-8880 http://www.sband.org/
Ohio	Butler County Bar Association	Butler County	$20 for an initial 30-minute consultation	No	Phone: (513) 896-6671 or (800) 543-0846 http://www.butlercountybar.org/
	Clermont County Bar Association	Clermont County	No set fees, but most lawyers charge $20 for first half-hour consultation.	No	Phone: (513) 732-2050 E-mail: cclaw@cclla.org http://www.clermontlawlibrary.org
	Cuyahoga County Bar Association	Cuyahoga County	$25 for an initial 30-minute consultation	Yes	Phone: (216) 621-2414 E-mail: info@cuybar.org http://www.cuybar.org/
	Columbus Bar Association	Franklin County	No set fees	Yes	Phone: (614) 221-0754 http://www.cbalaw.org/
	Geauga County Bar Association	Geauga County	No charge for an initial 30-minute consultation	No	Phone: (440) 286-7160

(continued)

State	Sponsoring Organization	Geographic Area Covered	Fee	Online Referral Service	Contact Information
Ohio (continued)	Cincinnati Bar Association	Hamilton County	$25 for an initial 30-minute consultation	No	Phone: (513) 381-8359 or (888) 628-2577 http://www.cincybar.org/
	Lake County Bar Association	Lake County	No charge for an initial 30-minute consultation	No	Phone: (440) 352-6044 E-mail: lcba@lcba-ohio.org http://www.lcba-ohio.org/
	Toledo Bar Association	Lucas County	$40 for an initial 30-minute consultation	Yes	Phone: (419) 242-2000 E-mail: diana@toledobar.org http://www.toledobar.org/
	Madison County Bar Association	Madison County	No set fees	No	Phone: (740) 852-9515
	Mahoning County Bar Association	Mahoning County	$15 for an initial 30-minute consultation	Yes	Phone: (330) 746-2933 E-mail: info@mahoningbar.org http://www.mahoningbar.org/
	Medina County Bar Association	Medina County	No set fees	No	Phone: (330) 725-9744
	Dayton Bar Association	Montgomery County	$25 for an initial 30-minute consultation	Yes	Phone: (937) 222-6102 E-mail: refer@daybar.org http://www.daybar.org/
	Stark County Bar Association	Stark County	$15 for an initial 30-minute consultation	No	Phone: (330) 453-0686
	Akron Bar Association	Summit, Portage, and Wayne Counties	$30 for an initial 30-minute consultation	No	Phone: (330) 253-5038 http://www.akronbar.org/
	Trumbull County Bar Association	Trumbull County	No set fees	No	Phone: (330) 675-2415

State	Bar Association	Coverage	Consultation Fee	Online Database	Contact
Oklahoma	Tulsa County Bar Association	Tulsa and surrounding areas	$20 for an initial 30-minute consultation	No	Phone: (918) 584-5243 1446 South Boston Avenue Tulsa, OK 74119 http://www.tulsabar.com/
	No statewide referral service is available, but the Oklahoma State Bar Association maintains an online list of member attorneys, searchable by geographic regions and area of practice, available at http://www.oklahomafindalawyer.com/.				
Oregon	Oregon State Bar	Statewide	$35 for an initial 30-minute consultation	No	Phone: (800) 452-7636 http://www.osbar.org/
Pennsylvania	Pennsylvania Bar Association	Statewide	$30 for an initial 30-minute consultation	No	Phone: (800) 692-7375 or (717) 238-6807 http://www.pabar.org/
Rhode Island	Rhode Island Bar Association	Statewide	$25 for an initial 30-minute consultation	No	Phone: (401) 421-7799 E-mail: rviau@ribar.com http://www.ribar.com/
South Carolina	South Carolina Bar Association	Statewide	$25 for an initial 30-minute consultation	Yes	Phone: (800) 868-2284 Columbia and Lexington Counties: (803) 799-7100 E-mail: scbar-info@scbar.org http://www.scbar.org/
South Dakota	South Dakota Bar Association	Statewide	Searchable database of attorneys online. Participating attorneys have agreed to charge a "reasonable fee" for a 30-minute consultation.	Yes	Phone: (800) 952-2333 http://www.sdbar.org/

(continued)

State	Sponsoring Organization	Geographic Area Covered	Fee	Online Referral Service	Contact Information
Tennessee	Knoxville Bar Association	Knox County	$25 for an initial 30-minute consultation	Yes	Phone: (865) 522-7501 http://www.knoxbar.org/
	Nashville Bar Association	Davidson, Sumner, Rutherford, Robertson, and Williamson Counties	No set fees	Yes	Phone: (615) 242-6546 http://www.nashbar.org/
Texas	State Bar of Texas	Statewide	$20 for an initial 30-minute consultation	No	Phone: (800) 252-9690 http://www.texasbar.com/
Utah	Utah State Bar	Statewide	$30 for an initial 30-minute consultation	Yes	Phone: (800) 698-9077 or (801) 531-9075 http://www.utahbar.org/
Vermont	Vermont Bar Association	Statewide	$25 for an initial 30-minute consultation	No	Phone: (800) 639-7036 E-mail: nredington@vtbar.org http://www.vtbar.org/
Virginia	Virginia State Bar Association	Statewide	$30 for an initial 30-minute consultation	No	Phone: (804) 775-0808 or (800) 552-7977 http://www.vsb.org/vlrs.html
Washington	King County Bar Association	King, Pierce, and Snohomish Counties	No set fees	Yes	Phone: (206) 623-2551 E-mail: lrs@kcba.org http://www.kcba.org/LRS/lrs.htm
	Kitsap County	Kitsap County	$35 for an initial 30-minute consultation	No	Phone: (360) 373-2426 E-mail: info@kitsapbar.com http://www.kitsapbar.com/
	Lewis County Bar Association	Lewis County	$30 for an initial 30-minute consultation	No	Phone: (360) 748-0430

State	Organization	Area	Fee		Contact
	Snohomish County	Snohomish County	$25 for an initial 30-minute consultation	No	Phone: (425) 388-3018 http://www.snobar.org/
	Thurston County Bar Association	Thurston, Mason, Grays Harbor, Lewis, and Pierce Counties	$25 for an initial 30-minute consultation	No	Phone: (360) 923-4844 http://olylaw.net/
	Tacoma-Pierce County Bar Association	Pierce County	$25 for an initial 30-minute consultation	No	Phone: (253) 383-3432 http://www.co.pierce.wa.us/PC/
	Clark County Bar Association	Clark, Cowlitz, and Skamania Counties	$40 for an initial 30-minute consultation	No	Phone: (360) 695-0599
West Virginia	West Virginia State Bar	Statewide	$10 for an initial 30-minute consultation	No	Phone: (304) 558-7991 http://www.wvbar.org/
Wisconsin	State Bar of Wisconsin	Statewide	$20 for an initial 30-minute consultation	No	Phone: (800) 362-9082 Madison: (608) 257-4666 http://www.wisbar.org/
Wyoming	Wyoming Bar Association	Statewide	No set fees	Yes	Phone: (307) 632-9061 http://www.wyomingbar.org/

Selected Bibliography & Further Reading

"**I**f I have seen further, it is by standing on the shoulders of giants " Isaac Newton wrote that in 1676. He was, of course, talking about physics. But the thought is just as appropriate to legal research. All attorneys owe an incredible debt to their peers who research and publish books, articles, and other works about the law. I'm no exception. My shelves are full of well-worn books that have been invaluable to me—both while I was writing this book and in my day-to-day work.

The following is a list of some of the materials that I used in my research. Many are written specifically for lawyers, so they can make for difficult reading. But don't let that scare you off. If you take your time, you shouldn't have much difficulty understanding the most daunting of them. And a few are surprisingly entertaining.

Most of the cases that are cited here can easily be found on the Web. Usually a Google search for the name or the citation will be enough to pull them up. But if that fails, you should be able to access them with FindLaw (www.findlaw.com), which is, in and of itself, an excellent source for all things legal. In most instances it's the best place to start any legal research project.

Chapter 1: Your Constitution

BOOKS

Garraty, John A., ed., *Quarrels That Have Shaped the Constitution*, rev. ed. (New York: Harper & Row Publishers, 1987).

Levy, Leonard W., *Origins of the Bill of Rights* (New Haven, Conn.: Yale Nota Bene, 2001).

Student Press Law Center, *The Law of the Student Press*, 2d ed. (Arlington, Va.: Student Press Law Center, 1994).

ON THE WEB

National Archives Experience: Charters of Freedom, www.archives.gov/national_
archives_experience/charters/charters.html.
Student Press Law Center, www.splc.org/.

Chapter 2: Your College

BOOKS

Bickel, Robert D., and Peter F. Lake, *The Rights and Responsibilities of the Modern University: Who Assumes the Risks of College Life?* (Durham, N.C.: Carolina Academic Press, 1999).

Olivas, Michael A., *The Law and Higher Education: Cases and Materials on Colleges in Court*, 2d ed. (Durham, N.C.: Carolina Academic Press, 1997).

CRITICAL CASES

Gott v. Berea College, 156 Ky. 376, 161 S.W. 204 (1913).

Chapter 3: Your Professor

BOOKS

Hollander, Patricia A., D. Parker Young, and Donald D. Gehring, *A Practical Guide to Legal Issues Affecting College Teachers*, 2d ed. (Asheville, N.C.: College Administration Publications, 1995).

Poskanzer, Steven G., *Higher Education Law: The Faculty* (Baltimore, Md.: Johns Hopkins University Press, 2001).

ON THE WEB

American Association of University Professors Legal Program, www.aaup.org/Legal/.

Chapter 4: Academic Dishonesty

BOOKS

Kilber, William L., Elizabeth M. Nuss, Brent G. Paterson, and Gary Pavela, *Academic Integrity and Student Development: Legal Issues, Policy Perspectives* (Asheville, N.C.: College Administration Publications, 1988).

Lathrop, Ann, and Katherine Foss, *Student Cheating and Plagiarism in the Internet Era: A Wake-Up Call* (Englewood, Colo.: Libraries Unlimited, 2000).

Mallon, Thomas, *Stolen Words: Forays into the Origins and Ravages of Plagiarism* (New York: Ticknor & Fields, 1989).

Whitley, Bradley E., Jr., and Patricia Keith Spiegel, *Academic Dishonesty: An Educator's Guide* (Mahwah, N.J.: Lawrence Erlbaum Associates, 2002).

ON THE WEB

Center for Academic Integrity, www.academicintegrity.org/.
Plagiarism.org, www.plagiarism.org/.
Purdue University Online Writing Lab, owl.english.purdue.edu/index.htm.

Chapter 5: Animal Rights

BOOKS

Francione, Gary L., and Anna E. Charlton, *Vivisection and Dissection in the Classroom: A Guide to Conscientious Objection* (Jenkintown, Pa.: The American Anti-Vivisection Society, 1992).

Sherry, Clifford J., *Animal Rights: A Reference Handbook* (Santa Barbara, Calif.: ABC-CLIO, 1994).

Singer, Peter J., *Animal Liberation*, 3d ed. (New York: Ecco, 2002).

Regan, Tom, *The Case for Animal Rights*, rep. ed. (Berkeley: University of California Press, 1985).

ON THE WEB

Animals Protection Institute, http://www.api4animals.org/.

Association for the Assessment and Accreditation of Laboratory Animal Care, www.aaalac.org/.

Public Health Service Policy on Humane Care and Use of Laboratory Animals, grants.nih.gov/grants/olaw/references/phspol.htm.

Rutgers University School of Law Animal Rights Project, http://www.animal-law.org/.

USDA Animal Care Home Page, www.aphis.usda.gov/ac/.

Chapter 6: Harassment & Discrimination

BOOKS

Dziech, Billie Wright, and Linda Weiner, *The Lecherous Professor: Sexual Harassment on Campus*, 2d ed. (Urbana: University of Illinois Press, 1990).

Sandler, Bernice R., and Robert J. Shoop, eds., *Sexual Harassment on Campus: A Guide for Administrators, Faculty, and Students* (Needham Heights, Mass.: Allyn & Bacon, 1997).

ON THE WEB

Association on Higher Education and Disability (AHEAD), www.ahead.org/.

Human Rights Campaign, www.hrc.org/.

Lambda Legal, http://www.lambdalegal.org.

U.S. Department of Education Office of Civil Rights, www.ed.gov/about/offices/list/ocr/index.html.

U.S. Equal Employment Opportunity Commission, www.eeoc.gov/.

Chapter 7: Student Records

BOOKS

Hammond, Robert, *Identity Theft: How to Protect Your Most Valuable Asset* (Franklin Lakes, N.J.: Career Press, 2002).

Rainsberger, Richard A., Eliott G. Baker, Dennis Hicks, Brad Myers, Jim Noc, and Faith A. Weese, *The American Association of College Registrars and Admissions Officers Guide to FERPA 2001* (Washington, D.C.: AACRAO, 2001).

ON THE WEB
Federal Trade Commission's Identity Theft Website, www.consumer.gov/idtheft/.

Chapter 8: Free Speech

BOOKS
Golding, Martin P., *Free Speech on Campus* (Lanham, Md.: Rowman & Littlefield, 2000).

O'Neil, Robert M., *Free Speech in the College Community* (Bloomington: Indiana University Press, 1997).

Shiell, Timothy C., *Campus Hate Speech on Trial* (Lawrence: University of Kansas Press, 1998).

CRITICAL CASES
Doe v. University of Michigan, 721 F.Supp. 852 (E.D. Mich. 1989).

Piarowski v. Illinois Community College, 759 F.2d 625 (7th Cir. 1985).

Chapter 9: Dormitories & On-Campus Housing

BOOKS
Bliming, Gregory, *The Resident Assistant: Applications and Strategies for Working with College Students in Residence Halls*, 5th ed. (Dubuque, Iowa: Kendall/Hunt Publishing Company, 1999).

Gehring, Donald D., ed., *Administering College and University Housing: A Legal Perspective* (Asheville, N.C.: College Administration Publications, 1992).

CRITICAL CASES
Moore v. Student Affairs Comm. of Troy State Univ., 284 F.Supp. 725, (M.D.Ala.1968).

Chapter 10: Disciplinary Proceedings

BOOKS
Paterson, Bent G., and William L. Kibler, *The Administration of Campus Discipline: Student, Organizational, and Community Issue* (Asheville, N.C.: College Administration Publications, 1998).

Pressman, Robert, and Susan Weinstein, *Procedural Due Process Rights in Student Discipline: An Update and Revision of the Procedural Due Process Section of School Discipline and Student Rights by Paul Weckstein* (Cambridge, Mass.: Center for Law and Education, 1990).

Silverglate, Harvey A., and Josh Gewolb, *FIRE's Guide to Due Process and Fair Procedure on Campus* (Philadelphia: Foundation for Individual Rights in Education, 2003).

Chapter 11: Cyber Issues on Campus

BOOKS

Hawke, Constance S., *Computer and Internet Use on Campus: A Legal Guide to Issues of Intellectual Property, Free Speech, and Privacy* (San Francisco: Jossey-Bass, 2001).

ON THE WEB

Center for Democracy & Technology, www.cdt.org/.
Electronic Frontier Foundation, www.eff.org/.
Electronic Privacy Information Center, www.epic.org/.

Chapter 12: Campus Safety & Security

BOOKS

Bordner, Diane C., and David M. Petersen, *Campus Policing: The Nature of University Police Work* (Lanham, Md.: University Press of America, 1983).
Powell, John W., Michael S. Pander, and Robert C. Neilson, *Campus Security and Law Enforcement*, 2d ed. (Boston: Butterworth-Heinemann, 1994).

ON THE WEB

Office of Postsecondary Education's Campus Security Website, www.ope.ed.gov/security/.
Security on Campus, Inc., www.securityoncampus.org/.

Chapter 13: The Police

BOOKS

Dash, Samuel, *The Intruders: Unreasonable Searches and Seizures from King John to John Ashcroft* (New Brunswick, N.J.: Rutgers University Press, 2004).

ON THE WEB

The American Civil Liberties Union, www.aclu.org/.

CRITICAL CASES

Miranda v. Arizona, 384 US 436 (1966).

Chapter 14: Alcohol & Parties

BOOKS

Drivers License Guide Company, *ID Checking Guide: United States and Canada* (Redwood City, Calif.: Drivers License Guide Company, 2004).
Gehring, Donald D., Christy P. Geraci, and Terry McCarthy, *Alcohol on Campus: A Compendium of the Law and Guide to Campus Policy*, rev. ed. (Asheville, N.C.: College Administration Publications, 1999).

Taylor, Lawrence, *Drunk Driving Defense*, supp. ed. (New York: Aspen Publishers, 1999).

ON THE WEB

United States Department of Transportation, National Highway Traffic Safety Administration, www.nhtsa.dot.gov/.

Chapter 15: Sex & the Law

BOOKS

Levesque, Robert J. R., *Adolescents, Sex, and the Law: Preparing Adolescents for Responsible Citizenship* (Washington, D.C.: American Psychological Association, 2000).

Posner, Richard A., and Katherine B. Silbaugh, *A Guide to America's Sex Laws* (Chicago: University of Chicago Press, 1996).

ON THE WEB

Alan Guttmacher Institute, www.agi-usa.org/.
National Center for Victims of Crime Stalking Resource Center, www.ncvc.org/src/.
National Sexual Violence Resource Center, www.nsvrc.org/.
Planned Parenthood Federation of America, www.plannedparenthood.org/.
Rape, Abuse, and Incest National Network, www.rainn.org/.

Chapter 16: Off-Campus Housing

BOOKS

Portman, Janet, and Marcia Stewart, *Renter's Rights* (Berkeley, Calif.: Nolo Press, 1999).

ON THE WEB

U.S. Department of Housing & Urban Development Renter's Kit, www.hud.gov/renting/index.cfm.

Chapter 17: Money Issues

BOOKS

Braitman, Ellen, *Dollars & Sense for College Students or How Not to Run Out of Money by Midterms* (New York: Random House, 1999).

Daskaloff, Alexander, *Credit Card Debt: Reduce Your Financial Burden In Three Easy Steps* (New York: Avon Books, 1999).

ON THE WEB

College Board's Guide to Residency Requirements, www.collegeboard.com/about/association/international/residency.html.

Equifax, www.equifax.com/.
Experian, www.experian.com/.
Smart Student Guide to Financial Aid, www.finaid.com/.
TransUnion, www.transunion.com/.

Chapter 18: Student Activism

BOOKS

Gora, Joel M., David Goldberger, Gary M. Stern, and Mort Halperin, *The Right to Protest: The Basic ACLU Guide to Free Expression* (Carbondale: Southern Illinois University Press, 1991).

Issac, Katherine, *Ralph Nader Presents Practicing Democracy: A Guide to Student Action* (New York: St. Martin's Press, 1995).

Shaw, Randy, *The Activist's Handbook: A Primer for the 1990s and Beyond* (Berkeley: University of California Press, 1991).

ON THE WEB

Protest.net's Activist Handbook, protest.net/activists_handbook/.

Appendix A: Debunking Popular College Myths

BOOKS

Bronner, Simon J., *Piled Higher and Deeper: The Folklore of Campus Life* (Little Rock, Ark.: August House Books, 1990).

Brunvand, Jan Harold, *Encyclopedia of Urban Legends* (New York: W.W. Norton Company, 2002).

ON THE WEB

The Urban Legends Archive, www.urbanlegends.com/.
Urban Legends Reference Pages. College, www.snopes.com/college/.

About the Author

Attorney C. L. Lindsay III is the founder and executive director of the Coalition for Student and Academic Rights (CO-STAR), an organization that offers free legal advice to university students. He is a nationally recognized expert on student rights and academic freedom. His syndicated column, "Ask CO-STAR," is distributed nationally on Knight Ridder/Tribune's College Wire Service. C. L. graduated from Denison University in 1993 and received his law degree from the University of Michigan in 1996. He lives in Bucks County, Pennsylvania.

About CO-STAR

The Coalition for Student and Academic Rights is a national, nonprofit network of lawyers who help college students and professors with legal problems. CO-STAR offers a full suite of services, including legal counseling, mediation, and on-campus educational programs. For more information, visit the CO-STAR website at www.co-star.org.